6

MASS COMMUNICATIONS
A World View

MASS COMMUNICATIONS
A WORLD VIEW

edited by ALAN WELLS

Newcomb College, Tulane University

 National Press Books

HN
90
·M3 W44

Library of Congress Catalog Card Number: 73-93347
International Standard Book Numbers:
0-87484-218-2 (paper)
0-87484-219-0 (cloth)

Manufactured in the United States of America

National Press Books
285 Hamilton Avenue, Palo Alto, California 94301

This book was set in Baskerville by Libra Cold Type. The
designer was Nancy Sears. Sponsoring editor was Alden
C. Paine and copy editor was Zipporah Collins. Michelle
Hogan supervised production.

CONTENTS

PREFACE

Mass communication is justifiably becoming a major topic of interest in American colleges. Students of journalism, mass communications, sociology, political science, and psychology are becoming sensitive to the far-reaching impact of the mass media on individuals and society at large. Courses quite naturally focus on current practices in the United States. This volume is designed to put such material in comparative perspective and thus shed new light on American media practices. It is recommended as a supplement to texts for mass communications courses. It is also designed as a resource for the growing number of courses dealing with international media. Perhaps no single volume can do justice to this topic; what is attempted here is the presentation of a sampling of geographic regions and issues, with the understanding that course instructors may provide supplementary reading of their own choice. The selective bibliography suggests possible sources.

The mass media in the United States are almost entirely commercial enterprises. Television is dominated by the three big networks, and newspapers are increasingly concentrated in chain and multimedia conglomerate operations. Both the electronic media and the press rely on advertising for their revenues. This pattern of ownership and source of funds shape the product that is presented to the public. Thus financial imperatives determine the type of programming offered. Government regulation by the Federal Communications Commission and the Federal Trade Commission may on occasion inconvenience the electronic media but it seldom threatens their basic structure and practices. The writings in this volume indicate that the American pattern is not the only, or necessarily the best, mode of operation.

The book is divided into two parts; the first provides material on overseas media systems, the second on international facilities and influences. Part I provides some criteria for judging our own system and suggests alternative methods of operation. It might be noted here that the Corporation for Public Broadcasting recently established in the United States manifests some of the characteristics of the British Broadcasting Corporation that are described in the introduction to section A of Part I. This section deals with Western countries with flourishing media systems that differ in major ways from the dominant media in the United States and with two totalitarian systems, those of the Soviet Union and China, that are both essentially controlled by their governments but reflect the differing societies in which they operate. Despite the urgings of some who are attacking the critical work of the press, it is not recommended here that the United States media likewise become quiescent government mouthpieces.

Section B of Part I is devoted to the mass media in the less developed countries of Africa and Asia. It also takes up a topic of crucial importance to the Third World, namely the potential of the media for enhancing modernization and economic development in poor countries. In these countries television often becomes a way of life for the population at large before mass transport, heavy industry, or even piped water arrives. But actual use of the media in the underdeveloped world usually falls far short of the glowing promises contained in theoretical discussions of media benefits.

Part II outlines in section A the facilities for international communication—the global cable system, the satellites, and the news-gathering organizations that utilize them. Section B deals with some aspects of international communication, including government propaganda and commercialism.

I am of course indebted to the authors and publishers who have permitted me to reprint their work: this is in essence their volume. I am also indebted to my students, who have demonstrated to me that the mass media in the United States cannot be studied in isolation and that the study of overseas media is both interesting and fruitful. In particular, Bob Lipson, Ann Quave, Mary Lou Portais, Mary C. McCarthy, and Thelma M. Williams have lent valuable assistance. My thanks also to Alden Paine and National Press Books, publisher of my volume Mass Media and Society (Palo Alto, 1972), who have encouraged work on a comparative volume. Maryknoll Communications kindly permitted me to draw on material from Picture Tube Imperialism? (Maryknoll, N.Y.: Orbis Books, 1972). Finally, I owe acknowledgment to Wilson P. Dizard, whose interesting book Television: A World View (Syracuse, N.Y.: Syracuse University Press, 1966) prompted the title for this volume.

Alan Wells

New Orleans
August 1973

PART ONE

MASS MEDIA SYSTEMS

Introduction and Theoretical Overview

The concept of mass media systems is a complex one. It is used here to mean the overall configuration of the hardware, personnel, and mode of operation of a country's mass media. The media for purposes of this book include newspapers, radio, and television. Because of their technological similarities the electronic media are often run on similar lines, frequently by the same people. In the United States, for example, the major television networks formerly were the major radio networks. They still are involved in radio, but diversification of that medium has muted their preeminence. Both radio and television are regulated by the Federal Communications Commission under the same broadcasting statutes, and both are funded by commercial spot advertisements. The press, on the other hand, often operates under a different set of principles. In this country, then, and in many others we are not dealing with a mass media system in any real sense, but with two or more separate media systems.

The media systems in a country usually reflect the economic, social, political, and even geographic conditions of the country. The study of media systems would be sterile, however, if it merely demonstrated how well they "fit" their social environments—for media systems are man-made and can be changed (within limits, to be sure). The central task in studying media systems is to determine how the type of system adopted influences the way the medium is used and how this in turn shapes its social impact. With this in mind, we turn to the ways in which media systems have been classified. Several characteristics relevant to a more detailed analysis of such systems are then suggested.

MEDIA SYSTEM TYPOLOGIES

Despite the complexity and variety of mass media systems, experts often urge the adoption of a simplistic scheme of classification—a bipolar view with the "free" United States system at the desirable end of a continuum, and totalitarian systems at the other. This approach has been a strong ideological weapon in the spread of American media enterprises overseas (see Schiller's article in section B of Part II). As Skornia (1965:181–82) has noted concerning television, this view is most evident in the trade journals:

> An editorial in Broadcasting magazine in March, 1955, told of the alleged victory of the American broadcasting plan, which has "prevailed in all democratic nations," over the so-called British Plan. The editorial concluded: "Henceforth the lexicon will change. It will be the 'American Plan' versus the 'Totalitarian Plan' until the latter collapses." Similarly, Advertising Age in November of 1959 observed that "Nations that have resisted commercial TV have made little progress." "Nations that have not resisted commercial TV have made rapid strides."

In the quote from Broadcasting magazine, commercial television is apparently assumed to have a monopoly on democratic virtue. Publicly financed systems such as the British are labeled "totalitarian!" Advertising Age implies that commercial television is causally related to national progress. There is little evidence that fully commercialized media are so beneficial.

The choice, however, is not limited to either "free" (private) or totalitarian (one variant of public) systems. Newspapers, for example, do not have to be either privately owned local commercial enterprises as in the United States or centrally controlled government mouthpieces as in the Soviet Union. Various alternative means of sponsorship—by political parties in multiple party states, labor unions, churches, etc.—may widen the choice beyond that between business and government control. Similarly, alternative systems of public control of electronic media are possible, and these may lead to cultural and informational programming that is free of either political or commercial interference.

The options for control of broadcasting, then, are three, and actual systems may be located anywhere between the pure types, as shown in figure 1. The United States system is not entirely free of political constraints, as the President's Office of Telecommunications Policy and the Republican leadership of the FCC remind us, while the Public Broadcasting System introduces the possibility of some inputs to the system responsive to the public. Even with political domination, as in the Soviet Union, sales functions may be served and cultural and information programming at least partially independent of political directives may be included. Nonetheless, programming tends to follow the dictates of broadcast control.

Adding a third control dimension to the bipolar continuum refines it considerably but still leaves us with a simplistic classification scheme for entire

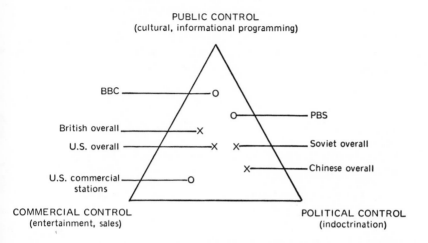

FIGURE 1. Types of Broadcasting Control

PUBLIC CONTROL
(cultural, informational programming)

BBC ———————————O

O——————————— PBS

British overall ———————X

U.S. overall ——————————X   X———————— Soviet overall

X———————— Chinese overall

U.S. commercial ——————————O
stations

COMMERCIAL CONTROL   POLITICAL CONTROL
(entertainment, sales)   (indoctrination)

media systems. Other classifications in the literature are therefore examined for a more useful one. Merrill and Lowenstein have recently proposed a three stage classification based on the differing characteristics of media audiences. They claim that

media in any nation grow from elitist to popular to specialized. In the elitist stage, the media appeal to and are consumed by opinion leaders, primarily. In the popular stage, media appeal to and are consumed by the masses of a nation's population, primarily. In the specialized stage, the media appeal to and are consumed by fragmented, specialized segments of the total population [1971:33].

Media systems, they find, pass through this orderly progression. Most systems in less developed countries are still in the initial elitist stage. When literacy is widespread and a large segment of the population has escaped abject poverty, the media shift to the popular variant, as they have in Europe, North America, Japan, Israel, and Australia (p. 36). With higher education, affluence, leisure, and sufficient market scale, the final stage is reached. Somewhat ethnocentrically, they claim that the United States is currently entering this stage, the first country to do so (p. 39).

This typology, of course, fails to take into account organizational factors or the way the media are used. It is based primarily on the pattern of growth experienced in North America, and it seems most appropriate for categorizing the printed media (although, as far as daily newspapers are concerned, the United States is probably moving away from the specialized stage). The electronic media in many underdeveloped countries never really have an elitist stage—cheap transistor radios, collective listening and viewing, and the importation of mass television fare make it unnecessary. Alternatively, as in China, ideological imperatives may ensure a mass audience (or none at all) from the outset.

Perhaps the most commonly used typology of media systems is that developed by Siebert, Peterson, and Schramm (1956). As interpreted by Wright

(1959:24), they "view the communication systems of the world as operating—more or less precisely—under four major theories," or perhaps styles would be a better term. These are the Soviet-communist, libertarian, social responsibility, and authoritarian patterns. Their characteristics are depicted in figure 2. This typology fails to discriminate well among the wide variety of communist and noncommunist systems (although in part this is inevitable in any typology), its social responsibility type is only emergent, and there is no consideration of

FIGURE 2. The Siebert–Peterson–Schramm Typology

Type Name	Control of Media	Programming Policy	Representative Countries
Soviet-communist	Government, Communist party	Emphasis on transmitting communist doctrine, mobilizing support for government, raising cultural tastes of masses	Soviet Union, other communist countries
Libertarian	Nongovernment	Emphasis on freedom from restraints on programming	Anglo-American and other western countries
Social Responsibility	Organizations responsive to public	Emphasis on transmitting public information and discussion of social issues, avoidance of harmful material	Anglo-American countries
Authoritarian	Public and private, subordinate to state	No criticism of government; censorship of programming	Early European countries, less developed countries

transferred systems of a colonial or neocolonial nature (such as extensions of international commercialism). The typology also ignores the crucial fact that some media systems are organized to make money, others merely to communicate to a public.

In his examination of contemporary European systems, Paulu begins with a western (free)-totalitarian continuum in mind. To him "the Western theory is that within practical limits all points of view should be heard, under the assumption that the best ideas finally will prevail." Censorship is used, he notes, to exclude "dangerous" material—which apparently includes any democratic questioning of commercial domination. "The totalitarian point of view," he continues, "is that the press should be used, as the Soviet Constitution declares, 'In conformity with the interests of the working people, and in order to strengthen the socialist system' " (1967:51). Such a typology is of little use in analyzing the European media systems. Paulu therefore turns to the classification scheme developed by Namurois (1964), which outlines four types based on different modes of control.

FIGURE 3. The Namurois Typology

Type	Control of Media	Representative Countries
State-operated	Operated by government ministry, department, or administrative agency	Most communist countries
Public corporation	Operated autonomously under state charter	Britain (BBC, ITA), France, West Germany, Belgium, the Netherlands
Public interest partnership	Operated by legally private corporations with state stock interests	Italy, Sweden, Switzerland
Private enterprise	Operated by private corporations with weak government regulation	United States, Japan's private stations, Luxembourg

As described and applied by Paulu (1967:51–76), the typology may be portrayed in the abbreviated form suggested by figure 3. While the typology depicted in figure 2 stressed the underlying philosophy of the media, the stress here is on the control of electronic media. It produces a much more discriminating set of criteria, merging the Soviet-communist and totalitarian types but separating out elements of both the libertarian and social responsibility categories. Their usefulness is in projecting program style from type of control. The private enterprise operation is unlikely to produce costly educational programming or curb the "consumption now" exhortations of advertising. The state-operated station or public corporation appears best suited for those tasks.

This classification, however, fails to take account of important differences within each type, as Paulu's exposition of media systems indicates. It is possible for a state-operated system to be either more or less centralized, either shrill or low-keyed in its programming. Thus stations in Yugoslavia, for example, have considerable autonomy in programming and budget allocation (Paulu, 1967:57). Among other state-operated systems, China's revolutionary use of the media (see the Liu article below) contrasts with Russia's quiescent and comparatively decentralized style of media use (see the Hopkins article below). Public corporations vary in their organization and programming imperatives (cultural, informative, educational, entertainment), and the degree of government intervention. They may prohibit or permit advertising. Partnerships exist between government and private entrepreneurs or (e.g., in Sweden) between government and a variety of political, commercial, and cultural organizations.

THE FIVE KEY ASPECTS OF MEDIA SYSTEMS

The Namurois classification by control appears to be adequate on this dimension. Control is a key factor in describing and analyzing media systems. Linked to control are the questions of finance, programming, target audience, and feedback mechanisms, and these, it is argued, are the other essential elements distinguishing media systems.

The options for financing the media range from advertising revenue to some form of subsidy, either private or through government tax support or a mixture of the two. License fees on electronic media receivers are commonly used to pay for broadcasting service. Half the world's countries (including most of Europe) employ this method.

Advertising practices vary widely in countries that raise revenues from this source. The United States pattern of commercial domination, in which up to a third of broadcast time and the bulk of newspaper space is used for advertising, is by no means the only style. Most European countries finance broadcasting with some advertising revenue, but commercial announcements are strictly controlled, and program sponsorship is often preferred to spot announcements. There are often fixed time limits for advertising that are more binding than the National Association of Broadcasters' code provisions in this country. In Germany, for example, only twenty minutes of commercials are permitted per day. Even East European broadcasting organizations carry ads, but the revenue derived is small and the products promoted are invariably those of state industries (Paulu, 1967:100–110). When advertising is limited in these ways, program content is less influenced by the advertiser.

Programming according to Tunstall (1970:9) may be directed to commercial, educational, cultural, or political ends, or to simple entertainment. Usually, of course, the broadcaster has a combination of such goals. All programs must be minimally entertaining if they are to hold the attention of their audience. Newspapers have parallel sets of goals and must also hold the readers' attention. Following the formulation of Merrill and Lowenstein (1971), target audiences may usefully be classified as elite, mass, or specialized.

The need for feedback is particularly crucial in educational programming of radio and television. It may take the form of field worker reports (which have been found most effective for specific projects), audience participation and local control (as in Yugoslavia), polls or rating systems, and evaluations by critics or sponsors. The latter two methods are most common in commercial systems where raw size of audience is often crucial. The former methods, although more cumbersome, are most useful where the main concerns are education and change.

FIGURE 4. Key Dimensions of Media Systems

Dimensions	Options
Control	State-operated, public corporation, partnership, private enterprise (with varying degrees of government regulations), institutionally sponsored
Finance	License fees, general taxation, advertising and taxation combination, advertising, private subsidy
Programming goals	Entertainment, education, sales, culture, political ideology, cheapest possible operation (utilizing foreign material)
Target audience	Elite, mass, specialized
Feedback mechanism	Reports from field workers, audience participation, polls and ratings, reports from critics and sponsors

A realistic classification of media systems, therefore, probably goes beyond the typologies of three or four categories. The five key dimensions of media systems outlined above are summarized in figure 4, and systems may combine these dimensions in dozens of ways. Primary questions to ask of a system are, therefore: How is the medium controlled? How is it financed? What is its purpose? Whom does it serve? How does it ascertain the effect it is having?

REFERENCES

Merrill, John C., and Ralph L. Lowenstein. 1971. Media Messages and Men: New Perspectives in Communication. New York: David McKay.

Namurois, Albert. 1964. Problems of Structure and Organization of Broadcasting in the Framework of Radio Communications. Geneva: European Broadcasting Union.

Paulu, Burton. 1967. Radio and Television Broadcasting on the European Continent. Minneapolis: University of Minnesota Press.

Siebert, Fred S., Theodore Peterson, and Wilbur Schramm. 1956. Four Theories of the Press: The Authoritarian, Libertarian, Social Responsibility and Soviet Communist Concepts of What the Press Should Be and Do. Urbana: University of Illinois Press.

Skornia, Harry. 1965. Television and Society. New York: McGraw-Hill.

Tunstall, Jeremy, ed. 1970. Media Sociology: A Reader. Chicago: University of Illinois Press.

Wright, Charles R. 1959. Mass Communication: A Sociological Perspective. New York: Random House.

THE VARIETY
OF MEDIA SYSTEMS

Introduction

The United States mass media system is commonly
characterized as private and commercial. True, it
transmits useful information to and entertains its
audience, but its main task, the one for which it
is rewarded, is to "deliver" audiences to the advertisers. Despite the presence of some outstanding
journalists and creative artists, and the occasional
educational and cultural use of the media, they
are run overwhelmingly as profit-making enterprises. Given this set of economic constraints there
is probably no real alternative to current practices:
the context in which media personnel work must
change if the nature of their product is to be upgraded.

　　　The commercial pattern in the United States
is sometimes claimed to be "natural" to politically
"free" countries. Evidence supporting this claim
is not very strong. When we examine the media of
other countries in the Western world, we find a
variety of systems each reflecting the traditions
and institutions of its country. Newly independent
and developing countries, which are often politically neutral, seldom have time to develop their
own media traditions. They therefore usually imi-

tate one of the existing systems of the "free" world. The model chosen may be that of the United States, but it is equally likely to be the British or French pattern, partly because those two countries once ruled widespread empires and partly because they demonstrate a viable alternative to the American commercial operation. For Americans who are seriously interested in reform of media operations, study of successful Western media systems (even if they obviously could not be adopted in whole) can suggest many alternatives. In addition, they provide the key to understanding Canadian media sensibilities, since that country's communication patterns and traditions closely resemble the British. The media systems in Britain, Western Europe, Japan, and the communist countries are outlined below.

THE BRITISH SYSTEM

The mass media in Britain and the United States developed more or less simultaneously, with both leading the rest of the world in use of the technological innovations they discovered. But use of the media in Britain took a radically different course from that in the United States.

Since Britain is a small country and was already heavily industrialized when the mass press began, distribution of newspapers was feasible on a nationwide scale. The early existence of a national railway network, which still operates today, made rapid transport of daily papers relatively easy and inexpensive. London was not only the nation's railroad center, but also the cultural, political, and economic capital of the island. Fleet Street there became and remains the locus of the national press.

Today there are about 140 daily papers in Britain (Hancock, 1970:15). The best known are the national papers, several of which are available on newsstands throughout the country. Unlike an American reader, the British consumer has a wide choice even though the total number of newspapers is low. The papers reflect various political persuasions and class differences, which still play a part in the British consciousness. They also reflect differing degrees of seriousness, from the ponderous intensity of the Times (circulation 432,000) to the tabloid sensationalism of the working-class-oriented Daily Mirror (about 5,000,000 circulation). The middle-class Daily Express and Daily Mail have circulations of 3,750,000 and 2,000,000 respectively (Hancock, 1970). All carry advertising, but there is less than in the American papers, because their higher circulation and national distribution preclude both the need for and the effectiveness of the local advertising that is so common in United States dailies. News is far more nationally (and internationally) oriented than in the typical American city paper. Because the government is centralized, little of importance is missed: there are no state legislatures to report on. Local news from outside of London is of little significance, as the low-keyed content of the more than one thousand local weeklies in Britain makes evident.

After a short and unsuccessful period of radio broadcasting operated by a manufacturing cartel, the British Broadcasting Corporation was set up as a government-licensed public (i.e., nonprofit) corporation. It was established for both technical and ideological reasons (see Wright, 1959: 34–38). Given the compactness of the country and its proximity to population centers on the continent, only three broadcasting channels were made available. The ideological commitment of the BBC was to raise the cultural standards of the mass audience.

For this purpose the three channels—designated the light program, home service, and the third program—were allocated to meet ascending levels of cultural taste. Programming ranges from light entertainment to serious music, drama, and debates (carried by the third program). The idea was to slowly upgrade all three stations while weaning more and more of the mass audience away from the light program offerings to the serious channels. This aristocratic domination continued until the 1960s, when transistor radios and the mushrooming of commercial stations (the English-language Radio Luxembourg and offshore "pirate" stations, which were outlawed in 1967) wooed away the young with popular music offerings. In reaction, the BBC has modified its serious, cultural-uplift image, devoting one of its present four channels to "pop" music. This channel commands 45 percent of audience listening time (BBC, 1972:45). Commercial radio under the auspices of the Independent Television Authority began broadcasting in 1973.

The BBC's radio broadcasting was noncommercial from the outset and was financed by an annual license fee on receivers. Television was similarly funded and was initially the sole preserve of the BBC. In the mid-1950s, the British government chartered the ITA to subcontract time on what was then a second television channel. In television, as in radio, the BBC has reduced its seriousness (some would say dullness) in response to this commercial competition. Since its revenues are still assured, however, it has not had to revert to the American style of inoffensive mass programming.

The BBC operates two national television networks, which draw a total daily audience of more than 27 million viewers (BBC, 1972:31). Although the central facilities are in London, regional branches of the BBC in Wales, Scotland, and Northern Ireland, together with three network production centers in England, contribute to national network programming. Local programming is produced by the three regional branches and eight local programming regions in England. These services are funded primarily from license fees on receivers, which amounted to more than 75 million pounds in 1971 (BBC, 1972:222). Formally, the government has considerable control over the operations of the BBC. But apart from requiring a daily report on Parliament and emergency prerogatives, there is a gentlemen's agreement of noninterference. Thus Paulu 1961:7–17) found that in its social and political context the BBC has been both independent and "responsive to national needs." But, in a different context, such a system might function less smoothly.

The Independent Television Authority has contracted with fifteen independent programming companies, each with a regional territory of operation. These companies air both their own programs and ITV network material (usually produced by one of the five biggest companies), as well as externally purchased programs. They sell advertising spots as in the United States, but advertising time is limited and spots are placed in natural program breaks. ITV's share of the total television audience was 54 percent in 1971 (ITA, 1972:173). Total revenues for the twelve-month period ending July 1971 amounted to a little over 100 million pounds (ITA, p. 178). Commercial television, then, is thriving, and the drive to the crass and mass style of programming is compelling.

Nonetheless, overall the British system differs quite radically from that in the United States. The daily press is national in scope, and broadcasting is much more deeply concerned with quality public service programming. Gould (1972) has argued that public television in the United States has much to learn from the BBC. It is able to put its audience first, to avoid an overreaching concern with profit, and to program selectively for audiences of differing tastes. Increasingly, though, the BBC is aiming at mass markets, and particularly at those in the United States. As Gould notes, this has been a quite successful venture in terms of growing sales and Emmy awards. If programming is designed for what the British call "mid-Atlantic" audiences, however, quality may suffer. For this and other reasons, all is not well with British television.

As recently as 1968, Trilling (1968) wrote in praise of British TV. She found programs often technically superior to their American counterparts, more true to life, and less condescending about the intellectual capacity of their audience. In part, of course, she was reflecting the euphoria of viewing television without constant commercial breaks. But she was also celebrating the quality of work that is possible when artists, writers, and newsmen are free of commercial control. In 1973, however, she claims (in personal correspondence) that declining standards make such praise unwarranted.

BRITISH-INFLUENCED SYSTEMS

The British media system has served as a model for other countries, particularly those in the Commonwealth or British spheres of influence, past and present. For example, the mass media in Israel are closer to the British than to the American pattern (although they display uniquely Israeli qualities). The Israeli press, like the British, is nationally oriented. Of the twenty-five dailies, ten are published in immigrant languages. Owing to direct and indirect party sponsorship, several papers are openly political and reflect the wide range of partisanship in the country. Because of the overseas ties of immigrants and the importance of world affairs to Israel's survival, international news receives considerable space. Unlike most of the "free world" press, Israeli newspapers undergo extensive military censorship on grounds of the constant threats to the country's security (see Lowenstein, 1969).

Radio in Israel (Kol Israel) has been under strict government control from the outset. Television was resisted for ideological and cultural reasons, but was finally introduced after the six-day war, to counter Arab broadcasting. Krosney (1969) recounts the difficulties experienced by the Israelis in programming for the newly conquered Arab population using an organization dominated by those who clearly put the needs of the Israeli population first. There are similarities with attempts to introduce "ethnic" programs on WASP-dominated stations in this country.

The two largest Commonwealth nations, Canada and Australia, both exhibit mixed media systems. In each, because of the size of the country, the daily press is city-based. Australian newspaper interests are conspicuous in their ownership of commercial television stations. All of the major cities have three commercial stations along with a network outlet for the public Australian Broadcasting Commission. Operating for exceptionally long broadcasting hours and on low budgets, these stations import much programming, primarily from Britain and the United States (see Green, 1972:44–52, 277–87). Canadian television is in a position similar to that of East Germany: it has a richer, more powerful neighbor transmitting television signals across its border within range of most of the population. The public Canadian Broadcasting Corporation and the independent network, CTV, fare poorly in their attempts to compete with south-of-the-border programming. The French broadcasting service in Quebec is the sole exception.

WESTERN EUROPEAN SYSTEMS

The countries of Western Europe exhibit considerable diversity in the way their media operate. Newspapers show this the least. They either are city-based or, usually in the smaller countries, have a national circulation. They are often politically partisan, usually commercial enterprises, and in a few cases represent extremely concentrated power bases. The most conspicuous of these is the German publishing empire of Axel Springer, which has a third of the country's circulation and has tried to gain control of a television network—so far unsuccessfully (Paulu, 1967:68). The greatest variability is with the electronic media, especially television. It is here that the Europeans break new ground.

The selection from Paulu's work reprinted here outlines two ways of organizing the broadcast media. The first uses the public corporation. The excerpt describes ORTF of France, which since the de Gaulle era has lost some of its stifling centralization and added a third channel (see Green, 1972: 132–43), and the highly innovative NOS organization in the Netherlands. The British, Germans, and Belgians also use public corporations, each in their own fashion. Germany began with nine regional corporations that later formed two national programming networks or pools (see Paulu, 1967:63–69; Green, 1972: 117–31).

The second type of broadcasting system (misleadingly called private corporations by Paulu) provides for joint government and private commercial control. Italy and Sweden, the countries reviewed in the excerpt, together with Switzerland, fall into this category. Since media in the Eastern European countries are state-controlled, the only countries following the American practice of exclusively private commercial broadcasting are tiny Luxembourg and minuscule Monaco and Andorra (Paulu, 1967:85).

THE JAPANESE MEDIA

Japan is the most highly developed non-Western country in the world. Its national economic growth in the twentieth century outstrips that of any other industrial power, and it has transformed itself from a war-devastated country in 1946 to an economic superpower in the 1970s. This has been achieved without the cultural dislocation or the reliance on Western capital that seems to accompany the developmental efforts of most other non-Western societies (postrevolutionary China excepted). The mass media reflect Japan's adoption (and often improvement) of Western technology, while at the same time maintaining considerable cultural autonomy.

By 1968, Japan's newspaper circulation per capita slightly exceeded that of Britain (both are considerably higher than the United States rate), while the ratio of radio and television receivers was only a little below that of the richest countries. All but 4 percent of Japanese households had television sets. The largest daily newspapers have national distribution, and three have circulations of over 5 million (Ishida, 1971:83). Like the programming of NHK described by Krisher in the article that follows, newspapers (except political party publications) tend to be strongly nonpartisan, indeed timid by Western standards.

NHK, as Krisher points out, is Japan's noncommercial public corporation. It operates on license fees that give it the world's largest television budget (well over $300 million in 1971) to devote to its two nationwide television and three radio networks. Four independent commercial networks vie for television advertising revenues of more than $600 million a year. (Green, 1972: 257–59). Each is linked to one of Japan's newspaper empires, although the networks now out-earn their parent enterprises.

THE SOVIET UNION, EASTERN EUROPE, AND CHINA

We have seen that public corporations and mixed systems largely avoid the commercial domination of broadcasting found in the United States while at the same time avoiding outright government control. Such systems, which serve their nations' cultural and educational needs, are usually ignored by media proponents in this country, who see only a choice between "free" (that is, corporate controlled) and "totalitarian" modes of operation. The disadvantages of the latter are indeed to be avoided. Our selections focus on systems in the communist bloc, but the same stifling effects can be expected wherever the government takes control of the media for political exhortation. The media are limited by this as surely as they are when abandoned to the marketers of soap, cigarettes, and corn flakes.

Political domination, even in the communist bloc, does not imply complete uniformity, as the selections here indicate. Tradition and the bureaucratic features of Soviet life result in a somewhat low-keyed mass product in the Soviet Union, while China's media have been intimately involved in the "cultural revolution" and are given to shrill exhortations.

The excerpt from Hopkins's book on Soviet media—which makes frequent comparisons with United States practices—first traces the role of the press and its current problem of serving the people and the party simultaneously. The mass press is not uniform. Rather it caters to the Soviet Union's many national and linguistic groups, while attempting to consolidate unification. Hopkins describes the party organization of the media and the way they are used for mass mobilization, moral and formal education, social criticism, entertainment, and, most recently, merchandising. In the final section Hopkins gives a brief outline of Soviet broadcasting—an activity that has provoked active criticism within the country. Programming has been poor and dissemination slow. Not until the 1960s did the government seriously set about the task of matching the best media use in modern industrial countries.

The media in the Warsaw Pact countries have been heavily influenced by Soviet media methods. East Germany was no exception. While the country was occupied by the Red Army after World War II, the media transferred from the totalitarian Nazi system to the Soviet model. Departures from Russian practices, however, are clearly evident. Like Czechoslovakia, East Germany had audiences of some sophistication, and it had to upgrade media performance in the face of competition from without. Broadcasting knows no political borders, as the Voice of America, Radio Free Europe, Deutsche Welle, and the BBC's overseas service fully recognize. East Germans have been strongly attracted to West German television (which is similar to Britain's modified commercial programming) so the Communist stations have had to improve their offerings. Although they have not matched the overall performance of affluent West Germany, they have presumably kept part of the audience for their best programs. Indeed, according to Colitt (1968), West Germans will often tune in to the East when the fare offered (for example, an outstanding children's program) warrants it.

In Czechoslovakia, prior to the Soviet invasion in 1968, journalists had been highly critical of Soviet policy and had temporarily "liberated" themselves (see Hamsik, 1971). Long outside the Soviet fold, Yugoslavia's media also deviate from the usual communist pattern. The country has eight broadcasting organizations and forty-nine stations, which enjoy considerable local control and autonomy (Paulu, 1967:57-58). Although the structure of the media in the rest of Eastern Europe largely conforms to the Soviet pattern, their content varies considerably. The East Europeans, for example, are occasional consumers of Western programming as well. Thus Poland takes "Bonanza" and British commercial programs along with Intervision material from the Communist bloc (see Green, 1972: 193-207).

China's use of the media, like its interpretation of communism, differs sharply from the Soviet pattern. Overtly political instruments, the media are now seen much more as a personal voice for Chairman Mao and a tool for exhorting the revolutionary masses, than as a benign channel for the party bureaucracy. The Chinese media were indeed drifting into the latter variant until the cultural revolution. As Broman (1969) describes it, Mao regained control by attacking the media and the party bureaucracy with a wall poster campaign. As his Red Guards gained ascendance, he was able to take command of the established communications channels. This later phase of the cultural revolution is described below by Liu. He indicates that the Maoist faction totally disrupted the media and succeeded in imposing an activist view of their use. But, now that the Red Guard has been disbanded, lower-keyed bureaucratic media patterns will probably be slowly reestablished.

REFERENCES

British Broadcasting Corporation. 1972. BBC Handbook, 1972. London: BBC.

Broman, Barry M. 1969. "Tatzepao: Medium of Conflict in China's 'Cultural Revolution.' " Journalism Quarterly, summer, pp. 100-104.

Colitt, Leslie R. 1968. "Television." Nation. November 11, pp. 508-10.

Gould, Jack. 1972. "What Public TV Can Be: Britain's BBC." Columbia Journalism Review, July/August, pp. 16-20.

Green, Timothy. 1972. The Universal Eye. London: Bodley Head.

Hancock, Alan. 1970. Mass Communication. London: Longman Group.

Hamsik, Dusan. 1971. Writers against Rulers. New York: Vintage.

Independent Television Authority. 1972. ITV 1972: Guide to Independent Television. London: ITA.

Ishida, Takeshi. 1971. Japanese Society. New York: Random House.

Krosney, Herbert. 1969. "TV Comes to Israel." Nation, October 6, pp. 339-43.

Lowenstein, Ralph L. 1969. "The Daily Press in Israel," Journalism Quarterly, summer, pp. 325-31.

Paulu, Burton. 1961. British Broadcasting in Transition. Minneapolis: University of Minnesota Press.

———. 1967. Radio and Television Broadcasting on the European Continent. Minneapolis: University of Minnesota Press.

Trilling, Diana. 1968. "An American Looks at British Television," Atlantic. February, pp. 70-76.

Wright, Charles R. 1959. Mass Communication: A Sociological Perspective. New York: Random House.

Public and Private Corporations: France, the Netherlands, Italy, and Sweden*

BURTON PAULU

BURTON PAULU is Professor and Director, Department of Radio and Television, University of Minnesota, Minneapolis. He is former president, vice-president, secretary, regional director, and member of various committees of the National Association of Educational Broadcasters. He has worked on a broad range of international broadcasting research projects and has also been a practicing broadcaster. He holds a Ph.D. degree from New York University, 1949. He is the author of numerous articles and several books including Radio and Television Broadcasting on the European Continent (University of Minnesota Press, 1967) and British Broadcasting in Transition (University of Minnesota Press, 1961).

HE PUBLIC CORPORATION

In some countries broadcasting is done by a public corporation chartered by the state. Such organizations normally are not subject to direct government supervision, although they receive policy guidance from a board of directors which often is appointed by the govern-

*Reprinted from Burton Paulu, *Radio and Television Broadcasting on the European Continent.* University of Minnesota Press, Minneapolis, pp. 58–63, 76–82. © 1967 by the University of Minnesota. Used by permission.

ment. Liaison with the state usually is through the ministers of posts, telephone, and telegraph, or education and culture. Although there always are some programming requirements and prohibitions, when the system works well the responsible minister resists pressures to regulate program content. Once the government has laid down basic policies, it usually allows the broadcasting organization much initiative and freedom, including the right to expend funds within the broad limits imposed by charter and license. Yet such corporations always are subject to some supervision and final review, and in extreme situations the state has authority to suspend their operations.

The examples of public corporations treated here are those in France [and] ... the Netherlands. ...

France

The creation of the Office de Radiodiffusion-Télévision Française (ORTF) in June 1964 was a consequence of widespread criticism of French broadcasting. Specific complaints about program service and inadequate personnel were accompanied by charges that French radio and television were dominated by the executive branch of the government. The main objective of the new organization, therefore, was to provide more autonomy for broadcasting. The ORTF, managing its own budget and running its own affairs, was to be governed in matters of broad policy by an administrative council with private as well as government members, and no longer was to be controlled by the minister of information, even though still to be under his tutelage.

The history of French broadcasting reveals that the role of the state has been dominant. A French law of 1923 gave the state a monopoly over radio and television.[1] Between 1923 and 1941, France was served by a combination of state stations operated by the Postal and Telegraph Authority and private commercial stations. Legislation enacted in 1944 following the liberation of France ended all private broadcasting, and Radiodiffusion et Télévision Française (RTF) came into being on March 23, 1945. A subsequent ordinance on February 4, 1959, provided the legal basis for French broadcasting until the recent act of 1964.

The act of 1964 was precipitated by strong criticisms of French broadcasting.[2] There were complaints that the RTF was controlled by the Ministry of Information; that it employed unnecessary and unqualified staff members because of pressure from members of Parliament; that some of the periodic strikes were really protests against government control of news programs; and that even simple projects required high-level—and thus delaying—financial approval. There were frequent changes of top management, coupled with wide-

spread press criticism of state control. This had been bad enough
when one party regularly succeeded another in power, but the long
De Gaulle regime tipped the scales consistently in one direction. One
critic asserted that between 1956 and 1959 French television did not
devote a single program to the Algerian revolt, and it was generally
agreed that during the 1962 campaign to amend the Constitution so
as to strengthen the presidency, the Gaullist position was enormously
favored by television.[3] Another famous incident occurred in February 1963 when the RTF canceled television interviews with Nikita
Khrushchev and Marshall Rodion Y. Malinovsky.

During the parliamentary debates on the new legislation, the
minister of information, Alain Peyrefitte, spoke very frankly about
the problems the reorganization was intended to eliminate.[4] He cited
two indications of inadequacy in the RTF: the loss of listeners and
viewers to stations in adjacent countries and the frequent strikes of
RTF staff. He then listed several basic defects in the present organization: unnecessarily stringent financial controls, particularly the
requirement for financial approval before all major expenditures;
bureaucratic weaknesses within the RTF; the development of small
power cliques which interfered with efficient operation; and the
susceptibility of the RTF to political pressure.

The solution to these problems, according to Mr. Peyrefitte,
was to give the broadcasting organization greater autonomy. There
apparently was permanent confusion about which decisions came
from the RTF and which came from the government. An example
was the Khrushchev-Malinovsky interview. This had been canceled,
he said, because Mr. Khrushchev, invited to record an interview for
February 7, 1963, commemorating the twentieth anniversary of the
Battle of Stalingrad, used the occasion to violently attack the government of West Germany and Chancellor Adenauer. Had this been
broadcast it might have been misunderstood in West Germany as an
expression of official opinion at the very time the French government was working for rapprochement with Germany. The solution,
therefore, was to make the broadcasting organization autonomous
so that no one could regard it as an official mouthpiece.

Alain Peyrefitte concluded by outlining "the three attributes of
autonomy" to be given the RTF. First was financial autonomy: Like
other French public enterprises the new ORTF would be free to
determine its budget, subject only to a posteriori review. Second
would be the substitution of tutelage (*tutelle*) for government control (*autorité*). Third would be the creation of an administrative
council, with both government and private members, to determine
basic policy, operations being left to the ORTF. In summary Mr.
Peyrefitte declared: "We hope this will constitute a break with the

past. The government-controlled RTF disappears, to be succeeded by an autonomous Office, free of government domination, administered by a Council which will guarantee its impartiality, under a distinguished president, and with a director general really responsible for the administration of the organization."[5]

During the three-day debate in Parliament the Gaullist majority showed some hesitation about surrendering state control of broadcasting because of the hostility of the press to De Gaulle. On the other hand the opposition alleged that, though this was a step in the right direction, the government would still have too much influence, in view of its power to appoint half the members of the administrative council, as well as to appoint and discharge the director general.[6] Nevertheless, the bill was passed by the National Assembly on May 28, 1964, by a vote of 276 to 181, and became law on June 27, 1964.[7]

The new statute describes the Office de Radiodiffusion-Télévision Française as a "public state establishment of industrial and commercial character," created to maintain a "national public service of radio and television" in order to "satisfy the public's need for information, culture, education, and entertainment."[8] Like other French state organs "of industrial and commercial character," the ORTF has an administrative council and is under the *supervision* rather than *control* of a minister. It is the minister of information who safeguards the ORTF's broadcasting monopoly; sees that its public service obligations are discharged; approves the budget jointly with the minister of finance and economic affairs; and checks the use made by the ORTF of its resources.[9]

A decree of July 22, 1964, set the administrative council at sixteen members, half representing the state, and the other half viewers and listeners, the press, the ORTF staff, and the public. All appointments are made by the government with private members chosen from lists drawn up by representative organizations. Council membership is for three years although the terms of office can be ended at any time at the mandate of the members representing the state.[10] This administrative council determines ORTF policy and budget. It also assures itself of the quality and morality of the programs; ensures the objectivity and accuracy of all information broadcast; and sees that the programs reflect the country's main trends of thought and opinion.* The director general and the two deputy directors are appointed by cabinet decree, rather than, as some members of Parliament had hoped, by the administrative council.[11]

---

*Statuts, Art. 4. It was Parliament that requested the council be responsible for ensuring not only the quality but also the morality of programs.

ORTF financing is from license fees, and by implication—although the law does not say so—advertising is prohibited.* Financial supervision is assured by requiring the minister of information to discuss ORTF financial plans with parliamentary representatives at least once every three months.[12] Nevertheless, the new law provides much more financial independence than did the old one, since the ORTF now is subject only to those controls normally prescribed for a national public undertaking. Accordingly, there now is only a posteriori rather than a priori financial reviews as before. Parliament wanted to insert in the law a guarantee for a right of reply by person considering themselves injured by materials broadcast. The government did not accept this proposal, but did instruct the director general to preserve recordings for examination by those who believed themselves wronged.

On July 22, 1964, the government published five decrees implementing the new legislation. One of them set up radio and television program committees, appointed by the minister of information. One third of the members of each committee represent public services, and are chosen after consultation with certain designated ministers; one-third are persons particularly competent in family, social affairs, and news problems; and the remaining one-third come from the arts and entertainment fields. These committees advise the broadcasting authorities on program policies. The director general does not have to follow their advice; but if he ignores it, production of the broadcasts in question may be held up until he has reconsidered his origina decision.[13]

Although the new law had the objective of releasing French broadcasting from government control, it still contains many provisions which the government could use to influence, if not control, the ORTF. Thus, the minister of information retains various supervisory prerogatives; the government appoints all the members of the administrative council, as well as the director general and the deputy directors; and Parliament maintains certain financial controls. There also is authority for the government to require the broadcasting of any statements or communications it considers essential, though these must be identified by source.†

The chances for government influence and control surely are

---

*But there is periodic speculation on a possible change of policy on this point, partly because of the ORTF's regular deficits. (*New York Times*, November 9, 1964, p. 10; *Variety,* November 17, 1965, p. 27; *Broadcasting,* February 1, 1965, p. 62.)

†*Statuts,* Art. 5. The last requirement was inserted to eliminate embarrassments like that caused by the cancellation of the Khrushchev interview since it distinguishes publicly between broadcasts made by the ORTF on its own authority and those made at government request.

less under the new law than under the old one, but such possibilities still exist. For example, during a parliamentary debate which took place the year following the enactment of the new legislation, the minister of information, Alain Peyrefitte—the same man who had told the National Assembly that the purpose of the new law was to free the ORTF from government control—stated that, in view of the virtual monopoly of the printed press by De Gaulle critics, television might properly provide a counterbalance by favoring the General.[14] Needless to say, the opposition parties did not accept this theory of the role of the ORTF. But during the presidential election of December 1965 the rival candidates were given air time as never before; and even though they still complained about their treatment, one foreign reporter wrote: "It is something quite new for French people to have five challengers for the presidency, during the lunch hour and at night, dominating the screen with an incessant attack on the regime."* . . .

The Netherlands

Broadcasting in the Netherlands is unusual for its division of program responsibilities among several private independent broadcasting societies, all coordinated by a public foundation made up of government and private representatives.[15] Between 1920 and 1926, in recognition of the social potentialities of radio, certain religious and political groups set up their own broadcasting organizations. Each obtained a concession from the government, and after an initial conflict, air time was divided under a law of 1930, the four larger groups getting equal shares whereas the smaller groups received a total of seven hours per week.

---

*London *Times*, December 2, 1965, p. 10; *Variety*, December 1, 1965, p. 23; *New York Times*, January 26, 1966, p. 5. . . .
    Rather than draw hasty conclusions about the influence of government on broadcasting from a literal reading of legal documents, one must examine these situations in their national settings. Thus, the BBC and the ITA are two public corporations generally agreed to be quite free of government control. Yet the British government may appoint or dismiss the governors of the BBC at will; revoke its charter for "reasonable cause"; assign or withhold radio frequencies and television channels; determine the amount of money payable by the Treasury to the Corporation; nationalize the BBC in an emergency; or revoke its license for unsatisfactory performance. The postmaster general may, if he wishes, dismiss members of the Independent Television Authority and review the Authority's accounts. The Television Act of 1964 devotes several pages to program standards; furthermore, under the terms of the act, the government has laid down strict regulations for advertising. The British government has the authority to initiate or veto programs on both BBC and ITA. The BBC license states that the Corporation, "whenever so requested by any Department" of the government, is to broadcast "any announcement . . . which such Department may request." (*1962 Licence*, Sec. 15 (3).) There is a similar requirement in the Television Act of 1964 which established the ITA. (*Television Act 1964*, Sec. 18 (1-4).) See also Paulu, *British Broadcasting in Transition*, pp. 15-16 and 39-40.

Early in 1947 the five organizations then in existence joined to found the Nederlandsche Radio Unio (NRU), and agreed to administer jointly their buildings, studios, technical equipment, and music and record libraries. The NRU also controlled such combined units as orchestras, choirs, and a drama repertoire company; standardized the conditions of employment and social benefits for all personnel; and assumed responsibility for regional broadcasting at home and liaison with broadcasting organizations abroad. Each society, however, remained responsible for its own programs, although machinery was set up for coordinating their output.

Television experimentation began in the Netherlands as far back as the 1920's, some of it under the auspices of the world-famous Philips electronics firm in Eindhoven.[16] After World War II experiments were resumed privately, being taken over in 1951 by the Netherlands Television Foundation (NTS), established in that year by the five broadcasting societies to coordinate television as the NRU did radio.

Although commercial television has been earnestly discussed in a number of European countries, the Netherlands is the only place where it led to the resignation of the Cabinet.[17] In 1961 a bill was introduced into the Dutch Parliament providing for a second television network with commercial support, after the pattern of the British Independent Television Authority. Parliament did approve a second television network, but only on a noncommercial basis. On November 12, 1962, the government introduced another commercial television proposal, this time suggesting that one third of the second network's programs be provided by the already existing noncommercial NTS, with a commercial concessionaire responsible for the remaining two thirds. When a third network was eventually set up, it would be assigned entirely to the NTS, with the commercial contractor then taking over all of the second network. Anticipating objections, such safeguards as profit limitations and requirements for high-quality programming were provided. But this proposal too was rejected.

Debates over commercial television in the Netherlands raised the same issues as elsewhere. There was disagreement about whether the introduction of advertising would raise or lower program quality. A lobby, known as OTEM, made up of various banks, newspapers, and industrialists seeking a commercial television concession, was organized to support the proposal. However, except for the few newspapers with financial interests, the press opposed commercial television, anticipating a loss of revenue and fearing that some of the smaller newspapers, holding minority viewpoints, might thereby be eliminated. The four larger broadcasting societies opposed the pro-

posal bitterly: they had entered radio forty years before in recognition of the social importance of broadcasting, and they did not
want to lose or share control now. At the same time, other groups
in the population objected to the current arrangements, feeling that
they were inadequately represented in the programming. An important factor on the side of commercial television was the favorable
audience reaction to TV Noordsee, the short-lived commercial station
which was suppressed in 1964.

On February 27, 1965, the Netherlands government resigned
after a week of crucial meetings could not produce agreement on
radio and television policy, including the possibility of advertising.[18]
At that point the Liberal party and some Protestant ministers were
advocating a limited form of commercial television, whereas other
clergymen, though willing to accept advertising, objected to having
private contractors produce any programs. Fears that the existing
broadcasting societies might be discriminated against were another
factor in the fall of the Cabinet.

In June 1965, the new government issued a memorandum on
broadcasting, which, after being debated in Parliament, led to the
promulgation, effective December 1, 1965, of a transitional radio
and television system, pending the passage of a definitive act.[19] It
continued the division of major program responsibilities among the
existing broadcasting societies, while opening the possibility of
licensing new organizations. In April 1966, a draft bill was submitted
to Parliament. This was passed in the Second Chamber on January 18,
1967, and in the First Chamber on February 28, 1967, and is expected to take effect not later than 1968.

The new law continues the country's traditional dependence on
broadcasting societies as the main source of programs, while reorgan-
izing the coordinating body and introducing advertising as a supplementary source of revenue.[20] General responsibility for broadcasting
rests, as before, with the Minister of Social Welfare and Culture.
Through a commissioner appointed by and responsible to him, he is
in ultimate control of programming, though he has no right of prior
censorship. In theory, this commissioner has extensive supervisory
powers: He can attend the meetings of the Netherlands Broadcasting
Foundation and its principal management (but not program) committees; he can inspect programs; and he has limited disciplinary
authority over the people who present them. It is expected, however,
that these powers will seldom be used.

The two previous radio and television organizations—the Netherlands Radio Union (NRU) and the Netherlands Television Foundation (NTS)—are merged into the Netherlands Broadcasting Foundation (Nederlandse Omroep Stichting, or NOS).[21] The president of

the Foundation is appointed by the crown on the advice of the
government, as are a quarter of the members of the general board.
Another quarter are appointed by various cultural and social organizations after consultation with the Minister of Culture, and the remaining half are nominated by the broadcasting societies. A Board
of Directors, consisting of the President and six members of the
Council (three from the broadcasting societies, two from the cultural organizations, and one representing the crown members) is
responsible for day-to-day decisions. They are assigned, respectively,
to general affairs, technical affairs, financial affairs, personal affairs,
regional broadcasting, radio programming, and television programming. There are separate program councils for radio and television,
one third of the members of each being nominated by the broadcasting societies, one third by the cultural organizations, and one third
by the government. The NOS coordinates over-all program output,
is in charge of broadcasting properties, directs domestic regional
broadcasting, and represents Dutch broadcasting in its relations
abroad, including the exchange of programs with foreign countries.

The new act liberalizes the conditions under which new and
minority groups receive air time. It categorizes broadcasting societies
according to size (over 400,000, 250,000, and 100,000 members,
respectively) and recognizes the claims of other interested groups,
such as churches and political parties, for occasional broadcast periods. To be eligible, an applicant society must meet certain standards: its main purpose must be to do radio or television broadcasting; it must be prepared to present a complete and balanced schedule
covering all kinds of subjects; it must not be commercially oriented;
and it must have at least 15,000 license holders as members or contributors. The NOS itself is directly responsible for at least 15 per
cent of the radio and 25 per cent of the television time, though its
maximum total is not to exceed 40 per cent. Most of the remaining
time is assigned to the large broadcasting organizations in the ratio
of 5:3:1, although there are guarantees of limited air time for some
other groups.

Six such societies are now active: the Algemene Vereniging
Radio Omroep (AVRO), of no definite leanings; the Katholieke
Radio Omroep (KRO), Catholic; the Nederlandse Christelijke Radio
Vereniging (NCRV), Protestant; the Omroepvereniging (VARA),
Socialist; the Vrijzinnig Protestantse Radio Omroep (VPRO), liberal
Protestant; and the newest society, the Televisie en Radio Omroep
Stichting (TROS), which was admitted May 11, 1966, and started
broadcasting October 1, 1966. These are very large organizations:
their total membership of more than two million constitutes 20 per

cent of the entire population of the country and more than 50 per cent of all Dutch families.*

The four main societies must devote some of their time to programs of general interest not limited to their specific points of view, including the news service and other general information programs. Time also is allotted to churches, which are authorized to transfer production responsibility to organizations appointed or created for that purpose. Some Protestant churches assign responsibility to the IKOR (the Radio and Television Commission of the Ecumenical Council of Churches), the CVK (Convention of other Protestant Churches), and the Humanist Confederation. The RKK (Roman Catholic Association) is responsible for Roman Catholic broadcasts. Broadcasting time also is allocated to the RVU (University of the Air), to the National Art Collections Foundation, and to the Foundation for the Promotion of Social and Cultural Aims via Television and Radio (SOCUTERA). Nine of the ten political parties represented in the Netherlands Chamber of Deputies are allowed to broadcast, including—since 1965—the small Communist party.

From 1924 to 1940, broadcasting was supported entirely by the broadcasting societies, which depended upon contributions from their members, but after World War II they began to share the receipts from receiver licenses with the Postal Administration. They also received some income from their program journals, all of which carry advertising. Under the new law, broadcasting budgets are submitted to the government through the responsible minister, and when approved, funds are allocated from the traditional sources listed above as well as from advertising.

The current Dutch system is too new to be judged. On paper, however, it has certain advantages over the previous arrangements. For one thing, it minimizes the role of the older broadcasting societies, making it possible for new groups, representing new interests and points of view, to become active. It simplifies coordination, by centralizing responsibility in a single organization. Finally, the additional income from advertising will provide more resources, particularly important as additional television program hours place even greater demands upon the producing organizations.†

*The *Manchester Guardian Weekly* characterized the five older societies as follows: "One staunchly Socialist, one properly Protestant, one militantly Catholic, one implicitly Conservative, and one (the smallest and some say the brightest) liberally non conformist." (February 4, 1960, p. 5.)

†Since the possibility of commercial support for broadcasting was the key issue that brought down the Cabinet in 1965, the new arrangement deals at length with broadcast advertising . . .

PRIVATE CORPORATIONS

Namurois describes the broadcasting organizations of Italy, Sweden, and Switzerland as "partnerships of public authorities and private interests."* Legally, these are private corporations in which the government, sometimes together with private interests, holds stock while reserving certain ultimate control powers. Thus, the government may take a part of the capital for itself; it may insist that private stockholders be nationals of the country; it may retain more voting power than its stockholdings merit; and it may control a certain number of seats on the board of directors, often sufficient to ensure a majority. Some of these companies—that in Sweden, for example—actually have provided some profit returns for private stockholders. The broadcasting organizations of Italy, Sweden, and Switzerland are examples of private corporations over which ultimate control is exercised, in theory at least, by their respective governments

Italy

The Italian Postal and Telecommunications Code stipulates that broadcasting services belong to the state, which may operate them directly or delegate them by special agreement.† Accordingly, Italy's first broadcasting organization, Unione Radiofonica Italian, a limited company, was set up in 1924 for six years. This was succeeded in 1927 by Ente Italiano Audizioni Radiofoniche, with a twenty-five-year franchise, which changed its name to Radio Audizioni Italia (RAI) in 1944. In 1952 the charter was rewritten to include television and extended to 1972. In 1954, with the inauguration of a regular television service, the name of the company was changed to RAI-Radio-televisione Italiana. The present concession gives RAI a monopoly of all radio and television broadcasting in Italy as well as control of program distribution by wire.

Legally RAI is a private corporation whose relations with the

---

*Such an organization, he says, is "a private corporate entity whose purposes are to serve the public interest, and which on that account enjoys the organic participation of the public authorities and is accordingly subject to regulations which depart somewhat from those of ordinary commercial or civil law." (Namurois, *The Organization of Broadcasting*, p. 78, hereafter cited as Namurois.) Terrou and Solal put Italian broadcasting in the category of "enterprises taking the form of commercial companies." (Terrou and Solal, *Legislation for Press, Film, and Radio*, p. 163, hereafter cited as Terrou and Solal.)

†The following reasons are given for the state broadcasting monopoly: It avoids the private monopoly which would result from the scarcity of wave lengths if broadcasting were done privately; it guarantees service to all parts of the country including lightly populated areas where private commercial broadcasting might not be economically feasible; and it provides better guarantees of impartial and objective programming than would private enterprise. (RAI, *This is RAI*, pp. 1-2; Namurois, pp. 79-82; RAI, *RAI*.)

Italian government are regulated by a contract. The majority of its shares belong to the Istituto per la Ricostruzione Industriale (Institute for Industrial Recovery, or IRI), the government agency administering most of the state's holdings in industrial, commercial, and banking concerns. The remaining shares are privately held.

RAI is constituted so that the government is assured of being able to control its policies and procedures. The majority of stock in the general meeting of shareholders must be held by the government agency, IRI, so that the government is certain of a majority of the votes. Thirteen of the twenty members of the board of managers are elected by that general meeting, and the other seven appointed by various government ministries. Although the board of managers may elect its own chairman and vice chairman (from its members), as well as the managing director and director general of the company, all these appointments must be approved by the minister of posts and telecommunications after consultation with the council of ministers. There also is a board of auditors presided over by an official of the state general accounting office. Furthermore, the constitution and rules of the company must be approved by the minister of posts and telecommunications, after consultation with the special parliamentary committee set up to supervise RAI.

In addition to these direct administrative controls, RAI is required to submit its program plans for quarterly approval by the Ministry of Posts and Telecommunications, which, however, is expected to be guided by a committee in determining cultural, artistic, and educational policies. The 1952 charter gives the government some controls over news programs, "which might prejudice international relations or the good name of the state, or general interest." There is a parliamentary committee of thirty members, representing both houses and all parties, whose function it is to ensure political independence and news objectivity. On the technical side, the Ministry of Posts and Telecommunications must approve in advance all major technical installations and alterations, as well as supervise their performance, although RAI operates its own transmitting facilities. Finally, financial, administrative, and accounting checks are provided by the Treasury, the Ministry of Posts and Telecommunications, and the state auditing office. (RAI revenues consist of the proceeds from license fees, as well as receipts from radio and television advertising.)

Internally RAI is departmentalized for administration, radio programming, television programming, news, radio engineering, television engineering, and foreign relations. There also are service departments for personnel, building, research, and technical studies, as well as the Telescuola Center. The latter, incidentally, has been given a measure of independence from other program activities since its head reports to the director general, rather than to the director of television programming.

In 1956, a private company challenged the RAI monopoly by applying to the Ministry of Posts and Telecommunications for permission to develop a commercial television service.[22] In the ensuing case before the Constitutional Court in 1960, the company argued that because the Italian Constitution of 1947 guarantees all men freedom of expression through all media, as well as freedom for the arts, sciences, and private enterprise, the state cannot monopolize broadcasting. In opposition, however, RAI maintained that the Constitution also authorizes the operation by the state, "in the general interest," of certain activities involving "essential public utilities" or "monopoly situations" which are "preeminently a public service." In its decision the court ruled against the private company, reasoning that because of the limited number of channels, television is in the "monopoly situations" category; that it is "preeminently a public service"; and that reasons of "general interest" justify a state monopoly.*

The decision also pointed out, however, that the monopoly status of RAI carried with it an obligation to make air time available to all points of view. Article 2597 of the Civil Code, in fact, requires that anyone operating a statutory monopoly is legally obliged to give equal treatment to all.[23] The court even went so far as to state that the situation required additional legislation to that effect.

In view of the potential for government control built into the RAI legal structure, it is important that the government leave the organization freedom of operation, if that is its intention. Some critics, however, have claimed that the Italian government often has gone in the opposite direction. Using its authority to name the principal RAI officers, the Catholic-oriented Christian Democratic party, long dominant in Italian politics, usually assigns these positions to party members. It also has been claimed that, in the years since the decision, neither the government nor RAI has done what it could to bring more points of view to the air.† But a review of RAI operations

---

*The decision applied to television broadcasting only, but it is likely the same reasoning would have been applied to radio if the RAI radio monopoly also had been questioned.

†One critic ended his analysis of RAI operations with this statement: "The conclusion to which an attentive observer is inevitably led on assiduous observation of the production of the Italian radio and television is then that a good technical and artistic level shadows but cannot hide the central problem of free expression, which remains unresolved. Only an independent Authority, directly responsible for its production and organizationally pluralistic can satisfy the requisites of objectivity and wealth of information, of cultural vitality and liberty, and of recreational shows of dignity and intelligence, which are the very foundations of a forward looking democratic society." (Cesare Mannucci, "Structure and Policy of the RAI–TV," *Gazette*, 11 (No. 1):67 (1965).)

leads to the conclusion that, on the whole, the system works well. The range of offerings is wide, and in addition to much fine educational and cultural material includes many political and controversial programs which the government would suppress if it wanted to. Perhaps the best comment was provided by the staff member who remarked that, while Italy's RAI may not be as free as Britain's BBC, in view of Italy's Fascist background, RAI is very free indeed, and is making steady progress in the right direction.

Four other corporations are directly associated with RAI. The first is ERI—Edizioni RAI-Radiotelevisione Italiana—RAI's own publishing company, which produces the weekly program guide, *Radio Corriere-TV*, and many program bulletins and brochures, in addition to small luxury editions of art books and similar publications. The second, SIPRA—Societa Italiana Pubblicita Radiofonica Anonima—of which ERI and RAI are the sole shareholders, handles all radio and television advertising. The third is SACIS—Società Per Azioni Commerciale Iniziative Spettacolo—the RAI agent for the rental and purchase of films for television; and it conducts all RAI negotiations with the commercial film industry, including the rental of feature films. The fourth, TELESPAZIO, created in October 1961, operates an experimental satellite receiving station and is responsible for the reception of signals for both telephone and television communications.

Sweden

Sveriges Radio is a limited-liability company with a monopoly of radio and television broadcasting in Sweden. Supplementing the Articles of Association which constitute the company is an agreement with the government about programming. Operation of the transmitters and connecting links, however, is a responsibility of the Telecommunications Administration. Sveriges Radio also is in charge of broadcasts for listeners abroad, as well as of the preparation of transcriptions for use in other countries.

Although broadcasting in Sweden grew out of the activities of various amateur radio clubs, it has been the monopoly of a single company since 1925.[24] Sveriges Radio, as it has been called since 1956, is a private corporation, in which, unlike the situation in Italy, the state has no stock. Ownership of shares must be one-fifth by the press; three-fifths by large national organizations and popular movements; and one-fifth by business and industrial interests. None of the shares are held by individuals. The board of governors consists of a chairman, ten other members, and ten alternates chosen to represent various cultural, social, administrative, economic, and technical interests. The government appoints the chairman and half the board members and alternates, the others being elected by the stockholders at the annual general meeting.

Conditions for broadcasting are governed by an agreement between Sveriges Radio and the government, which runs for five years and is automatically renewed in the absence of notice to the contrary. The government reserves the right to allocate license revenues through the Ministry of Communications, and to determine the number of broadcasting hours. Programs must inform, instruct, and entertain; be objective, impartial, and varied; and be presented with full regard for the potential of broadcasting in the cultural and social life of the nation. There is a government-appointed broadcasting council of twenty-four members which reports to the minister of communications once a year. It is to exercise retrospective surveillance over programs, and to make certain that Sveriges Radio lives up to the terms of the broadcasting agreement, but it has no powers of censorship, and it cannot give any kind of directives either to the director general or the board of governors. It also deals with complaints about the program service. Commercial broadcasting is prohibited, and, except for the right of certain state authorities to make announcements of great importance to the public, the corporation acknowledges no outside claims on program time.

Although the board of governors is the final authority within Sveriges Radio, it is concerned with general policy rather than day-to-day problems, ultimate responsibility for the latter being vested in the director general, who is appointed by the board. Under him are separate radio and television organizations, each with its own program director, as well as heads for music, drama, overseas broadcasts, publications, talks, administration, and technical services. The central news room, which provides basic material for both radio and television, reports to the director general.

To make long-range plans a government commission was appointed in 1960 to study the growth and financing of radio, its assignment being extended in 1962 to include television.[25] On April 7, 1965, the commission published a 750-page report, which soon came to be regarded as the Swedish counterpart of the British *Pilkington Report*. The committee recommended that Sveriges Radio be transformed into a foundation, the nearest practical equivalent in Swedish law to the public corporation encountered in many countries; that the board of governors be reduced to half its present size; and that the organization be generally streamlined. However, Parliament rejected the first two proposals. Various suggestions were made for restructuring the program departments: One was the further development of regional broadcasting centers, and another a compre hensive plan for three day-long radio services. In addition, a second television network was proposed beginning in 1968, although this will not begin until 1970. Special attention was given to educational programs for both radio and television. Other proposals concerned financial matters and it was suggested that, although advertising was barred, radio licenses be abolished and total costs borne by an increased television license.

The committee recommended against advertising, but the subject of commercial broadcasting came up during public discussion of the committee's report, partly because of the development of pirate stations in the vicinity of Sweden. There are pressures for and against commercial television and it would not be surprising to find it emerging in Sweden as it has in other countries. If the pressures for it become strong, however, Sveriges Radio probably would react sympathetically, in order to put itself in a position of influence and control. All things considered, Sweden seems an outstanding example of a country which allows its broadcasting services operational freedom, even though its laws contain the potential for government control.

NOTES

1.   François Pigé, *La Télévision dans le Monde—Organisation Administrative et Financière.* (Paris: Société Nationale des Entreprises de Presse, 1962), p. 58; Fernand Terrou and Lucien Solal, *Legislation for Press, Film, and Radio* (Paris: Unesco, 1951), pp. 179–186.

2.   London *Times,* March 9, 1961, p. 11; London *Times,* February 23, 1962, p. 10; London *Times,* May 16, 1962, p. 10; *New York Times,* February 8, 1963, p. 1; London *Times,* February 8, 1963, p. 8; *New York Times,* February 21, 1963, p. 8; London *Times,* February 12, 1963, p. 10; London *Times,* July 11, 1963, p. 8; London *Times,* April 24, 1964, p. 10; *Variety,* May 13, 1964; *Listener,* February 20, 1958, p. 309; *Economist,* March 2, 1963, p. 785.

3.   Wilson P. Dizard, *Television: A World View* (Syracuse: Syracuse University Press, 1966), pp. 143, 145.

4.   France. *National Assembly Debates,* May 26, 1964, pp. 1376–1379.

5.   *Ibid.,* p. 1379.

6.   London *Times,* May 22, 1964, p. 10.

7.   France. *National Assembly Debates,* May 28, 1964, p. 1509.

8.   *Office de Radiodiffusion-Télévision Française: Statuts, Régime Financier, Comités de Programmes* (hereafter cited as *Statuts*), Art. 1; "A New Statute for the French Broadcasting Organization," *EBU Review,* 87B:33–35 (September 1964).

9.   *Statuts,* Art. 2.

10. *Ibid.,* Art. 3.

11. *Ibid.,* Art. 6.

12. *Ibid.*, Art. 8.

13. *Décret no. 64-740 du juillet 1964;* Albert Namurois, *Problems of Structure and Organi* zation of Broadcasting in the Framework of Radiocommunications (Geneva: European Broadcasting Union, 1964), pp. 101–102.

14. *Le Monde,* May 4, 1965, p. 6.

15. "The Origin, Development and Present Organization of Sound and Television Broadcasting in the Netherlands," *EBU Review,* 48B:9–11 (April 1958); Namurois, pp. 46–47, 54; Terrou and Solal, p. 199; NRU Press Service, *The Netherlands Radio Union in the Evolution of Dutch Broadcasting* (Heuvellaan, the Netherlands, n.d.); Walter B. Emery, *Five European Broadcasting Systems,* Journalism Monographs No. 1 (Austin, Texas: Association for Education in Journalism, 1966), pp. 21–38. Information also was received from the Dutch broadcasting authorities.

16. *Televisie Nieuws,* No. 6:1 (1962).

17. A. J. J. Van der Made, "The Netherlands: Proposals for Commercial Television," *EBU Review,* 78B:35–36 (March 1963); "The Second Television Programme in the Netherlands," *EBU Review,* 89B:14–16 (January 1965); John Tebbel, "How Europe Fights Commercial TV," *Saturday Review,* August 1965, pp. 46–47; Pigé, pp. 84–86; *Televisie Nieuws,* No. 2: 4–5 (1962).

18. *New York Times,* February 27, 1965, p. 6; *New York Times,* March 3, 1965, p. 6; London *Times,* February 27, 1965, p. 8.

19. J. van Santbrink, "Legislation and the Broadcasting Institutions in the Netherlands, Part II: The Transitional System (1965) for Sound Broadcasting and Television in the Netherlands," *EBU Review,* 102B:53–59 (March 1967).

20. *Televisie Nieuws,* No. 4:1–4 (1967).

21. Information for this section was provided by the Dutch broadcasting authorities.

22. "RAI Monopoly Tested in the Constitutional Court," *EBU Review,* 63B:38–39 (September 1960); Paolo Greco, "Monopoly in Television Broadcasting Services and Freedom of Expression," *EBU Review,* 64B:29–34 (November 1960).

23. Cesare Mannucci, "Structure and Policy of the RAI-TV," *Gazette* 11 (No. 1):57–67 (1965).

24. Namurois, pp. 54, 82, 93, 108; *EBU Review,* 60B:23–24 (March 1960); Olof Rydbeck "Broadcasting in Sweden," *EBU Review,* 80B:6–10 (July 1963); Terrou and Solal, pp. 197–199; Sveriges Radio Aktiebolag (Articles of the Association).

25. Ingemar Lindblad, "The Future of Swedish Broadcasting," *EBU Review,* 92B:15–18 (July 1965).

What Public Television Can Be: Japan's NHK*

BERNARD KRISHER

BERNARD KRISHER is Newsweek's Tokyo Bureau Chief. He has been a Newsweek correspondent since 1962 and bureau chief since 1966.

I was first introduced to NHK, Japan's mammoth public radio and TV empire, on my arrival in Japan a decade ago and have more or less lived with it since and seen my children grow up with it. Even from a Western point of view—Japanese tastes are quite different from ours—one cannot deny that it is probably the best public television organization in the world. At its best it is superb and at its worst, still not bad.

The network maintains two TV channels, one general and the other educational, both operating eighteen hours a day and reaching 97 percent of the nation's 23 million TV set owners. The general network broadcasts its entire schedule in color; the educational channel telecasts three hours in color per day. In addition, NHK operates two nationwide AM radio networks and one for FM. The general network devotes 36 per cent of its schedule to cultural programs, 32.5 per cent to news, 22 per cent to entertainment, and 9 per cent

---

*Reprinted from the *Columbia Journalism Review,* July/Aug. 1972, p. 21–25, copyrighted. Used by permission.

to education; the educational channel, 80 per cent to education, 18 per cent to culture, and 1.7 per cent to news.

NHK's general programs appear on Channel 1 in Tokyo; its educational programs, on Channel 3. A typical day on Channel 3 begins at 6 a.m. with a middle-level English conversation course, followed by lectures on American history, industrial development, agriculture, a French language class, and a "Mother's Study Room." From 9 until 3:30, some twenty different twenty-minute programs are telecast for classroom use. After 3:30, there are French, English, German, Spanish, Russian, and Chinese language programs, violin lessons, general science programs, high-school correspondence course lectures, college-level lectures, and programs for the deaf and handicapped.

Channel 1's programs are geared to a wider audience, with prime-time cultural presentations which commercial U.S. TV might push into a Sunday afternoon slot. Most popular are the dramas, including a costly feudal-age costume series based on an ancient literary masterpiece. In the longer historical series, Japanese culture is stressed and all the violence is removed. Oddly enough, these less violent, low-key dramas are more popular with NHK's mature audiences than the more "exciting" *samurai* dramas on commercial TV. (Overall, however, in prime time commercial TV receivers usually exceed those watching NHK, except for news.)

NHK spares no cost to bring first-class *kabuki, noh,* and *bunraku* productions into millions of homes in prime time. It has its own 120-member symphony orchestra, the oldest and one of the finest in Japan. To introduce foreign culture, it regularly imports award-winning scholars for invitational lecture tours which are telecast and broadcast. These have included Ralph Bunche, Wernher von Braun, and, last year, John Kenneth Galbraith. In addition, the network sponsors and televises concert-hall events such as the New York City Ballet Company (in 1960).

On New Year's Eve, NHK features a three-hour talent show, now so important that a decision to invite a performer or drop one can make or break his career. The general network also has numerous "hobby" programs, from cooking to handicrafts and dressmaking. A current program with high rating teaches computer operation.

NHK's popular audience-participation *Japanese Folksong Festival* also should be mentioned. The show's master of ceremonies, Teru Miyata, will go to a local town, rent the city hall, import some talent from Tokyo, and recruit local performers. Before the show goes on the air, he will have thoroughly immersed himself in the lore and legend of the town or county, and then surprise the audience with his knowledge of local customs. Because the Japanese maintain a fantastic interest in customs and legends, the program boasts one of the highest ratings.

But what NHK probably is best at is news. On fast-breaking stories such as the 1970 hijacking of a Japan Air Lines' jet to North Korea, or a police siege of a mountain lodge where militant radical students kept the lodgekeeper's wife hostage for a week, NHK excels. In both cases movable color vans were at the scene in less than an hour, telecasting live with intelligent commentary. During the incident, which lasted for five days, TV cameras followed the plane almost from the moment of hijacking to the various airports where it stopped before moving to Korea. When the plane landed in Seoul, Korea, an NHK crew was waiting, and when the plane returned to Japan from North Korea, NHK telecast it.

NHK has no Cronkites, Huntleys, or Brinkleys. The announcers and commentators are not particularly attractive—they are rather serious-looking, unsmiling, self-controlled officials—and the news is always serious. Top attention is focused on what President Nixon or Prime Minister Sato said; a light feature rarely gets into the regular newscast. Economic-growth figures, passage of budgetary bills, and the like also get big play. (Japan has no Vietnam, no busing, no race problem, so "economics" is big news.)

As the news is spoken, Japanese ideogram headlines are superimposed on the screen. This is "to strengthen the impression on the audience," explains a news editor, adding that the Japanese language has so many words with similar pronunciation that unless one *sees* the word as well as hears it there is room for misinterpretation. Superimposed headlines often add greater detail or statistical information to the spoken report.

While U.S. and European stations cull much of their news from the wire services and newspapers, NHK's domestic news is all staff-reported: it has some 1,000 reporters in Japan—a larger news staff than any domestic newspaper or news service. "All our reporting is our own," says Shuji Tanuma, deputy director of news. "We feel it's too dangerous to depend on outside sources or even on the independent judgment of one announcer or newscaster. Our news is the result of organized and group reporting."

Nearly a dozen times a week, NHK also presents a unique Japanese TV forum called the *zadankai*, or roundtable discussion. Whenever a newsbreak occurs or a trend emerges—an assassination abroad, an earthquake, a famous novelist's suicide, an election, a moonshot—a variety of experts will be summoned to the NHK studios to discuss the subject. The most interesting *zadankai* is the *Political Forum* every Sunday morning, featuring representatives of the ruling Liberal-Democratic Party and the four opposition parties, including the Communist Party. The program not only gives NHK's vast audience an opportunity to see and hear the spectrum of politic views but serves another, hidden purpose—to keep the politicians of NHK's back. Another program allows listeners to let off steam and comment on programming.

Two very popular programs, *Hello, Madam* and *Notebook for Women,* feature well known newscasters and discuss topics of interest to housewives. There have been memorable thirty-minute or hour long segments where a camera focuses on a painter or calligrapher as he slowly creates a work of art, or a master at flower arranging or the tea ceremony, zen-like, shows his or her special skill, with rare, lengthy long moments of silence. *Sumo* tournaments, four times a year, run uninterrupted for hours, and special parliamentary debates are telecast in full, sometimes for ten hours at a time. No other network—public or commercial—anywhere in the world does that!

Since 1969, NHK also has been a formal part of Japan's national electoral process. The Ministry of Home Affairs sets a maximum TV time limit for candidates for each national office, then pays for the time—$66,667, for example, in connection with last year's upper-house elections. The candidate, in turn, pledges not to criticize other candidates by name in his talk, not to use the telecast to advertise his own business or profession, and not to endorse other candidates. Broadcast times are decided through lottery.

NHK commentators seldom are involved in controversy. They do not take positions; they simply "analyze" the news. The only sharp opinions NHK allows are those heard on roundtable discussion where one opinion can be immediately challenged by an opponent. NHK is so conscious of the vast public it serves that the former president, Hideo Nomura, even issued an edict that murder scenes could not be shown. The present president, Yoshinori Maeda, rescinded that, but the network is firm on the law and order issue. When novelist Yukio Mishima committed ritual suicide after attempting to persuade a group of Self Defense Forces members to revolt, NHK called him "Mishima," without the usual *san* (Mr.), relegating him to the status of criminal.

The lack of controversy on NHK—the network, for example, would never create a documentary like *The Selling of the Pentagon*— is attributed by one official to the belief that "the Japanese people expect balance from us—not advocacy." Kazushige Hirasawa, who has been an NHK commentator for twenty-three years and writes for the *Japan Times* and other publications, concedes that on NHK "I avoid advocacy. It isn't because I have been told to or because NHK is a semi-government or public corporation; I have no restrictions except my own self-restraint. I feel it is my job to explain, not advocate."

What NHK may lack in crusading journalism, it makes up in thorough and often lively documentaries on foreign countries and Japanese localities. One must also credit NHK with being far more internationally oriented than most Japanese and making them look beyond their limited *shima-guni* (island country). Nearly every two weeks a camera crew takes off from Tokyo to prepare an encyclopedic documentary on some distant country. "Recently I was quite impressed by an NHK documentary on Spain," Masumi Muramatsu, a book publisher and Japan's top simultaneous interpreter, told me. "I think it showed Spain with amazing neutrality. There was no brainwashing about Franco, nor were the cards stacked against everything the Government has done. I felt I was really brought up to date on modern Spain." At this writing a three-man team is spending 100 days in Africa to prepare six documentaries.

Since NHK produces all its own programs—some 700 a week—except for a very few imported foreign films and shows, it relies on computers to help producers schedule rehearsals and taping in its twenty-six Tokyo TV studios and another twenty-nine studios elsewhere. The computers also assign crews to the network's 217 black and white and 140 color cameras, sixty-seven broadcasting vans (which can be dispatched to most parts of the nation for fast newsbreaks within an hour), and its 176 videotape recorders. NHK even operates a completely automated studio where cameras can be focused and moved by remote control from an adjoining room.

NHK (for Nippon Hoso Kyokai, or the Japan Broadcasting Corp.) was founded in August, 1926, two years after the first radio signals were emitted in Japan, and it existed as the nation's sole noncommercial radio operation until 1951, when commercial broadcasting was introduced. In 1953 NHK introduced TV to Japan. The network now employs 16,560 persons—1,000 of them reporters and 300 cameramen. In fiscal 1971, NHK collected $336.5 million from the public—or an average of $922,183 a day. Its news budget alone for that period, not including salaries, came to $10.6 million dollars. Of this, $2.3 million went for coverage by its fifty overseas staff members in twenty-five overseas bureaus, including three in the U.S. A total of 125 spots comprising 82 hours, 41 minutes of satellite transmissions were telecast last year.

Ninety-nine per cent of the nation's TV set owners, with barely a protest, diligently pay NHK a fee of $1.05 a month if they own a black and white set; $1.55 for color. Indeed, perhaps the most fascinating aspect of NHK is the almost total acquiescence by the public to payment of its fees. "It is a cultural and historical phenomenon," explains sociologist Hidetoshi Kato. "Our people have been used to paying for broadcasting from the beginning, so everyone has accepted the concept that broadcasting and telecasting are something to be bought, like gas and electricity. There is no legal punishment if you don't pay your fee. There are thousands who don't pay; but the NHK collectors return month after month to persuade them to pay, and finally they get most of these holdouts."

Josaku Yamanaka, who is in charge of collecting fees, says that NHK presently maintains 23.2 million contracts (there are 28 million families in Japan), and only 150,000 to 200,000 persons—or 0.7 per cent of set users—refuse to pay. Even the Emperor, government offices, and NHK employees pay; only handicapped persons, hospitals, and schools are exempt. If reception is poor, NHK technicians attempt to improve it or instruct owners on how to adjust their antennas. NHK also helps settle disputes involving homeowners whose reception is hampered by new high-rise buildings—owners of the high-rises may be asked to erect special antennas and connect them, at their expense, to residents affected in their neighborhood.

At the same time, NHK ceaselessly investigates the life habits of the Japanese at its Public Opinion Research Institute, with the aim of improving its programming. In April, after a study which determined that many Japanese men don't return home until after 7 and go to bed after 10, the schedule was completely revamped, moving the major evening news program from 7 to 9 p.m., devoting the rest of the 9 to 10 p.m. period to news and commentary, and turning the 10 o'clock slot over to drama. Since few children are expected to watch after 10, the programs in this slot may begin treating more adult themes.

One reason why success has been so easy for NHK is that the public has grown up with and remained loyal to public TV, showing a rather condescending view toward the commercial product. Commercial TV is considered vulgar, and NHK, if not always terribly exciting, at least is never coarse or cheap.

NHK's pay and organizational structure are typically Japanese. Staff salaries are modest by U.S. standards, with payment largely based on seniority: a twenty-five-year-old employee earns about $3,400 a year, rising to $5,500 by age thirty-five and $6,300 at forty-five. An addition $15-a-month housing allowance is paid for the 35 per cent not lucky enough to live in the reasonably priced NHK apartments. Top brass and NHK elite employees, like NHK's top announcer, Teru Miyata, may earn as much as $20,000 a year.

Such a rigid bureaucracy—built on seniority, where young men wait decades before they can make waves and then may be too old to have much spark left—creates some stagnation. "NHK," complains

Keita Asari, one of Japan's most talented theatrical producers, "is a mammoth organization in the sense of financing and structure, where 3,000 capable young people are in despair. . . . It is an organization where no dreams and desires exist; only those who are tamed and domesticated have a chance at promotion. . . ."

Some TV critics, like Nobuo Shiga, also complain that NHK's programming is *kohei churitsu,* too fair and neutral; that its "stars" are bland; that "news commentators are talking machines without personalities." Intellectuals and TV critics aside, however, the majority of Japanese accept NHK's style—and NHK knows its audience.

Within its chosen parameters, NHK's independence seems assured. Its president is appointed by the Prime Minister, and the network theoretically is supervised by the Postal Minister, but it maintains considerable independence since its income flows directly from the people. Any government attempt to blackmail NHK into a point of view through financial pressure would surely arouse the public.

Thus the cosmopolitan president, Yoshinori Maeda—fluent in English, French, and Italian, a former newspaper executive, and a former Rome bureau chief of the *Asahi Shimbun*—could take a "high posture" in a recent controversy over capital funds and expansion of services to Okinawa. The Postal Minister tried to dismiss the request by asking Maeda to make economies. Maeda replied that this was impossible—and reminded him that the salary portion of NHK's budget was less than half that of the Postal Ministry's. The Postal Minister publicly rebuked Maeda. Nonetheless, more funds were forthcoming, and the incident didn't hurt Maeda. It only reinforced public confidence in NHK and enhanced the morale of NHK's staff, which tries to convince itself, and the public, that it is vital and independent—the finest public television institution in the world.

Media, Party, and Society in Russia*

MARK W. HOPKINS

MARK W. HOPKINS has been the Milwaukee Journal's
Soviet affairs specialist since 1964. Educated at Middle-
bury College, the University of Wisconsin, and Leningrad
University, he traveled extensively in the Soviet Union
for his newspaper in 1965 and 1967. For his reporting of
Soviet developments, he received an Overseas Press Club
Citation in 1968.

ver since their formative years after the
Bolshevik coup of 1917, the Soviet mass media have been cast as a
"people's press." Soviet newspapers, magazines, radio, and more recently television are the extensions of Everyman. They stand, they
are told, in the rank and file, amplifiers of workers' and peasants'
grievances and aspirations. Their strength, they are reminded, is
drawn from the people, a magical word in Soviet revolutionary tradition and present-day political lexicon that abstracts mankind's
virtues. Almost every issue of *Pravda*, official newspaper of the Soviet
Communist Party, carries a front-page photograph glorifying the com
mon man. The picture might be of a rugged Russian construction
worker against a backdrop of a new factory's steel-latticed super-

---

*Reprinted from *Mass Media in the Soviet Union* by Mark W. Hopkins, copyright © 1970,
by Western Publishing Company, Inc., reprinted by permission of the Bobbs-Merrill Company, Inc.

structure. It might show the soft, pastoral face of a young girl, her hair swathed in a surgical cap, her sparkling eyes intently focused on a chemist's flask. Whoever, the portrait is *Pravda*'s testament to the people, in a now mechanical exercise that is somewhat analogous to the American newspapers' puffs of local civic leaders.

In Soviet editorial offices, the sheer quantity of letters from readers, regardless of content, is considered a measure of the bonds between people and press. Not unlike his American counterpart, the Soviet editor counts it an accomplishment when he has successfully engaged faceless bureaucracy in the cause of a wronged individual. The Soviet journalist's professional ethics are saturated with his responsibility to the people. That Soviet mass media do not always play this role brilliantly, and that they indeed often undertake it with lackluster and even cynicism, does not obscure the fact that in theory they are allied with the masses.

What lends an unreal air to this commitment is the Soviet mass media's role as spokesman for the Communist Party. Even before the Bolshevik Revolution in November, 1917, the Russian revolutionist Vladimir Lenin wielded newspapers as instruments of political leadership and organization in the same way the partisan political press was used here before and after the American Revolution. A newspaper, Lenin wrote in his own revolutionary times, was needed "to concentrate all elements of political dissatisfaction and protest, to fertilize the proletarian revolutionary movement."[1] Joseph Stalin, during his quarter-century rule, made the Soviet mass media virtually a parrot of his thoughts by putting full weight on the partisan political nature of the press. In the hands of the Communist Party and Soviet state, he said, the newspaper was "the means to maintain contacts with the working masses of our country and rally them around the party and the Soviet state."[2] Nikita Khrushchev, though far more sophisticated than Stalin in techniques of persuasion, and more permissive of conflicting opinion, nonetheless had the Soviet politician's penchant for managing news. "As soon as some [Communist Party] decision must be explained or implemented," he told a conference of journalists in Moscow, "we turn to you, and you, as the most trusted transmission belt, take the decision and carry it to the very midst of the people."[3]

From the American vantage point, there is a conflict between the two fundamental roles of the Soviet press. American press theory is weighted with a journalist's obligation to stand somewhere between the people and the government, protecting the former from arbitrary power of the latter. So it seems the crudest hypocrisy for Soviet journalists to speak of their commitment to the people when Soviet mass media issue a torrent of government statements and interpretations of events with rarely a critical objection from journalists

themselves. The standard, not too profound American retort to this
arrangement is that the press cannot serve two masters simultaneousl
Either it is publicist for the government, or voice of the people. Criticism of political leaders then becomes one gauge of the American
mass media's worth as defender of the common man; and the Soviet
mass media's conspicuous refusal or inability to make any but the
most commendable and favorable statements about Soviet political
authorities seems at once proof of a kept press.

Soviet press theory squares the circle. It maintains, in harmony
with general Soviet political ideology, that the people and the govern
ment are one. They have no essential differences of goal. The government—specifically the Communist Party, which remains the
effective government in the Soviet Union—draws its power from
the people. Armed with principles of Marxism-Leninism, as the
Soviet rhetoric goes, the party directs and leads the people in the
building of a new society. If one accepts unanimity of Soviet government and people in objectives and attitudes, it follows that the Sovie
mass media simply circulate information in a homogeneous society.
Or to put it another way, as Soviet theorists do, if a state-owned pres
opposes the government, it simultaneously opposes the people, an
illogical act on the face of it.

To understand more fully Soviet press concepts, forgetting for
a moment what exists in practice, we must touch on Marxist thought
It contends among many things that a given society's institutions
evolve from its economic structure. Government, law, education,
commerce, and the arts are all fashioned by a dominant class. That
class in turn derives its power from ownership of the means of production, and maintains its superior status by manipulating all institutions. Thus, in contemporary Soviet press theory, the American mass
media are described as functionaries of capitalists. Being owners of
newspapers, magazines, radio, and television, capitalists easily manage
public opinion for their own purposes, according to the most bald
Soviet critique. By contrast, it continues, the Soviet mass media are
publicly owned and *a priori* identify with public interests. In the
somewhat stilted Soviet political vocabulary, this view may seem
hopelessly simplified and obsolete. "From the first days of its existence, the Soviet press has served the worker class and expressed the
thoughts and hopes of the broad masses of workers," Soviet journalists are instructed. " . . . The bourgeois press serves the class of capitalists. It is not concerned and by its very nature it cannot be concerned with the interests of the workers, with whom it has no ideological or organizational connections."[4]

The notion of ownership influencing mass media's performance
is by no means alien to American discussions of the press. Propon-

ents of publicly financed television fault commercial broadcasting for catering more to sponsors' wishes than to the needs of the public.[5] Nor is the idea uncommon elsewhere in the West. The publicly owned British Broadcasting Corporation is one ready and conspicuous example of an attempt to free the mass media from undue influence of narrow interest groups.

This, of course, was one stated goal of Bolshevik revolutionaries. But when we survey the structure and operation of the Soviet mass media today, it is apparent that something else exists. Instead of being the independent champion of that mystical and awe-inspiring force called the people, the press is bound to Communist Party and government bureaucracies which oversee the mass media to achieve certain objectives. These are not necessarily to the disadvantage of the mass of the Soviet Union's 239 million people. The Soviet press, for example, is enlisted in campaigns to educate people in basic hygiene. It disseminates information nationwide on new government programs, such as pension or educational reforms, that affect the lives of millions of Soviet citizens. But likewise, and to the disservice of the Soviet population, the mass media deliberately conceal or mis-interpret certain information. They offer virtually no facts or analysis, for instance, on how major decisions are arrived at in the Soviet polit-ical hierarchy. There is no attempt by the Soviet press to judge inde-pendently the qualities of men who direct the nation. Information about the world beyond Soviet borders emerges in the press decidedly and inevitably with a pro-Soviet bias.

This is to say that the Soviet mass media reflect a particular social system in which theory and practice do not always correspond. The Soviet political system falls far short of the democratic socialism that was once envisioned. Under the impact of Lenin's revolutionary doctrines and Stalin's totalitarian practices, Soviet society has been molded into a highly structured, minutely organized society focused on defined goals. The Soviet press, of course, has not been exempt from this process.

However, in assessing the Soviet mass media as they actually exist and function, two factors must be kept in mind. First, the Soviet press is, it should be obvious, one of many institutions in a vast and complex society, and necessarily interacts with all of them. This is not to ignore the fact that the Soviet press is first and fore-most beholden to the Communist Party and government bureaucra-cies, and that all Soviet institutions—government, law, education, industry, commerce, agriculture, and civic organizations—are inter-twined with the Communist Party apparatus. What takes place in Soviet society, however, is an interplay of forces within the estab-lished framework.

The Soviet printed press over the years has been one means by which a predominantly illiterate Soviet population was taught to read, and by which it has acquired much of the information necessary for daily living in a nation being transformed from an agrarian into an industrialized, urban society. Having aided in raising the educational level of its audience, the Soviet press was then challenged to alter its content to appeal to a far more sophisticated and discriminating readership than existed fifty years ago. . . .

As one other instance of the interplay of Soviet mass media with other social institutions, the Soviet press has often taken an active role in the dispensation of justice in Soviet courts. It is not uncommon in ordinary trials (excluding blatantly political trials) for Soviet newspapers to agitate publicly in support of or against the accused, prior to a court judgment. In recent years, however, the Soviet legal profession has turned particular attention to fair trial and impartial adjudication. With this turn in legal ethics, the Soviet press has been berated for generating mob passions and in fact interfering with justice.[6] The demand, if not yet the universal result, is that Soviet mass media assume a more responsible role in educating their audiences in the Soviet legal process.

As these various examples imply, the Soviet press does not exist in a vacuum, nor does it function purely as publicist for the Soviet political establishment. Being pervasive, as well as persuasive, in Soviet society, the mass media's structure and functioning are altered to some degree as other Soviet social institutions change. . . .

Soviet society, particularly its political leaders, places a premium on public harmony and unanimity, regardless of what private controversies or dissensions exist. National goals are characteristically formulated by the Communist Party hierarchy. The Soviet mass media and other social institutions are not always in harmony with particular policies. But where conflict exists, it is moderated if not concealed by the overriding quest of the leadership for public unity. Thus, the Soviet press, while it influences and is influenced by other organizations, offers less public documentation of the interaction than the American mass media. Still, it would be deceptive to say that the interplay is nonexistent simply because it is not always clearly demonstrated.

A second general concept germane to the Soviet press is the unpredictability of the mass media in society. Regardless of the conscious deliberations that went into the formation of the Soviet mass media, they do not always do what is expected of them. Indeed, they have produced unexpected consequences for Soviet social managers.

It takes no special knowledge to recognize that the effects of mass media anywhere are not wholly subject to scientific analysis.

In contemporary times, television has burgeoned into an industry of still incalculable consequences for the political and economic structures of modern, industrial nations. . . . Soviet political leaders have been no more capable of predicting the precise effects of mass media on popular thought and attitudes than anyone else. Generally, in fact, they have held a rather unsophisticated view of what roles the mass media play in society. For a good share of Soviet history, they have looked on the press as a bullhorn, ignoring its more subtle uses in mass persuasion and education, and seemingly unconcerned until recently with the process by which people become aware of and accept new values.

Meanwhile, the Soviet mass media have matured into large, sometimes unwieldy institutions, which within the framework of the highly integrated Soviet society can be said to have an existence of their own. In this view, the Soviet press is not simply a "transmission belt" carrying information and ideas from one point to another, as an apolitical piece of machinery. Rather, Soviet mass media create their own image of Soviet society, and they serve many different functions beyond those traditionally assigned roles as the people's voice and political house organ. . . .

THE SOVIET SCENE

The Soviet mass media are spread over a huge nation covering a sixth of the world's land surface, or about three times the area of the continental United States. The Soviet Union's sheer size has always presented formidable obstacles to development of an effective mass media network. It has meant enormous difficulties in distributing newspapers and magazines, in supplying newsprint and printing equipment—particularly in early years when the Soviet transportation system was small and backward. The Soviet geography has also made radio broadcasting and television costly means of communication. Both radio and television have been dependent in their growth, of course, on the progress of Soviet electrification. As a result, for decades, areas of the country were not reached at all by radio, and huge sections are yet beyond television broadcasts. Television, as highly as it is now prized by the Soviet government as an instrument of mass persuasion, certainly has been retarded because of the expense of constructing transmission systems, whether cables or relay towers.

Added to the Soviet land mass as a physical barrier to enlargement of the press network is the harsh climate of much of the country. This, too, has held back extension of the Soviet transportation system, including highways and rail and air lines, and of electrification, given their costs weighed against other national needs. Thus, dissemination of the printed press, and to some extent the growth of radio and television, have been restricted by conditions over which the Soviet government has no control, or which it has altered only at great cost. These are not profound observations. But in the continental United States we have grown accustomed to a well-developed transportation and distribution system. When discussing mass media, for one thing, we generally ignore the influence geography has on them. The obstacles that Alaska's geography poses to mass communication development are similar to those in a good share of the Soviet Union.

As in Alaska also, the Soviet population is concentrated in a proportionately small area. Only about 10 per cent of the Soviet Union's 239 million people live in Siberia and the far east. Approximately 70 per cent live in the western segment of the country, including the Urals region and the Caucasus. The grouping of the Soviet population obviously somewhat offsets the geographical problem. The bulk of Soviet citizens can be reached by the printed press and radio and TV broadcasting with a network that covers an area roughly equal to that of the continental United States. Of course, building a mass media system in this land area alone has been no minor undertaking; extending the system to encompass the remaining 30 per cent or so of the population has been the especially costly part, and was accomplished in slow stages.

What must also be kept in mind in surveying Soviet mass media is the multi-national character of the country. It is divided into 15 national republics, the Russian Federation being by far the largest. Many nationalities have their own autonomous republic or region within one of the 15 major republics. Of the total Soviet population of 209 million at the 1959 census (the most recent), 114 million, or a little over half, were Russian. There were about 37 million Ukrainians, the second largest nationality group; 8 million Byelorussians; and 16 other nationalities comprising a million or more persons. Beyond these, numbering in hundreds of thousands, sometimes in groups only of hundreds, were about 100 other nationalities.

A persistent and forceful policy of the Soviet government has been to unify these nationalities. Several particularly—Ukrainians, Estonians, Latvians, and Lithuanians—exhibit separatist tendencies to the present day, although their republics are politically and economically integrated with the entire Soviet structure. All the same, two forces are at play. The central government, the Communist Party, is constantly working at national harmony and stability among ethnic groups, which in times past especially has meant Russification of huge regions. On the other hand, various nationalities with old and deep cultural traditions seek to preserve their heritages.

What this has produced, as in the United States though for different reasons, is a multi-national press. All central publications and radio and television programs are produced in Russian, the official national language. However, each republic has its own native language newspapers, magazines, and broadcasting. These are by no means independent of the national government. Indeed, one of the ever-present apprehensions of the central party apparatus is that of native language publications encouraging, or at least not dispelling, nationalistic tendencies.[7] Therefore, whether a newspaper, for instance, is published in Russian or a native language, it is an integral part of the mass media network. Nevertheless, the operation of a national press system in a multi-national country causes certain difficulties. For one, much information, because it is originally transmitted in Russian, must be translated into 57 other languages for newspapers and 44 for magazines.[8] This carries with it the customary risks of distortion and misinterpretation. There is a more subtle issue. To minority nationalities, statements and proclamations from the central government must *sound* Russian, no matter how they are presented by the Soviet mass media. As a means of persuasion, the Soviet press then faces difficulties common to multi-national and multi-racial countries. They might be likened to the American newspapers' difficulty in reaching American Negroes. The newspapers generally are products of another sector of American society—the white middle class—and as a result, their content often is irrelevant to the Negro. The Soviet press, too, may well fail to reach segments of its audience because of cultural differences.

Whatever the Soviet mass media's success in communicating, the multi-national character of the Soviet Union unmistakably influences the performance and structure of the country's press. It ranks with Soviet geography and climate and population distribution as one of the given quantities. So, when we talk about the Soviet mass media in their habitat, it is a misconception to imagine *Pravda* against a background of Red Square and the Kremlin, just as it is misleading to think of the American press in terms of *The New York Times* or NBC-TV against New York's skyscraper silhouette. The Soviet mass media is simultaneously the 4-page, tabloid-size newspaper published in a cotton town in central Asia, the daily Ukrainian language paper in the republic capital of Kiev, the local radio station program in Russian coming from a loudspeaker in a student dormitory at Leningrad University, the Radio Moscow folk music hour drifting out of a shortwave set in the Siberian city of Irkutsk, or finally a color TV broadcast in Moscow itself.

THE SOVIET SYSTEM

To place Soviet mass media, secondly, into some sort of social milieu they function in an often corporate-like atmosphere. The general scheme is a government-managed press; analogously, it is a composite of several mass communications variants or offshoots operating in the United States. Traces of the American corporate public relations function can be detected in the Soviet mass media: the corporation house organ comes very close in terms of purpose and content to Soviet newspapers. Techniques of American advertising, as in the attempt to form opinion through repetition of slogans are present in the Soviet press system. The Soviet press also shares with the American religious and labor press the inclination to judge events from an ideological or class point of view. And in terms of general management and subordination of the mass media to a single directorate, the Soviet press is not unlike—searching for an approximate American counterpart—the United States military base newspaper. But such comparisons are somewhat deceptive right off. The Soviet mass media function in a considerably different political and cultural community than American, of whatever type. If it shares characteristics of a variety of American mass communications, the Soviet press all the same has its own personality traits and eccentricities.

A predominant one is its attachment to the Soviet political establishment. Through interlocking directorates, in which many Soviet journalists are simultaneously editors and Communist Party members, the mass media are in the first instance responsible to the party apparatus, from the very pinnacle to the base. The party appoints and approves newspaper and magazine editors, and radio and television broadcasting managers. Other arrangements further determine the roles and content of the mass media. A censorship agency checks the mass media, not as rigorously as in the past, but it is a restraining influence even if a given editor never seriously errs in his judgments.

There are also purely economic institutions and patterns in Soviet society that shape the press system. All printing plants, printing equipment, newsprint production and allocation, all means of communications (telegraph, radio, cable lines, railroads, trucking, etc.), all press distribution channels, and all communications industries (radio and TV manufacturers, for instance) are state owned. Their general and specific development is part of overall economic plans, along with steel production, housing construction, shoe manufacture, and thousands of other industries. Thus the mass media, like any Soviet enterprise, are intertwined in a vast economic system. Newspaper and magazine budgets are incorporated into a financial sheet of one or another Soviet organization, including the Communist Party. The same is true of radio and television broadcasting. There is no exact counterpart to such economic dependency among American mass media. Perhaps the closest is the American government, which publishes periodicals edited by government employees and printed on government presses at government expense.

Being wholly in the state sector, Soviet mass media are oriented in quite another direction than a press system, such as the American, which is financially allied to a private economy. For example, until the late 1950's, the Soviet press was almost oblivious to costs, to whether it was financially solvent or showed a profit. Even now, many Soviet newspapers are state subsidized, and the broadcasting industry is almost entirely government-financed. Hence, the motivation of Soviet journalists to satisfy audience tastes and demands comes from sources other than monetary. Or, to put it another way, Soviet newspapers have survived, even flourished in terms of circulation, far beyond the point where they would have withered and died in a competitive, private economy.

The Soviet mass media's primary or screening audience in the · past and present alike has been composed of Soviet political managers, the Communist Party apparatus of perhaps 200,000 or 250,000 members who alone among the party's complement of 14 million members function full-time as management for Soviet society. This is not to exclude other significant and influential groups in Soviet society, such as the government ministerial bureaucracy, the military, the industrial managers and economists. They, too, are special audiences of the mass media. Given their importance in Soviet economic and political affairs, they directly or indirectly affect the content and emphasis of the Soviet press. Soviet armed forces, for example, have their own mass media network, which concerns itself primarily with military affairs. A number of Soviet periodicals are devoted predominantly to problems of industrial management, economic theory, finance, and manufacturing.

However, the common denominator in Soviet society is the Communist Party apparatus. In that organization, lines of political and economic authority and responsibility intersect. The party's select politburo formulates major policy, in all spheres, foreign and domestic, political and economic. Clearly, the 11 politburo members are not autonomous. They react to events, as well as initiate policies. They refer, if not defer at times, to the Central Committee, a larger group of party members drawn from provincial party organizations, government administrative agencies, the military, and security police. The politburo works within the framework of reports and counsel from political and economic advisers. Nonetheless, the global decisions rest with the politburo. And multitudes of lesser decisions in the daily political and economic management of the Soviet Union are made in Communist Party committees, from the national Central Committee down to the republic, *oblast, raion,* city, and village levels.

In political matters, the politburo establishes guidelines of Soviet foreign policy, and often enough quite specific policies, much as the American President and his cabinet and advisers deal with foreign crises arising from wars, military provocations, international commerce and finance, and political coups. Within the Soviet Union, the Communist Party apparatus is the dominant and seldom-challenged voice in such inexact matters as cultural policy, literature, arts, and what in a broad sense are national purposes, values, and beliefs. Under these last falls the propagation of Marxism-Leninism as a philosophical interpretation of what makes society change and progress (or regress), of the relationship between the state and the people, the interconnection of economics and politics, of the artistic function in society, or the international function of socialism and communism among other social systems. Being the only Soviet political organization, the Communist Party exercises the power and prerogatives that American corporate management does *within* the corporation, or that the high command does in a military organization. . . .

A POLITICAL PRESS

In many ways, the Soviet journalist occupies a position similar to an American corporate vice-president for public relations or advertising. The Soviet newspaper, because of its involvement with the political system, has an overriding inclination to defend, explain, and promote management's—the party-government apparatus—policies and views. The Soviet editor, himself a member of the management team, is especially concerned that his publication win acceptance from his peers and superiors. This means, of course, that he constantly gauges shifts of thought and emphasis among those who make political and economic decisions, and tries to tailor his publication to parallel these changes.

The Soviet mass media's overall performance is always being judged by the Communist Party apparatus, among other audiences. In turn, the Soviet journalist corps is acutely sensitive to party reactions, much as the American advertising agency account executives are attuned to the likes and dislikes of clients. Or, to draw another comparison (indicated earlier), the Soviet mass media operate somewhat like the newspapers of the American labor unions or religious denominations. These publications, like the Soviet mass communications, are financially dependent on organizations that strive toward particular objectives shaped by a particular ideology. Editors of labor union newspapers are not only predominantly occupied with news and interpretations of the labor movement, but are inherently disposed toward promoting labor, and making value judgments in terms of what is good or bad for labor. Even given the American journalistic ethics that assign priority to factual, impartial reporting of an event, the labor press views developments within American society from a wholly different perspective than does, for example, the large metropolitan newspaper, which has a different audience and economic arrangement. Similarly, the religious press is allied with organizations propagating distinct systems of thought. The religious press, of whatever denomination, is at once a channel of information on theological matters, on administrative questions, and on purely lay issues. Editors of Protestant, Catholic, or Jewish newspapers may quite naturally vary in their interpretations of what is important, of what represents change or progress; but most are not fundamentally in disagreement with the philosophies of their sponsors. Within a general, changing framework of values and beliefs, and within a defined organization, the religious press is sometimes simply a mouthpiece. In other instances, it can be an innovator of ideas and critic of doctrine and authorities.[9]

The Soviet mass media perform in similar circumstances. But to these must be added the fact that the American religious or labor press operates in a pluralistic society. Other segments of mass communications in the United States reflect clearly different values and beliefs. Other special interests—political parties, business, government—as well as the mass popular press, continuously challenge narrow presentations or doctrinally distorted views of American society. The Soviet mass media for most of their history have not had to share the marketplace of ideas. Indeed, they have operated as if no market existed at all. In recent years, however, the Soviet press has started adapting to a sort of international pluralism of ideas. As world communications have expanded, and with development of global broadcasting via satellites, Soviet authorities have become aware of increasing competition from beyond Soviet boundaries. Somewhat like a religious press network, the Soviet mass media are confronted with dissemination of information within the Soviet Union by sources that take substantially different points of view. The most conspicuous examples are radio broadcasts by the United States and Communist China. International TV broadcasting presents even greater problems to Soviet authorities, in their own concern with purity of doctrine, as they look to the future.[10]

The Soviet government more rigidly and successfully restricts the interplay of different ideas among the Soviet people than a given religious organization can among its adherents. But denial of information is achieved only in a society which is severely repressive throughout. In recent years, the Communist Party has tended to emphasize the function of the mass media to counter foreign opinions and information rather than attempt to insulate the Soviet people from other worlds of thought.[11] This is not so much of its own choosing, but rather because in adopting some policies, and recording progress in some areas, the Communist Party has had to react to developments which were unforeseen or minimized. For example, after the Soviet government ceased jamming most foreign radio broadcasts in 1963, there was bound to be a change in Soviet mass media content, depending on the extent of penetration of foreign interpretations of events into Soviet popular thought.

Nonetheless, it is clear that the Soviet press is allied with a political order in Soviet society whereas, by contrast, the mass American press is an adjunct of an industrial order.[12] Therefore, evolution of the Soviet political system paces development of the mass media: the broad national objectives of the political structure simultaneously are those of the press. Soviet society's industrial, agricultural, military, educational, and cultural institutions interact with the mass media, as was proposed earlier, but these institutions also are part of the Soviet political order. The Soviet political structure, in this sense, is not simply the Communist Party apparatus, but the whole governing, decision-making bureaucracy. The central party has a commanding voice in this structure, as the board of directors does in an American corporation, or the chiefs of staff in the armed forces. Its authority has outer limits, defined not so much by regulation or law, though these are factors, but by past practice, by assessments of what is possible in given circumstances, and by generally accepted norms of administration and management. These in turn have been and are being shaped by those large forces operating in a given social structure, such as industrial development, urbanization, and rise of educational levels. The party's dominance in Soviet society has given the Soviet Union certain forms (collectivized agriculture, for instance, and nationalized industry), but the political structure, and the Communist Party apparatus specifically, has not therefore been immune from the effects of its own initiatives and accomplishments.

In this constant evolution and interaction of Soviet social institutions, the Soviet mass media take on assorted political responsibilities and duties. In Soviet writings, these are propounded as principles as American press theory describes performance of the mass media in their own political-economic circumstances. For instance, one Soviet reference for journalists[13] lists the following: (1) Party orientation (*partiinost*), which may be interpreted as conscious acceptance that the press is a politically partisan institution, and that it therefore expresses party philosophy and goals; (2) high level of ideology (*vysokaya ideinost*), which suggests that the mass media should be spiritually reinforced with the ideology of Marxism-Leninism, in perhaps the same way that the Catholic diocesan newspaper should not only reflect interests of the Church, but should be permeated with the spirit of Christianity; (3) truthfulness (*pravdinost*), an obligation to transmit information truthfully; (4) popular orientation (*narodnost*), which reminds the Soviet press of its responsibilities toward the masses, and simultaneously of the people's access to the publicly owned press; (5) mass character (*massovost*), which not only maintains that the Soviet press serves the masses, but functions amid them; and (6) criticism and self-criticism (*kritika* and *samokritika*), which calls upon the press to criticize failures and faults of the Communist Party, the government, and their agencies, as well as to criticize its own performance.

In Lenin's words, which are reprinted in virtually all Soviet discussions of mass media's functions, the press also is a collective propagandist, agitator, and organizer.[14] In the context of the times—the words were written in 1901—Lenin was arguing that a newspaper could be an organizational center of a political party, as well as an instrument of persuasion. To mention one more set of guidelines, the Soviet press has been given these characteristics: (1) differentiation, to serve various categories of readers, (2) purposefulness of content, especially in discussing problems of socialist development, (3) close association with readers by means of letters and news notes, and (4) organization of public affairs discussions.[15] These are all rather sweeping assignments for Soviet mass communications. It seems axiomatic, as with all large principles and purposes, that they can be interpreted to cover a multitude of sins and virtues.

How much criticism should there be, and toward whom should it be directed? When and how extensively should public discussions of government proposals be conducted? To what degree should the mass media side with the masses, if popular interests seem to conflict with Communist Party objectives (as clearly they did, to cite a gross example, in Stalin's blood purges before and after World War II)? One may say, in the Soviet context, that the political order answers these questions to its own satisfaction. But suppose the Communist Party apparatus exercises the most self-protective policies as far as mass media's performance is concerned. One danger, as the American government has discovered in far less expert and intense management of the news, is a "credibility gap." The mass media lose their effectiveness as molders and shapers of opinion. Or suppose press criticism of government policies is merely given lip service. As a society becomes more complex and less subject to close central command, which is the observable process in the Soviet Union, the lack of vigorous public criticism of policy implementation permits error to multiply.

In other words, given its general principles and its alliance with the political order, the Soviet press must constantly strike a balance among conflicting responsibilities. When national goals, for example, are clearly set and their achievement is imperative (victory in war is an instance), a dissenting, critical press performs a disservice. However, when uncertainty arises, or when alternative objectives of roughly equal merit exist, the mass media may be useful as an independent judge. That is the American viewpoint. The American mass media are regularly more the critic of national policy than the Soviet. The rationale is that public exposure and critical analysis of government decisions, among others, will reveal human flaws and right the wrongs. Needless to say, governments look on this press function with mixed feelings. They would prefer mass media to be constructively critical, or even to promote national policy.[16] The Soviet political order can and does of course enlist the mass media in its causes, far more comprehensively than the American. But Soviet authorities, too, value the critical function of the press. . . .

RADIO MOSCOW AND THE BLUE SCREEN

Soviet broadcasting fought with the printed media well into the 1960's for a place of influence and prestige. Perhaps because there was no commercial motivation as in the United States to analyze and dissect the psychological effects of radio and television, or perhaps because sociological studies were discouraged under Stalin or, finally, perhaps because political bureaucrats were slow to acknowledge the new electronic media—for one or a combination of these reasons, radio and television remained stepchildren among the mass media. A probing analysis in *Kommunist*, the Communist Party's leading theoretical journal, observed in 1965:

There is an effort being made to discover the possibilities of home television, to establish its esthetic nature under socialism, to determine its role in society. On the one hand, there is the traditional hierarchic point of view which assigns home television a modest role among the means of propaganda. The press, film and radio have accumulated considerable experience and long ago became a part of everyday life. But the home television is a novelty. Thus an "inertia of attitudes" or a form of "table of ranks" interferes with giving television the role it ought to occupy. On the other hand, some conclude that television should replace all means of propaganda and even art.[17]

If this sort of dispute over television existed in the mid1960's, recognition of the effects and impact of electronic media had not progressed very far in the Soviet Union. There had been a good deal of discussion and a good many assertions made about the extraordinary value of television and radio in political and cultural education; all of which may have been beside the point until radio and then gradually television broadcasting were formed into a national network reaching most or large segments of the Soviet population. But even in the mid-1960's, programming remained relatively lackluster.

The *Kommunist* critique discussed the faults of television. Programs lacked variety, announcers and commentators were mechanical in their presentations, television repeated what had already appeared in newspapers, major issues were treated superficially, far too few professionally trained and experienced television journalists were engaged in producing programs, television showed little talent as public critic. A Moscow television viewer, not untypical of the Soviet audience's reaction to television programming, had much the same attitude when a Soviet correspondent, disguised as a TV repairman, conducted an informal survey. "There are some shrewd people in television," the viewer noted. "If one channel's got a lecture, without fail the other one has a round-table discussion."[18] A Moscow scientist, in the same opinion survey, sympathized: "When the poor devil, the television viewer, gets through all the debris of form to the content, it turns out that all the while there was nothing there for him."[19]

Part of the complaint with television particularly, since it is the newest mass communications medium in the Soviet Union and arouses the most controversy, is that Soviet programming has adopted the content and style of the printed media. In this it has failed, the criticism goes, to develop its own character and, in what would seem the simplest of all, to entertain as well as inform. A TV critic writing in the national newspaper *Sovetskaya Kultura* quipped: "After studying television programs for the past few weeks and using fourth grade mathematics, we calculated the percentage of entertainment value of television broadcasts at 6% to 7%."[20]

The common theme, clearly, in judging Soviet broadcasting is its lack of imaginative, professional, and varied content. Criticisms may exaggerate to some degree, as blanket assessments often do. Relatively popular radio and television programs are aired in the Soviet Union. The Leningrad TV station inaugurated a series for young people that in *Pravda*'s opinion was lively and stimulating and "does not shun acute and controversial problems."[21] Another Leningrad program called "In Our Circle" brought together a family (actors), who discussed domestic problems and issues of popular concern. In one of the first attempts to survey audience likes and dislikes, a sample of nearly 2,000 TV viewers gave high ratings to sports programs (such as broadcasts of soccer games), to concerts and variety programs, and such audience participation shows as KVN—the Club of Cheer and Wit, in which viewers and studio panels of university students engage in a test of knowledge.[22]

However, despite streaks of success, Soviet radio and television do not on the whole seem to earn praise from authorities, communicators, or audiences. That is not altogether an original state of affairs. In the United States, radio and television have equally harsh critics. The issue in each country is to some extent the same. Should broadcasting—especially television—educate and inform, or entertain? American television is predominantly an entertainment medium, although in very recent years both the large commercial broadcasting networks and educational television have produced public affairs, documentary, and investigative programs of high merit. Soviet radio throughout its history has been considerably devoted to purposeful entertainment. Readings of plays and broadcasts of concerts were to lift the cultural level of the population. A smaller portion of time was given over to dissemination of information. In the early 1960's, Radio Moscow's domestic programming of 545 hours broke down this way: 55 per cent of the time was allocated to music; 16 per cent to news; 10 per cent to social-political information; 9 per cent to literature and drama; about 7 per cent to programs for youth; and the rest a mixture.[23] Central Television similarly has leaned to entertainment, though not all of the light variety. In 1962 or so, when Central Television broadcast 64½ hours a week, 22 per cent were taken up by films; 19 per cent, literature and drama; 18 per cent, music; 17 per cent, news; 14 per cent, programs for youth; 8 per cent, social and political information; and 2 per cent miscellaneous.[24]

A representative day of Radio Moscow—the listings for June 28, 1968—began at 8:45 a.m., with one of a series of talks on health, continued with a program on literature and then a talk by the first secretary of the Moscow City Communist Party organization. Other programs included a concert from Bucharest, Rumania, a report on the Supreme Soviet, a broadcast on "The Forest in Our Life," songs about Lenin, a program about high school graduates, sports news, commentary, and a review of international events. Programming ended after midnight with music. On the same day, Moscow television's Channel 1 (of four channels) began its broadcast schedule at 5 p.m. with a children's program, then offered a sports review, a concert from the Black Sea port of Odessa, and a soccer match. The broadcast day concluded at midnight with news and music. Channel

3—devoted largely to educational programs—offered during seven hours of programs, "Chemistry in the National Economy," a physics lecture for correspondence students, and German, English, and Russian lessons for high school students preparing for university entrance examinations.[25] Channels 2 and 4, broadcasting six hours each, from 6 p.m. to midnight, presented films, and a variety of discussions, interviews, and news programs.

There is no question that the educational potential of Soviet television is recognized. As in the United States, TV offers a means of mass instruction without the relatively expensive facilities of universities and institutes. On a practical level, television can be the channel for introducing technology, industrial production methods, farm skills and equipment, and construction techniques. It can partly shape a life style, by displaying fashions, work habits, architecture, and art, for example. And it can contribute to the formation of popular attitudes with films, dramas, discussion forums, lectures, and the like. . . .

Years of Development: Radio

"Our country," begins a Soviet chronological history of radio broadcasting, "is the mother of radio."[26] Without delving into rival claims for radio's invention, it is paradoxical that with the technical knowledge at hand broadcasting expanded as slowly as it did in the Soviet Union. Alexander Popov, the nineteenth-century Russian scientist whom Soviet historians credit with demonstrating the first crude radio receiver in 1895, the year that Guglielmo Marconi sent a brief message by wireless, was experimenting in radio two decades before the Bolshevik Revolution. Russia, like other industrializing nations of the time, was mastering wireless communications. The means of voice transmission was accessible shortly before World War I, although the first experimental voice broadcast was not made in Russia until 1920 and the first broadcasting station did not go into operation until 1922.[27] By the time the new Bolshevik government in Moscow was bringing civil war to a close in 1920 and turning its energies to political and economic reconstruction, American entrepreneurs were beginning to form the great empires that were to direct broadcasts to nearly one out of every two American homes by 1930, and two of three by 1935.

In the Soviet Union, radio broadcasting did not reach the American level of 1930, in terms of total receivers, until the early 1950's. Yet, radio broadcasting was admirably suited to needs of the Soviet political bureaucracy. Its potential for disseminating information rapidly over large areas was hailed by Lenin in 1920. A Communist

Party directive of 1925, in endorsing a national Society of the Friends of Radio, noted the "significant role which radio should play as a powerful means of agitation and propaganda."

However, two factors retarded radio broadcasting in the Soviet Union. One, implicit in Lenin's vision of all of Russia listening to a "newspaper read in Moscow,"[28] was the equation of radio broadcasting with the printed word, rather than the recognition of radio as a fundamentally different medium of mass communications. This was not an uncommon attitude anywhere. After all, wireless transmission was originally used to relay dot-dash messages. In the Soviet Union, however, once the attitude became entrenched in the central bureaucracy, it was difficult to change. And although the potential of radio was exploited for cultural education—broadcasting of concerts, for example—radio tended to be viewed as a public address system for the printed word. So, even into the 1960's, the volume of radio broadcasting was frequently described in terms of newspaper pages.[29]

The second obstacle to radio's development was the large initial investment necessary to reach even the more populous western expanses of the Soviet state. Given at least a basis for a printed media network in the early 1920's, the new Bolshevik government easily leaned to expansion of that, devoting only secondary attention to radio. Indeed, there perhaps was no realistic choice from an economic standpoint. Radio required a developed electrical power system, which the Soviet Union lacked. Soviet electrical energy production in the mid-1920's was about a twentieth of American output. Radio demanded a whole new industry, from the ground up, to manufacture receivers and transmitting equipment, not to mention continuing large investment in research and development. It was still an experimental form of communications, and although its potential was recognized, its actual benefits and uses remained hazy. Moreover, in the war-ruined Soviet economy, there were more immediate needs than the wide-scale construction of a radio network.

What was lacking then was a motivation in the Soviet Union, equal in force to the commercial stimulus in the United States, to enter into extensive radio broadcasting. The fact that radio could, if developed, reach millions of illiterate people did not weigh heavily enough. First of all, illiteracy predominated in rural Russia among the peasants, and among national minorities in central Asia and the Caucasus. Although the central leadership was intent on establishing political management among these millions, as development of the printed media showed, the problem was absence of electrical power for radio precisely in regions where illiteracy was greatest. Second, the formation of corps of political agitators to deliver lectures and read newspapers aloud to the illiterate provided oral communications as effective perhaps as radio broadcasting.

In sum, radio was perhaps too young to draw the full support of the Soviet political leadership, the Soviet state too big and its population too dispersed in the provinces to make radio feasible and, finally, there were existing mass media alternatives to radio. The result was laggardly growth of the broadcasting industry, while newspapers were assigned the chief responsibility for educating, mobilizing, and informing the masses. . . .

From the very beginning, the Soviet broadcasting system used both standard radio receivers and diffusion networks by which broadcasts were carried over telephone lines to loudspeakers. Where communications lines already existed, it was much less expensive to install loudspeakers than radios. The result was that Soviet broadcasting was predominantly a loudspeaker network until the mid-1950's. . . .[But] in the late 1950's and the early 1960's, the number of radios gradually exceeded loudspeakers. Thus by 1966, the loudspeaker network contained nearly 36 million units, while the number of radio sets had increased to 38 million.[30] But Soviet statistics must be accepted cautiously. In early 1968, *Pravda* reported 48 million radio receivers in the Soviet Union, and *Izvestia* gave a figure of 42 million "operating receivers."[31] These are large differences, and one must conclude that Soviet authorities do not know accurately how many radios or loudspeakers are actually in use.

In the early years, there was not much importance in statistics separating radio sets from loudspeakers. Central and local programming were picked up by both networks. In the 1950's however, as cold war intensified between the Soviet Union and the United States, radio receivers became objects of propaganda battles. With determination, the United States transmitted into the Soviet Union, and with equal determination, the Soviet government tried to jam broadcasts. The loudspeaker network was outside this conflict since obviously Voice of America and the BBC could not break into it. Soviet jamming of most foreign radio broadcasts ceased in 1963 (though it was resumed on a selective basis in 1968, after the Soviet-led invasion of Czechoslovakia). But both before and after that, production of standard radio receivers showed steady expansion. The proper question is why the Soviet government should deliberately reorient its broadcasting system more to radio receivers and away from loudspeakers, knowing full well that this simply compounded the problem of foreign ideological influence. The apparent reason, although it is not explicitly stated in Soviet sources on broadcasting, is that the economics of reaching a mass audience called for a radio receiver network. The revival and growth of Soviet communications industries after World War II meant cheaper and more reliable sets: the number of transmitters increased from 100 in 1950 to 407 in about 1962, and to "more than" 430 in 1968.[32] Not all of these were stations originating programs. In fact, the majority were relay stations for Moscow and regional broadcasting centers. Nevertheless, they provided the technical means for airing programs without stringing lines for loudspeakers.

To summarize, the present-day Soviet radio system is made up of networks of an estimated 42 to 48 million radios and 39 million loudspeakers. They receive from more than 430 stations and relay transmitters, which broadcast a total of 1,200 hours daily (central and local) in Russian and national languages. Through one or the other, Central Radio in Moscow, broadcasting on long, medium, and shortwaves, reaches virtually the whole Soviet population.

In the countryside, where the loudspeaker system still predominates among about 45 per cent of the population, the government has almost a monopoly of broadcasting. In urban areas, however, where standard radio receivers are more plentiful, Soviet programming competes with stations broadcasting from other Communist countries and from non-Communist countries in western Europe, as well as from the United States.

Of the four Soviet programs (the equivalent of American stations), Programs 1 and 2 of Central Radio carry the major load of news and information. Program 3 is mainly music and literature, while Program 4 is edited for far eastern sections of the country.[33] In addition to the four central programs, local radio stations originate their own broadcasts to supplement central studios. Along with these broadcasts, received on standard radio receivers, the loudspeaker network is equipped to handle three programs in towns of 300,000 or more people, and either two or three in smaller communities.[34]

The actual listening audience, as contrasted to nearly 100 per cent availability of a receiver for Soviet citizens, is unknown to anyone, in or outside the Soviet Union. Registration of radio receivers at one time provided Soviet authorities with a fair count of potential listeners. When licensing of radio sets was abolished, evidently around 1960,[35] the only guides to the radio audience size were estimates of receivers which, as mentioned, have not been too reliable. Subscription fees—a form of registration—apparently are still paid for the use of loudspeakers and thereby provide a more accurate count of these facilities (and also defray costs of an otherwise state-subsidized broadcasting system). In any case, there remain the problems of measuring listening audiences at various times in various parts of the country.[36] So far, Soviet mass communications researchers have done little to measure radio audiences and listenership. All that Soviet authorities know is that the radio broadcasting network is technically capable of reaching all but a fraction of the Soviet population.

Years of Development: Television

The same imprecision applies to the Soviet television audience. At the beginning of 1966, when the Soviet Union counted nearly 16 million television sets, the potential audience was estimated at 50 million viewers,[37] or three viewers to the set. Thus, in early 1968, when there were 23 million television sets, the number of viewers was possibly 70 million. The television network was said to broadcast 900 hours daily (central and local) over an area containing 124 million of the 237 million population.[38]

Even if these estimates of viewers are only approximately correct, they symbolize the concerted growth of Soviet television in recent years. If the 1930's were Soviet radio's spawning period, the 1960's have been television's era of expansion. Before that, television was virtually unknown in the Soviet Union. This, too, is paradoxical. The first experimental television transmission was made in the Soviet Union in April, 1931, and "regular" TV broadcasting began on March 10, 1939, in Moscow, where 100 very small screen sets received a slow-motion 30-minute program.[39] By the beginning of 1941, 400 television sets had been produced and the Communist Party had ordered construction of television stations in major Soviet cities.

World War II temporarily canceled these plans. At the war's end, the Soviet inventory of television sets was down to 200 and by the end of 1950 had reached only 15,000.[40] In the following decade, the pace of development gradually stepped up. At the start of 1956, there were about 1.3 million sets, and 4.8 million at the end of 1960.[41] Meanwhile, from the two television stations (in Moscow and Leningrad) of prewar years, the television broadcasting network grew to 18 stations at the close of 1955 and 275 in 1960, the latter figure including about 100 programming centers plus 175 relay facilities. The viewing audience by then was estimated at 20 million,[42] or about 10 per cent of the population.

One cannot say that postwar development of television was negligible. Yet it is evident that, despite its recognized effect in shaping attitudes and disseminating information, television had a low priority in Soviet planning. Had Soviet political authorities really been convinced of television's use and value, they could have directed a faster pace of growth. The technology was available. Research and development before World War II had given the Soviet Union a base on which to build. Investment funds, though acutely scarce in the

1950's, could have been taken from other sectors of the economy had Soviet leaders wanted to construct a TV network. However, the allocations were not made, and the conclusion must be that central planners simply did not believe television communications were sufficiently important when measured against the needs of heavy industry, the military, agriculture, and the like. And, too, the fact of established and growing printed media and radio broadcasting weighed against making huge investments in television.

Around 1960, however, thinking began to change. A Communist Party directive of that year declared that "Television opens new and great opportunities for daily political, cultural and esthetic education of the population" but that "Soviet television is still far from fully used. . . ."[43] The directive went on to criticize the specific shortcomings of television, and to outline a plan for improvement, including better trained staff and more imaginative programming. With this political imprimatur, and with somewhat less strain in the economy, the central planners began a rapid expansion of television. Three years after the 1960 directive, the Soviet Union had double the number of television sets—10.4 million—produced in the whole fifteen postwar years up to 1960. Within five more years, the total was up to 23 million. Simultaneously, the transmitter network was extensively added to. From the 100 TV stations in 1960, the system counted 125 programming centers in 1967.[44] The network of standard relay stations, to carry central programs nationwide, expanded from 175 to just under 780 at the start of 1968. With this growth, Soviet television broadcasts went to large rural areas in the western Soviet Union, and to the urban regions of Soviet central Asia, Siberia, and the far east.

Indeed, the most notable facts of Soviet television development have been the advances toward a national network, making use of cables, relay transmitters, and artificial earth satellites to reach distant points, and the construction of a major programming center in Moscow for the network. Initially, in the 1950's, programs of Central Television in Moscow were received directly only on sets within range of the Moscow transmitter, and indirectly by rebroadcasts of filmed programs over regional stations. By 1965, cables and relay stations linked most of the Soviet Union west of the Urals—that is, an area about the size of the United States—to Central Television. One coaxial cable extending nearly 2,000 miles from Moscow hooked up Simferopol in the Crimea, Sochi along the Black Sea, and the capitals of the Caucasus republics, Tbilisi, Yerevan, and Baku. By the end of 1967, large areas of the central Asian republics had been included in the national network. All of the expansive Kazakh republic was scheduled to receive Moscow television during 1968.[45]

These communications have been supplemented by a series of artificial earth satellites to relay television programs, telephone conversations, telegrams, and photographs from western regions to Soviet Siberia, the far east, and parts of central Asia. Between 1965 and the beginning of 1968, seven satellites of the *"Molniya"* (meaning "Lightning") series had been placed in orbit. As these trials were made, 20 ground stations were being constructed to receive central TV broadcasts bounced from the satellites. After some years of experimentation, the satellite relay and its *"Orbita"* system of ground stations began regular operations in the fall of 1967 and were said to transmit Moscow television programs to more than 20 million viewers.[46]

The programming center for the developing national TV network is in Moscow at the Ostankino station. It consists of a 1,750-foot tall tower rising over the Soviet capital and modern studios and equipment for both black and white and color television. Similar large complexes were scheduled to be built in Leningrad and Kiev in 1968. For the immediate future, Ostankino will be the prime developer of Soviet color television, which was inaugurated in October, 1967, in Moscow. One thousand color sets were produced for initial broadcasts. The Soviet television industry was scheduled to manufacture 15,000 more color sets in 1968, and move to an annual rate of 200,000 in 1970.[47] From this, it was apparent that color TV remained of secondary importance in the Soviet Union until at least the 1970's. Only Moscow, Kiev, and Leningrad, and gradually other major population centers— 39 cities in all in 1970—were to get color broadcasts. Programming was scheduled to increase from 6 hours a week in 1968 to 20 hours in 1970.[48]

Of more significance has been the addition of channels to the Soviet TV network. Until 1964, there were two channels in large cities, and only one elsewhere. Central Television added a third in 1964, and a fourth in 1967; a fifth, the color channel, was established when the Ostankino station began broadcasting. With the new channels, Central Television was broadcasting 28 hours daily in 1968, and was supposed to increase to 50 hours in 1970.[49] By comparison, central programming totaled 8 hours daily in 1959, as Soviet authorities turned to more rapid development of television.[50]

The Broadcasting Network

Like many broadcasting systems in the world, the Soviet network is regulated and managed by the government. The early arrangement, for four years from 1924 to 1928 when radio was making its entry, was a so-called "joint stock company" of four agencies, including the Russian Telegraph Agency and the People's Commissariat for

Postal Services and Telegraph.[51] In 1928, however, the post office and telegraph commissariat was given full management of radio broadcasting, and in 1953, the network was given over to the Ministry of Culture. Then, with the growth of television, the present Committee on Radio Broadcasting and Television was established in 1957 as one of numerous agencies in the Council of Ministers' apparatus.

The committee consists of four sections—editorial departments for radio, a separate editorial apparatus for television, a combined editorial staff for local radio and television programming, and finally a conglomeration of departments, including reference libraries, correspondent networks, and technical services. As with Soviet newspapers, the main editorial departments are broken down into subsections, nine for the radio network and eight for television. And some of these in turn have various special departments. For example, the radio network's main editorial staff for political propaganda is made up of subdepartments for Marxist-Leninist propaganda; industry, transport, and construction; agriculture; youth broadcasts; and satire and humor. The equivalent section for television has subdepartments for economics, international affairs, culture and daily services, natural sciences and technology, sports, and the "latest news." Both radio and television also have separate departments for music programming, for literature and drama, programs for youth, and for Moscow City broadcasting.

There are slight differences of editorial structure for radio and television. The radio apparatus has a separate staff for the "latest news" department and another for exchange of programs with republic and *oblast* radio stations. Within each network, Moscow's studios dominate the systems, somewhat as American broadcasting networks focus on New York offices and studios. While Central Television does much of its own programming for national distribution, the Moscow television center produces both programs for broadcast in the Moscow area and films and documentaries for reshowing in the provinces. For example, the national television network distributes up to 800 various types of programs a year to the 125 television centers, while the Moscow studios produce up to 1,500 for showing by local stations.

Subordinated to the state Committee for Radio Broadcasting and Television which manages the whole broadcasting network, are 157 republic and *oblast* committees attached to local government organizations, and about 2,500 city and *raion* radio editorial staffs. Local broadcast committees function as subsidiary management of a national network, rather than as supervisors of independent television and radio stations. Like the printed press, broadcasting editoria offices also are supervised by Communist Party organizations, which through their sectors for press, radio, and television counsel and instruct as to program content.

If we were to sketch the Soviet broadcasting network, we would find a central management overseeing program content of 157 subsidiaries (or local management), the whole network employing about 50,000 people. Editorial staffs of central broadcasting departments range from 30 to 150 persons each, including editors, correspondents, commentators, producers, and technical staffs. By contrast, a republic committee for radio and television numbers about 1,200 people in all, and an *oblast*, from 60 to 150.[52]

The amount of local radio broadcasting varies as does the size of the staff. In the Soviet republics, local stations air from 12 to 15 hours a day of local material, while in *oblasts*, they broadcast from 1 to 3 hours. For example, a recent annual programming of Leningrad's television studios included 4,330 hours of broadcasts, of which 1,620 were local programs, 1,610 were exchange and film programs, and 1,100 originated in Moscow and other cities. Or, to put the relation another way, in late 1964, when Moscow television was broadcasting 11 hours daily, the total volume nationwide of broadcasts was 850 hours daily. The 2,500 radio editorial staffs in cities and *raions*, using relay transmitters, broadcast from 20 to 30 minutes of locally originated programs up to three times a week. At other hours, Central Radio transmits through the local broadcasting facilities.

Most television programming seems to be concentrated in the large TV studios in Moscow, Leningrad, and capitals of the Soviet republics, although there are a total of 125 programming stations in the country.

In addition to domestic programming, Soviet radio and to some extent television engage in international broadcasting. Both the Central Radio and Central Television editorial organizations have separate departments to handle international broadcasts and exchange of programs. By and large, the exchange takes place between the Soviet Union and eastern European nations within the framework of the International Organization for Radio and Television Broadcasting (composed in 1966 of 24 nations), and of Intervision and Eurovision. However, the Soviet government judiciously limits exchange. And given the short broadcasting range of television, Soviet authorities have no great concern at the moment over unwanted foreign TV broadcasts as it has had with shortwave radio transmissions. When in 1963 Soviet television viewers saw the funeral of President John F. Kennedy in Washington via Telstar, for example, it was by consent of the Soviet government.

Soviet communicators envision the day, however, when satellites will relay TV programs directly to the home television set, by-passing existing ground stations which at present function as the "gatekeeper." In an interview early in 1968, for example, the Soviet Minister of Communications observed: "Quite probably in the future television programs relayed by earth satellites will go directly to home television. Then we will be able to televise broadcasts in practically every place on our planet."[53] There are impressive technical obstacles in the way of worldwide television broadcasts via satellite from one nation to another, directly to the home sets. The political seem just as formidable. But Soviet communicators are beginning to think of the day when they can portray the Soviet Union to millions of people by television, and when foreign TV broadcasts may reach the masses of Soviet citizens. International Soviet radio broadcasts already have reached sizable proportions. In 1968, Radio Moscow was beaming 150 hours of programs abroad in 57 languages every 24 hours. These broadcasts are skillfully edited to appeal to specific audiences. Indeed initial Soviet research in radio audience tastes was done by Radio Moscow with listeners in North America.[54]

An example of Soviet foreign broadcasting is Radio Peace and Progress, which began operating in 1964. It broadcasts a little over 15 hours a day, in eight languages, and mainly to western Europe, the United States, Communist China, and India. Although its staff of 60 uses Radio Moscow facilities, Radio Peace and Progress is ostensibly a "public organization" of the Union of Journalists, Press Agency Novosti, and other Soviet quasi-official agencies. As such, it does not speak authoritatively for the Soviet government as does, for example, TASS, although it de facto represents Soviet policies.[55] In return for the foreign broadcast activities, The Soviet government contends with the fact that both Russian and native language broadcasts of Communist China, the United States, Great Britain, Japan, west European and Scandinavian countries are received in the Soviet Union. International broadcasts by radio and conceivably in the future by television represent the most serious challenge to the Soviet political bureaucracy's monopoly of broadcast information within the country. In recent years, the Soviet mass media and political authorities have increasingly warned of the influence of foreign broadcasts on attitudes in the Soviet Union. The problem essentially was whether to prohibit foreign broadcasts by jamming networks, or to counter them. Especially since 1963, when most jamming ceased, the Soviet press has been directed to the second course. Thus, in 196. as the post-Khrushchev Soviet leadership developed a noticeably "harder" cultural policy, the Communist Party's leading theoretical journal *Kommunist* warned of an extensive anti-Soviet propaganda campaign engineered in western countries, chiefly the United States:

Bourgeois propagandists try to use the foreign radio, press and tourism as channels for injecting alien views into our midst. . . . It is essential to study the tactics of hostile propaganda and actively combat them. . . . But there is often little information, insufficient commentary and details in our newspapers and on radio to help understand current policies. In our time, when radio receivers are in almost every home, to ignore this or that event, to fail in pointing it out from the standpoint of socialist ideology means to give "freedom of action" to the falsifications of bourgeois propagandists. . . . More than that, it is important not only to correctly explain this or that fact, but it is essential to do it promptly. One must admit that bourgeois information agencies have achieved great efficiency, reacting quickly to everything occurring in the world, while we sometimes are late.[56]

One interesting effect of foreign broadcast competition seems to be a modification of Soviet communications behavior. When the Soviet government enjoyed a virtual monopoly of the airwaves, there was little motivation to program with the listener's tastes in mind. Indeed, Soviet broadcasting was considered essentially a medium of cultural education and entertainment. The attempted penetration of the Soviet Union by foreign broadcasts was temporarily deflected with massive jamming networks. Eventually this became politically untenable. How could the Soviet Union establish its place as a civilized, confident nation among nations, engaging in commerce, tourism, and political negotiations, and at the same time shielding its citizenry from the outside world? The two activities were incompatible. And, in effect, Soviet communicators were pressed to modernize the mass media to conform to the Soviet Union's international stature as a world power. About this same time, in the early 1960's, the reborn Soviet sociology was applied to mass media, among other areas, in an attempt to put Soviet communications planning on a more rational, scientific basis. This is not to say that foreign propaganda and news broadcasts were the primary motivation for reassessing and updating Soviet broadcasting. But they have been a strong stimulant, among several that would include a rising educational level, a conviction on the part of the political bureaucracy that the Soviet mass media were not reaching the public, and a better trained journalist corps that is also aware of foreign broadcast content and techniques. The total result was that Soviet television and radio underwent a process of expansion and improvement in the 1960's, in preparation for greater stature in the 1970's.

NOTES

1.   V. I. Lenin, *Sochineniya* (35 vols., 4th edn., Moscow, 1941-1952), Vol. 5, p. 9. For the American history of the press as political spokesman see, for example, Edwin Emery, *The Press and America: An Interpretive History of Journalism* (Englewood Cliffs, N.J.: Prentice-Hall, Inc., 1962), Chapters 6 and 10. All translations from the Russian are by the author.

2. T. M. Reshetnikov, *Partiya o pechati* (Sverdlovsk, 1934), pp. 16–17.

3. *Pervyi vsesoyuznyi sezd zhurnalistov: stenograficheskoi otchet* (Moscow, 1960), pp. 11–12.

4. N. G. Bogdanov and B. A. Vyazemskii, *Spravochnik zhurnalista* (Leningrad, 1965), p. 2

5. See, for example, Hyman H. Goldin, "Commercial Television," in *Public Television: A Program for Action—The Report and Recommendations of the Carnegie Commission on Educational Television* (New York: Harper & Row, Inc., 1967), pp. 227–234.

6. See, for example, Nikolai Prusakov, *"Prioritet zakona," Zhurnalist*, No. 3 (March, 1967), pp. 43–45. A deputy chairman of the Russian republic's supreme court, Prusakov asserts that judges must be spared inaccurate and emotional reporting of trials in progress if courts are to render fair decisions.

7. A Communist Party Central Committee statement criticized the Turkmen republic press, for example, for failing to give the "necessary attention to propagating the ideas of proletarian internationalism and friendship of the peoples of the USSR." See *Sovetskaya Pechat*, No. 2 (February, 1964), p. 2.

8. *Pechat SSSR v 1966 godu* (Moscow, 1967), pp. xviii and xix.

9. For discussion of the religious press, see Martin E. Marty, *et al., The Religious Press in America* (New York: Holt, Rinehart and Winston, Inc., 1963), pp. 51–52 and pp. 101–109. These pages focus especially on problems of editorial freedom within church organizations.

10. See, for instance, A. Yakovlev, *"Televideniye: problemy i perspektivy," Kommunist*, No. 13 (September, 1965), pp. 70–80, in which he discusses expansion of international television broadcasting, and then foresees the "open clash of two ideologies in the airwaves."

11. See, for example, D. P. Goryunov's report to the 1966 National Journalists' Conference in *Vtoroi sezd zhurnalistov SSSR*, supplement to *Sovetskaya Pechat*, No. 11 (November, 1966), pp. 15–16.

12. This interpretation is adapted from a stimulating essay by Jay W. Jensen, "A Method and a Perspective for Criticism of the Mass Media," *Journalism Quarterly*, Vol. 37, No. 2, pp. 261–266. See also Theodore Peterson, "Why the Mass Media Are That Way," in Charles S. Steinberg (ed.), *Mass Media and Communication* (New York: Hastings House Publishers, Inc., 1966), pp. 56–71.

13. Boganov and Vyazemskii, *Spravochnik zhurnalista*, pp. 37–49.

14. *Lenin o pechati* (Moscow, 1959), p. 139. The exact sentence: "A newspaper is not only a collective propagandist and a collective agitator, but a collective organizer as well."

15. See *"Nauchnaya konferentsiya po problemam zhurnalistiki,"* in *Sovetskaya Pechat*, No. 2 (February, 1966), p. 56. The characteristics were suggested by A. Mishuris, of Moscow University's School of Journalism, at a Moscow conference on laws of the development of the press in socialist society.

16. The late President John F. Kennedy, for example, acknowledged the valuable role of a critical press in a democratic society. But, as all Presidents in the age of mass communications, he saw the press as a means of rallying public support for his policies. See, for example, Theodore C. Sorensen, *Kennedy* (New York: Bantam Books, Inc., 1966), p. 349.

17. *Kommunist*, No. 13 (September, 1965).

18. *Zhurnalist*, No. 4 (April, 1967), p. 39.

19. *Ibid.*

20. *Sovetskaya Kultura*, September 9, 1965, in *Current Digest of the Soviet Press*, Vol. XVII, No. 39, p. 11.

21. *Pravda,* September 14, 1965.

22. *Zhurnalist,* No. 12 (December, 1967), p. 44.

23. *World Communications* (2nd edn., Paris: UNESCO, 1966), p. 367.

24. *Ibid.,* p. 368.

25. *Pravda,* June 28, 1968.

26. Gleizer, M. (ed.), *Radio i televideniye v SSSR: 1917-1963* (Moscow, 1965), p. 3.

27. *Spravochnik zhurnalista,* pp. 173-174.

28. Quoted in L. N. Fedotova, *"Stanovleniye reportazha na radio,"* p. 17.

29. See, for example, *Sovetskaya Pechat,* No. 6 (June, 1965), p. 1, where 1,200 hours of daily program are equated with "about 300 4-page newspapers of a large format."

30. *Narodnoye khozyaistvo SSSR v 1960 godu* (Moscow, 1961), p. 576, and *Ezhegodnik bolshoi sovetskoi entsiklopedii* (Moscow, 1967), p. 89.

31. See these newspapers for May 7, 1968.

32. *World Communications,* pp. 33 and 364; *Pravda,* May 7, 1968.

33. See Gayle Durham Hollander, "Recent Developments in Soviet Radio and Television News Reporting," *Public Opinion Quarterly* (Fall, 1967), pp. 362-364, for this information, and for amount of news programming on radio and television.

34. *World Communications,* p. 367.

35. V. N. Yaroshenko, *"Izucheniye radioauditorii,"* *Vestnik Moskovskogo universiteta, Seriya XI, Zhurnalistika,* No. 1, 1966, p. 29, mentions "abolition of subscriber fees," in the context of radio development in the early 1960's. For evidence that subscriber fees still seem to apply to wired loudspeakers, see *Zhurnalist,* No. 5 (May, 1967), p. 28.

36. *Ibid.,* pp. 29-30.

37. *Kommunist,* No. 13 (September, 1965), p. 70.

38. TASS International Service, May 5, 1968, and *Pravda,* May 7, 1968.

39. Gleizer (ed.), *op. cit.,* pp. 60 and 86.

40. *Forty Years of Soviet Power* (Central Statistical Board, Moscow, 1958), p. 265.

41. *Ibid.,* and *Narodnoye khozyaistvo SSSR v 1960 godu* (Moscow, 1961), p. 576.

42. *Sovetskaya Pechat,* No. 5 (May, 1960), p. 25.

43. *Sovetskaya pechat v dokumentakh,* p. 136.

44. *Ezhegodnik* (Moscow, 1962), p. 78, and *Pravda,* May 7, 1968.

45. *Kommunist,* No. 13 (September, 1965), p. 70, and *Pravda,* May 6, 1968.

46. Moscow Radio, April 12, 1968, translated in *Foreign Broadcast Information Service (FBIS),* April 15, 1968, p. D5; *TASS International Service,* December 27, 1967, in *FBIS,* December 29, 1967, pp. BB18-19.

47. Washington *Post,* May 16, 1968, p. 23.

48. *Izvestia,* August 11, 1968, and *Zhurnalist,* No. 10 (October, 1968), p. 38.

49. *Zhurnalist,* No. 12 (December, 1967), pp. 16-17.

50. *Sovetskaya Pechat,* No. 11 (November, 1959), p. 37.

51. This section, unless otherwise noted, is based on *Spravochnik zhurnalista*, pp. 181–186 and 212–215.

52. *Ibid.*, pp. 184–185.

53. *Ekonomicheskaya Gazeta*, No. 19 (May, 1968), p. 23.

54. See Yaroshenko, *"Izucheniye radioauditorii,"* p. 27. In an elementary survey, American listeners who wrote to the American Department of Radio Moscow were sent postcards asking listeners to note preferences for various programs.

55. See Associated Press dispatch from Moscow, January 17, 1968.

56. Translated in *The Soviet Press* (Madison, Wis.: University of Wisconsin Press), Vol. V, No. 1, 1966, pp. 7–9.

Mass Communication and Media in China's Cultural Revolution*

ALAN P. L. LIU

ALAN P. L. LIU is Assistant Professor of Political
Science at the University of California, Santa Barbara.
Dr. Liu was born in China and came to the United States
in 1961. He holds a doctorate in political science from
Massachusetts Institute of Technology. He was formerly
Research Political Scientist in the Center for Chinese
Studies, University of Michigan, and is the author of
Communication and National Integration in Communist
China.

The Cultural Revolution in Communist China has dealt a severe blow to the nation's mass media, the hardest hit being the printed media. Almost all major national and regional newspapers have either been suspended or reorganized and given new names. Professional journals have suffered a decimation. The publishing of all types of books has stopped in order to print the little red books of quotations from Mao's writings and editorials of the chief ideological journal, *Red Flag*. The Chinese film industry has been under Mao's attacks since 1964 and is now turning out mostly documentaries about the Cultural Revolution and the army. The sole survivor in this turmoil is the radio network. In fact, radio has become a crucial Maoist tool of mobilization.

*Reprinted from *Journalism Quarterly*, Summer 1969, pp. 314–19. Used by permission.

The thesis of this article* is that the destruction of the mass media in China in the Cultural Revolution resulted from the conflicts among three factors.

First, the personality factor of Mao Tse-tung who conceived of mass persuasion in an anti-intellectual and anti-institutional framewo and whose conception of mass persuasion was based mainly on peasant mobilization.

Second, the modernization factor, focusing on the wide gap between the urban and rural areas, that limited the effectiveness of printed media which, in turn, reinforced Mao's lack of confidence in the capability of mass media to heighten the political consciousness of the peasant masses.

Third, the policy (or power) factor, emphasizing the debates among Party propaganda officials in the late 1950s over the strategy of mass persuasion, that provided Mao with an opportunity to manip ulate one group against another in the Cultural Revolution. These three factors help explain the destruction of mass media and the paralysis of the Party propaganda apparatus.

MAO TSE-TUNG'S CONCEPTION OF MASS PERSUASION

Based mainly on his experiences with peasant mobilization, Mao conceived of mass persuasion as essentially mass emotional arousal by simple political agitations. To Mao, mass political consciousness coul be easily activated by intensive oral exhortations and mass organization. His emphasis was on immediate actions, in a ground-swell fashion, that storm one target at a time. To put it schematically the motivational aspect of Mao's concept of mass persuasion was emotional arousal and the instrumental aspect mass campaigns.[1]

Consequently Mao tended to suspect routinized persuasion by the elaborate propaganda organizations, mass media and the educational system the Communist Party established after 1949. For one thing, all these institutions emphasized a gradual, intellectually sophisticated and culturally diversified approach to mass persuasion that seemed to relegate the Maoist approach of oral agitation and mass campaign to the background. These institutions, to Mao, tended to erect barriers between his personal leadership and the masses—

* Research for this article was supported by the Center for Chinese Studies, University of Michigan. A large part of the research was done at the Center for International Studies, M.I.T., as part of a project on international communication sponsored by the Advanced Research Projects Agency of the Department of Defense (ARPA) under contract #920F-9717 and monitored by the Air Force Office of Scientific Research under contract AF 49(638) – 1237.

barriers which provided the intellectuals an opportunity to revise and sabotage his programs of mass mobilization.

Moreover, both for the consolidation of his power and the larger goal of industrialization, Mao had a radical design to arouse the political consciousness of the Chinese peasantry. Consequently he tended to judge the success or failure of the Communist Party's overall propaganda efforts on the single issue of heightening the ideological consciousness of the masses in rural China. The destruction of the printed media testified to Mao's dissatisfaction with their incapability to penetrate deeply into the rural areas.

MODERNIZATION AND MEDIA

Over the years, the growth of the mass media in Communist China was impressive. Yet in analyzing media growth in any developing country, one must distinguish growth as a result of fundamental modernization in society (e.g., growth of literacy, urbanization, political participation) from that as a result of arbitrary distribution by the political leadership.[2]

As Table 1 shows, arbitrary distribution contributed greatly to the growth of the media. Overall growth was most marked in two campaigns of agricultural collectivization: the 1955-56 campaign of "agricultural producers cooperatives" and the 1958-59 "People's communes." Among the media we see that press growth was lowest, for the press required more fundamental modernization, like literacy and urbanization, than oral media like radio to enable it to grow steadily.

Perhaps the most dramatic example of the conflict between arbitrary distribution of media and the underdevelopment of rural China is the development of mass media in the Great Leap Forward in 1958. At the beginning of the campaign all media were arbitrarily distributed to rural areas with fantastic speed, presumably ordered by Mao. But then after the failure of the Great Leap, the media quickly retreated to their pre-1958 state.

Table 1 shows that the 11,124 wired broadcasting stations (radio diffusion exchange) reported in 1959 were reduced to 1,975 in 1964. This represented, however, a moderate increase over that in 1957. Among the 11,124 stations reported in 1959, 1,689 were said to be county stations and 9,435 commune stations. Apparently the 9,435 stations at commune level were closed after 1960. These so-called commune stations consisted largely of a few loudspeakers connected with an ordinary radio. Cadres spoke to peasants through a microphone plugged into the radio. At the peak of the commune

TABLE 1. Growth of Radio, Film and Press in Communist China*

Year	Radio (Wired) Stations / Speakers		Film Cinema/Mobile Team		Press Titles	Circulation (Average)
1950	51	2,000	641	522	382	3,010,000
1951	183	6,100	724	734	—	3,400,000
1952	327	16,200	746	1,110	276	10,000,000
1953	541	31,800	779	2,154	—	—
1954	577	47,500	815	2,723	260	—
1955	835	90,000	868	3,742	265	12,000,000
1956	1,490	515,700	938	4,400	352	—
1957	1,700	993,200	1,030	6,692	1,429	15,000,000
1958	6,772	2,987,500	1,386	8,384	1,884	30,000,000
1959	11,124	4,570,000	1,758	9,212	1,427	21,000,000
1960	— (no data) —		—	—	1,455	20,932,177
1961	—	—	—	—	—	—
1962	—	—	—	9,000	—	—
1963	—	4,500,000	—	9,000	—	—
1964	1,975	6,000,000	2,000	12,000	—	—

*Statistical information in this table is from a variety of sources. Readers are referred to the author's *Radio Broadcasting in Communist China*, *The Film Industry in Communist China* and *The Press and Journals in Communist China*, all published as research monographs by the Center for International Studies, Massachusetts Institute of Technology.

movement, these so-called radio stations were set up in the fields where peasants labored. The Maoist dogma of increasing productivity by enhancement of ideological consciousness was carried to the extreme. The peasants resented this intensification of political regimentation. Furthermore such a radical decentralization of radio propaganda was inefficient. Hence the commune stations were abandoned after 1960, and the rural radio stations were, once more, concentrated at the traditional center of communications, the county towns. The 1,975 rural stations in 1964 corresponded to the number of counties in China that were inherited from the Manchu dynasty and maintained through the Nationalist period.

The phenomena of arbitrary media distribution and rural underdevelopment are also shown in the growth of the press in the same period. Table 1 shows that after the peak of 30 million circulation in 1958, circulation steadily went down. There is reason to believe that the number of newspapers also declined. In 1960 three provincial Party leaders stated that from now on quality instead of quantity would be emphasized.[3] This seems to suggest that press as well as radio underwent consolidation after the arbitrary distribution in

1958–59. The most significant indication of this was the report in 1963 that provincial newspapers were publishing rural editions to replace county newspapers. Yet even these supposedly high quality rural editions had a difficult time being accepted by rural residents, and rural Party cadres were the first ones to reject these papers for lack of interest in their content.[4]

Growth patterns of film projection units as shown in Table 1 are similar to that of radio. Arbitrary distribution of the mobile film-showing teams in 1958 was rectified after that time, and their number declined until growth started again in 1964. However, two things must be made clear. First, growth in 1964 resulted from a major government effort to divert urban film-showing teams to rural areas. Second, coverage of these teams in rural areas remained thin. A 1965 report stated, "The rural film-showing network is still weak. There are too few film-showing teams, far from satisfying peasants' demands."[5]

As the many accusations launched against former propaganda officials in the Cultural Revolution revealed, Mao Tse-tung interpreted the retreat of the mass media after the failure of the Great Leap not as an indication of rural underdevelopment but of sabotage by intellectuals and propaganda officials within the Party. But failure of the Great Leap did not shake Mao's faith in mass mobilization of the peasantry. The economic crisis of 1960–61 temporarily compelled Mao to stop distributing media arbitrarily in rural areas, but he was determined to revive it in the future.

In 1963 two circumstances precipitated Mao's decision to reassert himself. One was that the country had sufficiently recovered from the disasters of the Great Leap and was on the eve of embarking upon a new comprehensive industrialization program. The other was a debate among propaganda officials and intellectuals on proper strategy of mass persuasion giving Mao an opportunity to set one group off against another.

POLICY DEBATE ON PROPAGANDA

Ever since the late 1950s propagandists and intellectuals in Communist China have been debating propaganda strategy. The main issue was whether propaganda would be more effective by intensifying or reducing Party exhortations and regimentation. In analytical terms, the former stand emphasized penetration from above and the latter, identification from below. The former relied on mass campaigns and was bent on politicizing all types of media content. The latter relied on media and educational institutions and advocated a diversified approach to propaganda. Mao was for the former stand that called for intensification of exhortations and regimentations.

The debate further involved three basic issues of propaganda and national integration. The first one concerned the overall symbol of appeal that the Party should use to achieve national integration. Specifically this debate concerned the choice between the manipulative symbol of "class struggle" and the identitive symbol of "whole people (chuan-min)." Chou Yang, the former deputy director of the Propaganda Department of the Party Central Committee, was accused by the Maoists in the Cultural Revolution of advocating the policy of changing "literature and art for workers and peasants" to "literature and art for the whole Chinese people." The second issue concerned the allocation of resources in propaganda to purely "political" or "knowledge" matters. The latter included presumably nonpolitical subjects like science, technology and general social sciences. Once more, Chou Yang was accused of emphasizing "knowledge" at the expense of "political" type of propaganda materials. The third issue concerned the proper propaganda tactics for different social groups. There was, for example, the suggestion that a sophisticated and intellectual approach for political propaganda should be directed to literates in general. Similarly there was the view that mass campaigns were no longer an effective propaganda instrument and that the Party ought to give the illiterates and semi-literates more opportunities for education and allow them time to develop gradually a genuine political consciousness. These views were certainly incompatible with Mao's anti-intellectual and anti-institutional approach to mass persuasion.[6]

So far as the above debate was concerned, the Great Leap Forward in 1958 was a victory of the Maoists that emphasized further political regimentation and penetration. The subsequent economic crisis had temporarily discredited the Mao group. Those who emphasized identification were called in by the Party leadership to help the regime to tide over the crisis. That is why from 1961 to the early part of 1963, there was a conspicuous "liberal" trend in the art and literature of Communist China. The propagandists and intellectuals who were opposed to the Maoist strategy of penetration now took this opportunity to launch veiled attacks on Mao's leadership.

To Mao these attacks published in the Party press and journals were proofs of his earlier suspicion of sabotage and revision of his policy by intellectuals and some officials in the propaganda apparatus. For power considerations and for the realization of his new scheme of mass mobilization in 1963, Mao had to eliminate these real or imaginary "class enemies."

THE GREAT PURGE

Starting in 1963 Mao repeatedly accused the mass media in China, especially newspapers, journals and books, of resisting his demand for mass mobilization in rural areas. In 1964 Mao criticized the members of the All-China Federation of Literacy and Art Circles severely:

The majority of journals and publications of this federation (with few exceptions) basically did not implement the Party's policy in the past fifteen years. These people had become bureaucratic officials and would not go down to be near workers and peasants. They did not portray socialistic revolution and construction. In recent years they have even fallen near the edge of revisionism. If they are not seriously rectified, then there is bound to be a day when they will be made into an organization like the Petofi Club.[7]

From January 1965, Mao started his stage by stage purge of the overall propaganda apparatus in China. His first target was the Ministry of Culture in which several prominent Chinese intellectuals held important positions. In the process Mao set one group off against another, utilizing factions among the intellectuals and propagandists. Thus Mao first cast out the famous novelist-minister Sheng Yen-pin and three well-known deputy ministers. Mao then installed Lu Ting-i, then Director of the Propaganda Department of the Party Central Committee as the new Minister of Culture. Of the five new deputy ministers, four were of military and Party bureaucratic background. But Lu was only temporarily used by Mao to purge other intellectuals. Lu's own career was to be terminated soon.

Mao's purge of propaganda apparatus headquarters, the Propaganda Department of the Central Committee of the Party, was interesting. He started from below and pulled down the whole structure by a few major strikes. The first one was staged in Shanghai in November 1965, when a Shanghai newspaper suddenly attacked propaganda officials of the Peking Municipal Party Committee. When the Peking group found out that it was Mao who organized the attack from Shanghai, it grew panicky and soon collapsed.

Mao then turned to the Propaganda Department's heart. In May 1966 the Department's organ, *People's Daily,* the most authoritative newspaper in Communist China, was attacked by the army newspaper, *Liberation Army Daily,* for erring on the problem of the primacy of ideology over professional competence. The military was eventually brought in to reorganize the *People's Daily.* In July of the same year, Lu Ting-i and four deputy directors of the Department were purged. In a few months, the Propaganda Departments of eight provincial Party committees were purged (Shantung, Kiangsi, Kiangsu, Chekian, Fukien, Szechuan, Kweichow and Tibet).

The downfall of so many Party propaganda officials naturally affected publications originally controlled by these officials. The hardest hit were those formerly controlled by the Peking Municipal Party Committee. All of its journals were suspended. Some of its newspapers were reorganized and some suspended. Important newspapers like the *China Youth Daily* of the Young Communist League and *Chinese Workers' Daily* of the All-China Federation of Labor Unions, originally organs of major mass organizations, were suspended after their organizations were dissolved.

Since the newspapers and journals in Communist China were largely urban bound, Mao could suppress them with impunity; the rural areas were not much affected. By suppressing these media Mao also deprived the intellectuals and the purged propaganda officials of a potential medium of expressing their opposition to his leadership.

Replacing the suspended publications was a large number of tabloids published by various Red Guard organizations. These two- or four-page papers contained little that one would consider news, but they did contain substantial though conflicting revelations about the internal power struggle. They were designed primarily to discredit Mao's opponents by sensational exposé. These papers also provided the youthful rebels an opportunity to participate in the power struggle, and their morale was heightened.

In suppressing the media, Mao made one exception, he kept the radio open, for the broadcasting network is the only mass medium substantially effective beyond the urban centers. Important Central Committee decisions, now under the Maoist faction control, were broadcast one day earlier before the newspapers printed them in full. In addition radio served as the signal for Red Guards everywhere to start demonstrations and parades.

In the meantime Mao Tse-tung instituted the type of propaganda technique that he had long wished: the total politicization of the media content, as shown in radio programs and documentary films; the transformation of the press into simple propaganda pamphlets such as the Red Guard "newspapers"; and in the large-scale use of mobile oral agitation teams such as the so-called "Mao Tse-tung Thought Propaganda Team" composed of workers and peasants.

A recent press report stated that the mobile agitation teams had involved "several million people" and had "permeated almost every factory, school, hospital and government agency."[8] The most likely unit that can take the command responsibility is the army whose Party and indoctrination apparatus has remained intact.

CONCLUSION

In the last analysis, the destruction of much of the mass media system in Communist China illustrates the larger problem of building modern institutions in a developing nation. Any new institution in such a nation must withstand two violent onslaughts. One is the lack of modern social conditions on which to plant the root of institution. The other is the stresses and strains of a political leader's personality. In industrial nations, modern institutions like the mass media and voluntary organizations deeply rooted in society are able to remain independent of the shocks of political leader's idiosyncrasy. But the mass media in Communist China did not acquire such a capability.

NOTES

1.   To a large extent Mao's concept of mass persuasion stemmed from the single experience of the peasant movement in Hunan in 1927 which Mao reported in the famous "Report of an Investigation of the Peasant Movement in Hunan," *Selected Works of Mao Tse-tung,* Vol. 1 (Peking: Foreign Language Press, 1965), pp. 23–59.

2.   In the case of some Middle East countries, Lerner noted: "Radios distributed gratis by government facilitate 'social control' rather than 'individual participation'; they also explain why most Arab countries show an excess of radio-listeners over urban literates," in Daniel Lerner, *The Passing of Traditional Society* (The Free Press of Glencoe, 1964), p. 67.

3.   *Jen-min Jih-pao* (People's Daily), Jan. 11, 1960.

4.   *Nan-fang Jih-pao* (Southern Daily), Jan. 27, 1963.

5.   *Jen-min Jih-pao* (People's Daily), Jan. 12, 1965.

6.   These issues of debate were not gathered from a single source. They were mentioned here and there in the press, particularly in the press accusations against Chou Yang. The reader is referred to the following issues of the *People's Daily*: July 15, 1966; July 17, 1966; July 20, 1966; July 22, 1966.

7.   *Jen-min Jih-pao* (People's Daily), June 6, 1966.

8.   New York *Times*, Dec. 9, 1968.

THIRD WORLD SYSTEMS: IMITATION AND INNOVATION

Introduction*

This section examines the mass media in the under-developed countries of Africa, Asia, and Latin America from two perspectives—"what is" and "what could be." What are the existing media in these countries like, and what is the potential for using the media to break free of economic stagnation and backwardness? This second expectation has not been demanded of media in the developed countries, so it is quite likely that their media systems are not suitable to the poor countries' needs. I therefore conclude with some speculation about the ideal media system for Third World countries.

The first three articles deal with the media in Africa and Asia. They demonstrate the paucity of media compared to the rich countries, the colonial heritage, and contemporary operational problems. William Hachten outlines the diversity of Africa and its media. This continent has undergone rapid decolonization in the last two decades,

---

*Part of the material below is drawn from my article "Communications and Development: The Relevance of Media Content," Sociological Quarterly, 12, winter 1971. Used by permission of the publisher.

and considerable postindependence turmoil. The mass media, which are concentrated in the cities, have similarly undergone transition. Radio—the primary communicator—has been decolonized and expanded. It is now usually operated as a branch of government. Many countries, however, still broadcast in the colonial mother tongue, since it is the only language widely understood by the multilingual African peoples. The style and content of broadcasting also reflect the past, as often as not. The press show a coexistence between weak European transplants and even weaker African newspapers. Both suffer from the effects of low literacy rates. Television is scarce and serves mainly as a trinket for Africa's few nouveaux riches.

The Asian press, described by John Lent, suffers too from poor resources and limited readership. In addition, it is strongly circumscribed by government censorship and harassment. Although not generally controlled or owned by the state, as they are in the communist bloc countries, newspapers are far from "free" in the Western commercial use of the term. Adnan Almaney's article describes in detail the government press control in Egypt, which culminated in 1960 in nationalization. This may well be the trend of other Third World countries. Latin American media and United States influence on them have been dealt with elsewhere (Wells, 1972). The overall problem of global commercialization is discussed by Herbert Schiller in the last section of this volume.

COMMUNICATION AND DEVELOPMENT

Several prominent students of the mass media in less developed countries (Lerner, 1958; Schramm, 1964; de Sola Pool, 1966) have written of the mass media's potential for stimulating economic growth. The electronic media in particular can bypass the need for mass literacy, providing a developmental input that was unavailable to rich economies in their formative stages. Wide recognition of this has led to attempts to integrate communications into general theories of development. But media experts disagree on the extent to which the media actually fulfill developmental needs, and they have formed what may be called positive, negative, and neutral orientations or theories that are held implicitly—and sometimes simultaneously.

Positive theories are the most common in the literature. They state that increasing the availability of mass media stimulates economic development. This view coupled with the imperative to use the media for organization and mass exhortation characterizes the communist theory of media use (de Sola Pool, 1963:241). The United Nations also officially adopts a positive view, since it recommends minimum targets for the expansion of newspaper, radio receiver, cinema seating, and television receiver densities for all countries irrespective of economic level (Unesco, 1961:17). This is in part an attempt to extend basic human rights—in this case, the right to full dissemination of ideas—that are considered to be developmental.

Many prominent Western scholars apparently follow such positive views, although usually in a more cautious and guarded fashion. Lerner, for example, sees the new media as crucial in breaking down traditionalism and effecting "radical changes" in the psychological qualities of the masses (1958, especially chap. 11). Changes in the communication system, he notes, correlate highly with other behavioral changes (1960:133) and trigger the process of modernization (1963:348), which he assumes is necessary for economic growth. Similarly, Deutsch sees mass media development as an element of modernity and "social mobilization," which is considered a necessary, albeit not sufficient, condition for economic development (1966:213).

Negative theories hold that expansion of the media in developing countries produces, on balance, pernicious effects. When such a view is held by policy makers in these countries it has been described as "disillusionment" (de Sola Pool, 1963:236–38). It often results when the media instill unrealistic material demands in the masses, a phenomenon noted by Lerner (1958:5, 13, 231, 326). But these negative theories also reflect the failure to produce beneficial results, such as usable job training and general education. A few scholars warn that specific media may inherently have misanthropic effects in poor countries. For example, de Sola Pool (1966:108) has advised against an expansion of television, largely on the basis of its high operating and hardware costs. Ignoring such economic drawbacks, McLuhan holds that the psychic effects of television are dangerous even in developed countries, while radio is a disruptive force in poor countries (see Stearn, 1967:301).

Neutral theories posit that media development has no significant effect on economic development, or that it is merely a product of economic well-being. This is the stance of the developmentalist, who ignores the media as a causal variable. Cross-national studies have confirmed that there is a strong correlation, if not a causal relationship, between media development and economic level, urbanization, industrialization, and literacy (Unesco, 1961:17). Lerner suggested in 1958 that urbanization was a precondition for media development, but after a decade of rapid media expansion the evidence is less clear (Schramm and Ruggels, 1967:58). Media development may be limited, but not strictly determined, by such socioeconomic factors.

The presence of three competing theories on the link between mass communications and economic development is evidence that at least two are inappropriate or that all three are too simplistic. The fact that the media are part of the experience of their audience precludes the absolute validity of the neutral theory, which reflects only the vagaries of measuring media effects. The task, therefore, is to reconcile the positive and negative theories. This can be done, in part, by focusing on the uses to which media are put and, contrary to the tenets of McLuhan and his followers, on their content.

The mass media are widely thought to have a powerful modernizing potential. Their idealized uses range from the enhancement of "freedom of information" (Unesco, 1961:15) to diffuse nation-building tasks and the provision of "modern" role models (Schramm, 1964:37–38). The relationship between efficient performance of these tasks and economic development is not very clear. However, two of the more specific idealized uses mentioned by Schramm (1963:38) appear to be directly relevant to economic growth: the media should teach necessary skills that are more "advanced" than those currently held; and they should extend the effective market by stimulating the demand for consumer goods. Both of these programming goals are fulfilled to a degree, even if the audience is often unaware of what it is learning. Similarly, the unconscious teaching potential of "merely entertaining" programs is often unrecognized by media planners. The development outcome depends both on whether skill training keeps pace with consumer yearnings and on which sector of the economy is stimulated.

The media have a great potential for teaching productive skills and complementing formal education, especially since formal educational resources are typically scarce and unevenly distributed in the underdeveloped countries. Compared to massive educational reform, the task of improving media distribution—which in many countries is already relatively advanced—is fairly simple and inexpensive. This use of media, however, is not as easy as market stimulation, in part because it has not been widely practiced in the developed countries: there is no readily available pool of expertise in basic skill training via the mass media on which the poor country can draw. From Western research findings, however, it is apparent that a two-way communication system reinforces this type of learning (Katz and Lazersfeld, 1955). Such findings are widely applicable feedback programs have been used successfully in India and Jordan (radio forums) and in China and the Philippines (see the chapters on these countries in Lerner and Schramm, 1967). For efficient feedback, programming has to be as local as possible (Schramm, 1964:123), however, which raises costs and may negate the nation-building efforts of the media.

The teaching of basic skills can be aided by what has been termed the multiplicative effect of communications (Schramm, 1967:17; Oshima, 1967). Oshima calls for a selective approach to development, one that emphasizes experimental projects in all sectors of the economy. Successes would then be disseminated widely by the media. This could clearly be useful for some organizational innovations, but it would do little more than provoke envy of demonstrated innovations that required extensive capital investment. For example, it would seem useless (or worse) to demonstrate the benefits of tractor plowing to a poor farmer who can barely feed his draft animals.

The media in Western countries have been effective in inducing consumer demands through advertising techniques. It has been proposed that commercial underwriting and control of mass media in the underdeveloped countries will similarly spread the benefits of an active market (de Sola Pool, 1966:108). But commercial control may preclude or greatly limit the wider educational uses of the media. As Schramm (1964:131), Lerner (Lerner and Schramm, 1967:104-5) and others have warned, what the masses are induced to want must correspond to what they can conceivably get. The sector of the economy that employs the most people and serves mass rather than elite consumer needs is the one that should receive the media's market stimulation attention. Such, unfortunately, is often not the case. But stimulating the market for luxury goods only increases expectations and inequalities, thus acting in a counterdevelopmental manner. There is nothing intrinsically beneficial about the media; it is how they are used that counts. They are no panacea for a society's ills.

Wilbur Schramm's article at the end of this section outlines how mass media can be used as communications tools by the planners of social change. He deals with agricultural plans in India, television and radio forums elsewhere, health campaign uses in Asia, literacy drives, and the media as a support for formal education. He stresses throughout that such media campaigns must be adapted to local social and cultural conditions. Unfortunately, this good advice is seldom taken, as a considerable number of reports reveal. Simmons, Kent, and Mishra (1968), for example, show that people are reached by media, especially by radio, even in the urban slums of poor countries, and they give the media high credibility. But they receive virtually no news that can be classed developmental. In recent years there has been a very rapid and global expansion of television, but, like radio, this medium is seldom used for developmental purposes. Instead it is generally used to sell consumer goods to the few who can afford them. Ugboajah (1972), for example, has noted that African media are predominantly beamed at Westernized urban elite groups, and valuable traditional inputs are ignored. This misuse of the media, or at least the failure to capitalize on their developmental potential, is in part due to the style of media operation that is adopted. This in turn is influenced by outside pressures, the topic of the last section of this volume.

DEVELOPMENT NEEDS AND MEDIA SYSTEMS

It seems reasonable to infer that the type of media system adopted by a less developed country will influence programming. Thus the nature of the broadcasting organization, its support structure, and the regulatory constraints imposed on it are important, though often overlooked, determinants of content.

Since the media are invariably operated by a small group of people, they always have a manipulating potential. Indeed, unless information is broadcast at random it must first be evaluated and condensed. No matter how carefully this selection is made, a slant is given to the reportage of human events. Thus the problem of manipulation is a matter of degree. The United Nations General Assembly no doubt recognizes this, but it has resolved that "freedom of information is one of the basic freedoms and that it is essential to the furtherance and protection of all other freedoms." To disseminate information freely there should be "a diversity of sources of news and opinion" (Unesco, 1961:15). Yet a poor country cannot afford such diversity: its task is rather to guide its population along developmental tracks.

Several factors are of crucial importance in relaying developmental messages successfully by electronic media. First, the messages must reach their target audience, be correctly received, and be acted upon. This is by no means automatic, as recent studies on rural Brazil and Colombia indicate (see Grunig, 1971; Whiting and Stanfield, 1972), even though the spread of radio and television sets has been much more rapid than was expected from the low economic levels of these countries (see Simmons, Kent, and Mishra, 1968; Wells, 1972:chap. 5). Public availability or subsidization of receiver sets seems essential. Secondly, the media need to involve the audience in national concerns, instead of merely relaying the orders of the government elite (Schramm, 1964:37–38). Finally, programming is most effective if it is consciously planned to have a developmental impact.

As conceived here, developmental needs center about the creation of an austere and hard-working, but also contented and self-asserting, population. Although mass media planners in the less developed countries have attempted to use the media for a wide range of educational purposes (see Maddison, 1971, for example), they have not achieved this aim. It demands the formulation of attainable life-styles and aspirations, and these may be developed only under conditions of relatively equalitarian nationalism and cultural autonomy.

The developmental impact of the media can therefore be maximized by their use as teaching devices and multipliers, and by the propagation of an ideology conducive to the stimulation of indigenous mass markets. Advertising should stress items that use existing resources and play down the desirability of cosmopolitan consumer goods. Even if we concede the "end of ideology" in the West, we should recognize that in the Third World it has scarcely begun. Packaging the developmental ideology in nationalistic rhetoric (as has been done to a degree in Japan and China) may make it effective. To be believed, the ideological exhortations must be accompanied by structural changes, including some distribution of the benefits accruing from past sacrifice. Nationalism permits appeals to both sacrifice for one's country and the redefinition of modernism. The latter is difficult in a world of international communications, but it is nonetheless essential if consumer styles are ever to be applicable to the masses in underdeveloped countries.

What system is best suited for radio and television (which are usually held to have the most developmental potential) in these countries? The American model calls for private ownership of broadcasting facilities and financing through advertising revenue. The audience is treated as a market for advertisers, and programming is geared to maximizing the number of buyers. Educational programming is of low priority, since it is expensive to produce and generates low (or no) advertising revenue. Although the commercial pattern may stimulate consumer buying, it was not explicitly designed for maximizing economic growth. The adoption of this package by a less developed country inevitably involves some external financing and programming (sold at bargain-basement prices, having already met production costs in its rich country of origin). The latter, of course, portrays North American or European settings and values. Because international corporations are likely to be the heaviest advertisers (and giant international advertising agencies tend to predominate in the Third World) external rather than indigenous economies are more often stimulated.

If a choice is to be made then, the so-called totalitarian model (as described by Almaney in Egypt) may better suit developmental needs. The media can be nationalistic and project indigenous life-styles in their programming, and they can be used extensively for educational purposes. Such a system, however, is clearly expensive, and its political domination is likely to inhibit all but token feedback mechanisms. Its political indoctrination may become counterdevelopmental. In addition, it is likely to be dull and fail to provide the entertainment and cultural outlet required for a better life in poor countries.

Fortunately, the choice is not limited to these two alternatives. Media control could well be exercised by a public or private corporation as in Europe or Japan. This might avoid both full commercialization and political domination, thereby keeping the media flexible for developmental tasks. Financing might be supplied by license fees, although these might unnecessarily slow the dissemination of receivers. A poor country might well consider advertising as a supplementary source of revenue if commercials are limited to indigenous mass products. The best sources of funds, however, would be general taxation or special excise taxes on foreign and domestic luxury goods.

Programming goals should be primarily educational and cultural. Programs should include general information and specific projects, such as literacy, hygiene, population control, and agricultural drives. This type of programming has not been employed much in developed countries, so the poorer countries must pioneer it. School programming in rich countries has generally been supplemental rather than direct. A few projects such as Italy's "Telescuola" literacy drive may be suggestive for less developed nations (Dizard, 1966:210–13, 233; Paulu, 1967:170–81). Locally produced formal education and skill training materials should take high priority. Cultural fare that is entertaining can be programmed to enhance national unity and promote indigenous life-styles. Under no circumstances should cheap imported programming be used to fill air time, for there is no logical reason for broadcasting twenty-four hours per day.

The poorer nations would do well to eschew elite audiences and aim first at the masses. Special programs can be devised later to reach specific segments of the population (farmers, tradesmen, teachers, mothers, etc.) if the media offer the cheapest or most effective method of reaching them. Such projects can be successful only if they do not aim at maximizing audiences, and if they are not programmed in competition with more exciting or less demanding fare (for example, a soap opera or a sports event). If positive results are to be achieved, much more attention must be paid to feedback than is exhibited in Western broadcasting.

The options for less developed countries, therefore, go beyond a simple choice between two or four media systems. Unfortunately, short-term financial considerations and external pressures may lead to the adoption of "free" commercial media systems that are entirely unsuited for developmental uses. In terms of the five criteria discussed in the introduction to Part I, these are generally private corporate enterprises, controlled from outside, and financed by advertising; they program to entertain and sell goods to cosmopolitan elites, and are not very concerned with feedback. Such systems are a waste of a poor country's broadcasting resources. The less developed country should instead devise its own system, keeping developmental ends in mind.

REFERENCES

Deutsch, Karl W. 1966. "Social Mobilization and Political Development." In Jason L. Finkle and Richard W. Gable, eds., Political Development and Social Change. New York: Wiley.

Dizard, Wilson P. 1966. Television: A World View. Syracuse, N.Y.: Syracuse University Press.

Grunig, James E. 1971. "Communications and The Decision Making Process of Colombian Peasants." Economic Development and Cultural Change, 19, No. 4, pp. 580–97.

Katz, Elihu, and Paul Lazarsfeld. 1955. Personal Influence. Glencoe, Ill.: Free Press.

Lerner, Daniel. 1963. "Toward a Communication Theory of Modernization." In Lucian W. Pye, ed., Communications and Political Development. Princeton, N.J.: Princeton University Press.

——— 1960. "Communication Systems and Social Systems." In Wilbur Schramm, ed., Mass Communications. Urbana: University of Illinois Press.

———. 1958. The Passing of Traditional Society. New York: Free Press.

Lerner, Daniel, and Wilbur Schramm, eds. 1967. Communication and Change in the Developing Countries. Honolulu: East-West Center Press.

Maddison, John. 1971. Radio and Television in Literacy. Paris: Unesco.

Oshima, Harry T. 1967. "The Strategy of Selective Growth and the Role of Communications." In Daniel Lerner and Wilbur Schramm, eds., Communication and Change in the Developing Countries. Honolulu: East-West Center Press.

Paulu, Burton. 1967. Radio and Television Broadcasting on the European Continent. Minneapolis: University of Minnesota Press.

Schramm, Wilbur. 1964. Mass Media and National Development. Stanford, Calif.: Stanford University Press.

———. 1963. "Communication Development and the Development Press." In Lucien W. Pye, ed., Communication and Political Development. Princeton, N.J.: Princeton University Press.

Schramm, Wilbur, and W. Lee Ruggels. 1967. "How Mass Media Systems Grow." In Daniel Lerner and Wilbur Schramm, eds., Communication and Change in the Developing Countries. Honolulu: East-West Center Press.

Simmons, Robert E., Kurt Kent, and Vishwa M. Mishra. 1968. "Media and Developmental News in Slums of Ecuador and India." Journalism Quarterly, winter, pp. 698–705.

90

de Sola Pool, Ithiel. 1966. "Communications and Development." In Myron Weiner, ed., Modernization: The Dynamics of Growth. New York: Basic Books.

———. 1963. "Mass Media and Politics in the Modernization Process." In Lucian W. Pye, ed., Communications and Political Development. Princeton, N.J.: Princeton University Press.

Stearn, Gerald E., ed. 1967. McLuhan: Hot and Cool. New York: Dial Press.

Ugboajah, Frank Okwu. 1972. "A Traditional-Urban Media Model: Stocktaking for African Development." Gazette, 18, no. 2, pp. 76–95.

Unesco. 1961. Mass Media in the Developing Countries. Paris: Unesco.

Wells, Alan. 1972. Picture Tube Imperialism?: Development and Television in Latin America. Maryknoll, N.Y.: Orbis Books.

Whiting, Gordon C., and J. David Stanfield. 1972. "Mass Media Use and Opportunity Structure in Rural Brazil." Public Opinion Quarterly, spring, pp. 56–68.

Mass Media in Africa*

WILLIAM A. HACHTEN

WILLIAM A. HACHTEN is Professor of Journalism and Mass Communications at the University of Wisconsin (Madison). He holds a doctoral degree from the University of Minnesota. He has conducted field research on mass media in tropical Africa (1965) and returned in 1968 for further research on a Fulbright-Hayes fellowship. He is author of The Supreme Court on Freedom of the Press and Muffled Drums.

NTRODUCTION

Mass communication in Africa is so diverse as to be astonishing. It is a Sudanese camel driver jogging along listening to Radio Cairo on a small transistor radio; a Ghanaian civil servant reading the *Daily Graphic* while drinking a shandy at Accra's Ambassador Hotel; a Wolof man sitting with a group of his fellow Senegalese watching an experimental television program in Dakar.

Or it is a white South African reading the *Rand Daily Mail* on a bus carrying him to his office in bustling Johannesburg; a radio blaring out to the teeming Moroccan crowds in the labyrinth of the Fez medina; a band of tribal Africans intently watching a flickering motion picture projected from a mobile cinema van in a remote corner of Zambia.

---

*Reprinted from William A. Hachten, *Muffled Drums: The News Media in Africa*, pp. xiii-xv, 6-7, 14-32. © 1971, Iowa State University Press, Ames. Used by permission.

It may be also a correspondent for *Time* magazine catching a jet plane at Nairobi airport to cover a reported coup in a minor central African nation, or a Hausa man in his mud hut in the feudal north of Nigeria listening to the news from Radio Nigeria in far-off Lagos.

The news in Hausa on Radio Nigeria is always preceded by a brief recording of a Hausa drummer. This is appropriate, for over much of Africa the drum has long been an important traditional means of communication and is still widely used today. In Africa's expanding modern sector, the news media—newspaper, radio, television, magazines—may be regarded as the new drums of Africa. But the news media are as yet "muffled drums"—they are too few and inadequate for the great tasks expected of them and they are often harassed and controlled by self-serving interests. The new drums reverberating printed and electronic messages are still too weak technologically, economically, or politically to carry very far. Their messages often are distorted, garbled, and muted. The new "talking drums" do not speak clearly and effectively to the millions of new Africans. Yet in both the colonial period and the years since independence, the press and broadcasting have played an increasingly significant role in the dissemination of news and public information.

If a particular culture can be viewed as a system of communication, as Edward T. Hall has suggested in *The Silent Language,* then Africa as one of the most culturally diverse regions of the world has such problems of cross-cultural communication as will challenge the new talking drums for many years to come.

Leaders of the more than forty, mostly fragile national structures of that vast continent have been struggling against painful odds during the 1960s to establish politically stable societies while dealing with the age-old problems of poverty, disease, ignorance, and ethnic rivalries. In the tortuous drama that President Julius Nyerere of Tanzania has called the "terrible ascent to modernization," the news media of communication have a part to play. As yet, however, this role is neither clearly defined nor adequately performed. The news media as social institutions have had a brief and tenuous existence and they are still very much at the mercy of harsh economic and political restrictions.

"Mass media of communication" is a somewhat misleading term when applied to the news media in Africa. In any country the pervasiveness of mass media is directly related to economic and educational levels and most African nations are, by Western standards, still poor and illiterate. The mass media as we know them in America and Europe are all present there in uneven patterns, but they (except for radio) do not reach any large numbers of people, much less the "masses." At best, they mostly reach the educated minorities in the cities.

Newspapers are read by those few interested and literate Africans who are able to buy or borrow a copy and who are fortunate enough to live in a place, usually the capital, where newspapers are available.

Broadcasting reaches more people, usually those in urban areas who own or have access to radio or television sets and are interested enough to use them. Radio has much the largest audience since it does extend into the hinterlands.

Clearly, in this least developed of all continents (Africa has been called "the continent that God kept in reserve") the mass media are the least developed of any comparable area of the world. This does not mean they are unimportant; while only a small fraction of today's Africans are consumers of mass communications, this is the fraction that is shaping Africa's destiny. Many of Africa's vexing problems are related to breakdowns in communication and tied to the fact that so many Africans are not in touch with their leaders nor with the cities whence come new ideas and the concepts of the modern world.

But though audiences are small, mass communications are important to Africans because they can help speed the processes of development and national integration and bring the continent into a fuller participation in the modern world.

A mass media system is also a kind of mirror image of a nation's political and economic structure. Each is sensitive to the other. Newspapers, radio, television, and other media do not operate in a vacuum; their content, their reach, their freedom, and their audiences are determined by the context of the nation in which they operate. . . .

African peoples, in spite of their great linguistic and ethnic diversity, have been communicating among and between themselves in a wide variety of ways for a long time. In fact, the sheer range and variety of human or interpersonal communication on that immense continent offer a challenge to contemporary communications scholars.[1]

Mass communications, however, are not indigenous to Africa. A crucial element in the development of mass communications in Africa—both past and present—is the nature and extent of European influences. Differences in colonial experiences help explain differences in media systems.

The important component of any definition of mass communications is modern technology. To have *mass* communication, a message must be amplified or reproduced many thousands of times. This requires printing presses, newsprint, radio and television transmitters and receivers, and cinema projectors and theaters. These came from Europe with the Europeans. Initially, press and broadcasting facilities

were largely established for the convenience and use of the colonizers
and the few European settlers who followed. In most places Africans
were excluded or were at best an eavesdropping audience. Only in a
few areas have Africans historically produced their own newspapers
and these were based on European models.

Colonial rule was, by and large, the source of each country's
modern political institutions and the peculiar economic conditions
still markedly inhibiting local media growth. What happened before
independence profoundly affects the news media today even though
new African governments have tried to shuck off all vestiges of
colonialism. Since independence, the Africans have been converting
these "foreign" communication instruments to their own uses and
purposes. . . .

WINDS OF CHANGE

Throughout most of Africa, decolonization has been rapid. Before
1950, only four African countries were independent. But the strong
wave of nationalism that washed over the continent after World War
II forced the European colonial powers to grant independence to
most of their African possessions. Political freedom was carried on a
north wind into Africa. In 1956 Tunisia, Morocco, and Sudan gained
their independence. For the sub-Sahara, freedom dawned in 1957
when the British colony of the Gold Coast became the independent
nation of Ghana under its charismatic leader, Kwame Nkrumah. In
the years that followed—1960, 1962, 1964, 1965—the list of former
colonies lengthened rapidly: Nigeria, Senegal, both Congos, Tanganyika (now Tanzania), Cameroon, Uganda, the Ivory Coast, Kenya,
Zambia, Malawi, and even Gambia. Botswana and Lesotho, surrounded by white-dominated territories, won their independence
in 1966. In all, 35 new nations emerged in the decade between 1956
and 1966. Of the 43 major national states (most of whose boundarie
were inherited from Berlin's arbitrary mapmakers in 1885), the great
majority today are ruled by African governments. The principal
exceptions are in southern Africa—the Portuguese territories of
Angola and Mozambique, South Africa, Rhodesia, and South West
Africa—where white minorities impose their rule over African
majorities. The big news story out of Africa during the late 1960s
was the expanding guerrilla warfare backed by independent black
nations against the white man's redoubt in southern Africa. With it
was a growing fear of a racial war of ominous proportions. In the
unstable Africa of today, mass communication systems are as shaky
and volatile as the shifting political and social structures themselves.

Since 1965, military coups d'état overturned thirteen African governments, including the militantly "African socialist" regime of Nkrumah in Ghana and the federal republic of giant Nigeria. Other African governments toppled by their own army or police forces were Congo (Kinshasa), Dahomey, Burundi, Central African Republic, Upper Volta, Congo (Brazzaville), Mali, Sudan, Sierra Leone, Libya, and Somalia. These coups were not isolated events; they were only the latest of an increasing number of political upheavals that have scarred the young lives of at least thirty of the thirty-nine independent African-governed states. At the decade's end, civil wars persisted in Sudan and Chad, as a devastating war ended in Nigeria.

Nevertheless, today every African nation has some kind of news media system. As a continent, however, Africa is more poorly endowed with newspapers, radio, cinema, television, books, and publications than any other comparable area in the world. . . .

THE CONTINENT'S MEDIA FACILITIES

The news media . . . are sparsely scattered in irregular configurations as are the other underpinnings of modernity—railroads, paved highways, telephones, automobiles, industrial installations, shiny cities with jet airports, and Inter-Continental hotels. They tend to be concentrated in the larger capitals ringing the outer fringes of the continent: Dakar, Abidjan, Accra, Lagos, Cape Town, Johannesburg, Nairobi, Algiers, and Rabat.

In quick summary for the entire continent, excluding the United Arab Republic (which is usually considered in the Middle East), only about 175 daily newspapers circulated about 2.7 million copies daily; some 98 radio stations broadcast to 12.5 million radio receivers; 32 television stations transmitted to roughly 428,000 receiving sets; about 525 weeklies and fortnightlies had a combined circulation of more than 3.8 million; about 5,000 indoor motion picture theaters had about 1.3 million seats and an estimated weekly attendance of 3.7 million; and some 3,800 local libraries contained almost 14.8 million books.

Also, major world news services were available in most African countries and there were more than 27 local or national news services.[2]

These facilities are grossly insufficient to serve the almost 300 million people living in over 44 countries and islands, especially considering that two nations, South Africa and Nigeria, have a disproportionate share of media facilities. For example, just the 21 daily newspapers of South Africa account for 30 percent of all daily newspaper circulation in Africa.

(It must be noted that in developing nations, all social statistics are unreliable, and at best, approximate. This is especially true in mass communications. As in other parts of the *Tiers Monde,* the developed world's vast underbelly that cuts a wide swath through Asia, the Middle East, Africa, and Latin America, the mass media are growing unevenly and sporadically in Africa. Little wonder statistics and records are unreliable. New newspapers appear suddenly and established publications unexpectedly vanish. Determining the number of readers, or of radio and television sets in use, is almost guesswork in nations where reliable census data are nonexistent. Even data carefully assembled by Unesco and other United Nations organizations are often inaccurate to begin with or become quickly outdated. Newspaper sales fluctuate greatly and broadcasters often have only a hazy notion of how many people are listening.)

In several places independence brought a dramatic and accelerating growth of some media, particularly radio and television, but in general, mass communications have continued to lag well behind other world areas, with the partial exception of the Middle East and South Asia.

Only radio increased significantly during the sixties. Daily newspaper circulation and cinema facilities (mostly indoor) did not keep pace with population increase even though Africa's population was not soaring as fast as in some areas of Latin America and Asia. Overpopulation is one problem that Africa does not as yet generally share with other regions of the Third World. But its population is increasing faster than that of industrialized nations.

African media, with the exception of radio, are also well below the bare minimum standards set by Unesco for "adequate communications." The UN organization has suggested as an immediate target that a country should aim to provide for every 100 of its inhabitants at least ten copies of daily newspapers, five radio receivers, two cinema seats, and two television receivers. (According to Unesco, this arbitrary yardstick was established in order to measure the insufficiency of media *facilities* in developing nations. It tells us nothing about media *content* or *effects*.)

Most African nations, as well as many in Latin America and Asia (some 100 states and territories in all) fall below this very minimal "minimum" level in all four of the mass media. These countries have a combined population of 1,910 million or 66 percent of the world's total.[3] . . .

The number of radios in Africa is the bright exception (4.3 sets per 100 people) and is fast approaching the Unesco minimum. Radio has an estimated audience of 50 million. Television, because it is still in its infancy, is the only other mass medium that has grown significantly over the past five years or more, and in 1965 had.an estimated audience of 1.8 million.[4] More recently, however, television expansion has slowed.

There seems little doubt that daily newspapers and other publications have not been growing commensurate with broadcasting. This uneven growth of the news media in Africa can be explained in part by certain inherent characteristics of the news media themselves as they relate to the African setting. . . .

The pervasive dearth of modern mass communications adds to the burdens of those striving to modernize the continent, for printed pages, electronic broadcasting signals, and flickering film images are not merely divertisements or entertainment. Communication, whether mass or interpersonal, is intimately connected with the whole social fabric of a nation. As a nation moves from a traditional to a modern style of life, its means of news communication change accordingly, and often dramatically, from traditional or oral means to modern or media means. The need for news and public information increases as well. The news media perform an essential function in thus servicing a modernizing society, and each particular news medium has its own assets and limitations.

RADIO BROADCASTING

Radio demands first attention because of its wider acceptance in the African environment. Since it was first introduced in the years between the World Wars, mainly as a "news from home" service for the European populations, radio broadcasting has made far more progress than the press toward becoming a real *mass* medium in Africa.

The earliest radio broadcasting was in South Africa, which had the largest concentration of Europeans. The first radio station was opened at Johannesburg in 1920, followed by others in Cape Town and Durban. Kenya, in 1927, became the second country, and the first in tropical Africa, to initiate radio broadcasting. The earliest programs from Nairobi were designed for English settlers, but later broadcasts were transmitted in Kikuyu, Swahili, Arabic, and Hindustani.

On the west coast, radio on wired services began in Sierra Leone in 1934, on the Gold Coast (Ghana) in 1935, and Nigeria in 1936. In the latter year the British colonial government decided to develop radio in the British colonies as a public service. Because of this early emphasis, radio in the former British territories is still far ahead of that in other areas.[5] Radio in French Africa lagged behind and has never really caught up. While the British had a policy of establishing radio in each colony, the French, with their more centralized colonial administration, long relied on Dakar, Brazzaville, and Paris to provide radio signals for the far-flung regions of French West Africa and French Equatorial Africa. Broadcasting from Dakar began in 1939 but Radio Abidjan did not become an established satellite of Radio Dakar until 1951. Furthermore, radio under French colonial rule was always *French* radio; there was little effort to provide either broadcasting in vernaculars or any indigenous programming.

In most places, radio as a means of reaching the Africans was an afterthought. The government of Southern Rhodesia, for example, started a broadcast service from Salisbury in 1932 for European listeners in Southern Rhodesia, Northern Rhodesia, and Nyasaland. It was not until 1946 that facilities were established in Lusaka to broadcast to Africans of the three territories in Nyanja, Tonga, Lozi, Ndebele, Shona, and English.[6]

Before World War II, only seven tropical African territories possessed transmitting facilities. At war's end, fifteen had them. As new independent nations burgeoned, so did radio, for the new governments have fostered its development as their number one mass medium.

In 1955 Africa counted 151 transmitters; by early 1960 the same stations reported 252 transmitters (60 percent shortwave, the balance medium wave); by 1964 the number was up to 370 transmitters, with 43 African governments involved in broadcasting.[7] However, the number of programming services, a total of 98 in 1965 tended to be concentrated in a few nations: Angola, 16; Congo (Kinshasa), 8; Mozambique, 6; Nigeria, 7; and South Africa, 15.

The great increase in radio receivers—from 350,000 to almost 12 million in ten years—was due largely to the development of the low power drain radio receiver, popularly known as a transistor radio. Light and portable, radios were no longer dependent on an electricity power source and were comparatively inexpensive. Not surprisingly, in just the five-year period from the end of 1960 to the end of 1965, radio sets in use increased 140 percent. Even at that, Africa's 11,826,000 radios still represented only about 4 percent of all the radios outside the United States and Canada, and these were disproportionately located in Algeria, Morocco, Nigeria, and South Africa.

Throughout Africa radio is recognized as the least expensive and most effective way of reaching people, particularly the illiterate tribalized African living in the bush. No wonder, then, radio in Africa is virtually always a function of government. At independence, the new African governments quickly brought radio fully under the official umbrella if it was not there already. In Kenya, for example, radio and television, both public corporations, were combined as the Voice of

Kenya within the Ministry of Information. In the effort to Africanize programming, some stations discharged most European personnel and ended the long practice of relaying BBC news broadcasts.

Every government on the continent (including the remaining colonial regimes) gives radio a high priority in government information programs, is expanding technical facilities to reach the more remote areas, and is increasing internal coverage and programming to take advantage of radio's potential to mobilize public opinion.[8] Another marked trend is the increase of programming in the indigenous languages.

The advantages of radio in the African milieu are, perhaps, obvious: it easily overcomes great distance; it is, thanks to transistors, cheaply and easily received; listeners need not be literate; and, it is said, since Africans cling to their oral traditions, the spoken word offers the best results. Unquestionably, there is evidence of widespread use of radio in the rural and still-traditional areas.

Radio broadcasting, unlike the press, has surpassed markedly the position it held in colonial times. In fact, Africa, some feel, will not go through a newspaper age, as did Europe and America enroute to the electronic age of radio, television, and movies. Instead, it will proceed directly and fully into widespread adoption of the electronic media before newspapers and literacy are well established. Others reject such a McLuhanesque future for African media and argue that the printed word and literacy are essential to the modernization process and cannot be bypassed.

Tom Hopkinson, an authority on Africa and its press, wrote: "In the western world, the pattern has been newspapers, radio, television. In Africa and much of Asia, the first contact the ordinary man has with any means of mass communication is the radio. It is the transistor which is bringing the people of remote villages and lonely settlements into contact with the flow of modern life. For the tribesman entering the money economy, the transistor now ranks as his second most coveted possession, ousting the bicycle—a wrist watch still being the first priority."[9]

Impressive gains notwithstanding, radio is not without its problems. The pervasiveness of radio broadcasting varies from country to country rather markedly. It is furthest advanced in the south of the continent, in North Africa, and in English-speaking countries. Progress has been only fair in middle Africa, and despite transistors and universal government broadcasting, many gaps are still to be filled. Often the coastal city areas are blanketed by radio signals, but the hinterland is sparsely covered.[10] For economy reasons, broadcasting is widely used domestically, but shortwave transmissions in the tropics are severely affected by solar interference (sunspots) from October to April. The sunspot problem can be solved only by substituting frequency modulation (FM) broadcasting in combination with medium-wave booster services, an expensive changeover new governments cannot afford.

In spite of its potentialities, radio is not yet effectively reaching enough Africans in the bush. To do so requires broadcasting in a variety of languages which adds to the cost while reducing the efficiency. Radio may jump the literacy barrier, but the listener must understand the language coming out of his transistor set and at any given time a majority of listeners usually does not. Even now, much broadcasting is in English and French, and such programming is often European-slanted and irrelevant to the interests of many African listeners. In the Ivory Coast, for example, I observed that all but 6 of 175 hours of weekly radio broadcasting were in French.

Even though some nations claim both nationwide broadcasting capability and large numbers of rural listeners, African radio is still mainly an urban medium. USIA surveys often provide the best information available on local media habits. In a December 1960 survey in four West African cities, the USIA found that three out of four persons interviewed in Accra, Lagos, Abidjan, and Dakar listened to a radio and most of these had access to radio in their own homes.[11] These data analyzed against the low number of radio sets per 100 population for each country as a whole suggest that radio is mainly an urban phenomenon.

A later USIA survey in 1964 found that the total of regular radio listeners (at least several times a week) averaged about 60 to 65 percent in four of the five capitals surveyed (Abidjan, Accra, Lomé, and Douala) and ran up to 89 percent in Dakar. The report found "listening drops off in the hinterland cities and especially in the bush areas. The number of regular listeners is no more than 15 percent in the bush areas of the Ivory Coast, Togo, and Cameroon, within 30 miles of the capitals."[12]

Another problem is finding supporting revenue. The usual European device of raising it by license fees is subject to serious limitations. For one thing, in many countries the number of sets is small; for another, the administrative machinery required to collect fees is rarely available. This, coupled with the fact that transistors are frequently smuggled in and sold on the black market, has made it very difficult to collect either one-time or periodic fees. Commercial broadcasting is usually officially discouraged; most governments consider radio an educational and informational medium of too great a potential and too serious in purpose to be given over to commercial exploitation. However, some government-run radio stations have recently started to carry commercials to help defray expenses. Essentially, the usual financial support for radio comes from three sources: some license fees, a little commercial advertising, and large direct subsidies from the government.

The colonial experience has left its imprint on radio. The BBC influence pervades broadcasting in anglophonic Africa, most markedly in the presentation of news rendered in the curt, reserved style of the BBC. In the first years of Nigeria's highly professional Radio Nigeria, news shows not only sounded like the BBC, but approached that admirable British network in scope and reliability.

Unquestionably, radio has become the major channel by which news reaches the African public. All stations transmit regular news bulletins and a few provide bulletins every hour.

News on radio is almost always *official* news, not unexpected where radio is invariably government radio. Major sources for the news broadcasts are Reuters and Agence France Presse, as well as a local national news agency. Few stations have very extensive news-gathering staffs of their own. News is selective: comings and goings of government leaders receive a good deal of attention as do activities relating to national development. There is little negative news such as crime, strikes, unrest, or conflict of any kind. Government policy in several nations prohibits reporting any news that reflects badly on the nation. For example, Radio Maroc carries no news that might damage even slightly the image of King Hassan, the Kingdom of Morocco, or the Arab World.

The USIA survey in West Africa found

radio to be not only the most widely used mass medium but also the one most frequently used to get the news. Radio is even more important than word-of-mouth communication as a source of news in the cities. However, radio news is still far less important than word-of-mouth in the bush areas, except in rural Senegal, where the government has made a special effort to spread radios. In addition, radio is also considered the most trustworthy by those who use more than one medium. . . . Newspapers generally run far behind radio and word-of-mouth as a source of news, although they are used by a significant proportion of the people in the bigger cities, especially in Ghana.[13]

Earlier field surveys tended to corroborate these findings on the central role of radio in African news communication.

Another USIA poll asked adult urban Africans in Abidjan and Lagos: "To know what is going on elsewhere in the world, how do you personally get your information?" Radio was named by 77 percent in Lagos and 68 percent in Abidjan; friends and relatives were cited by 56 percent and 50 percent. Newspapers were listed by 60 percent in Lagos and 52 percent in Abidjan.[14]

These results indicate not only the importance of radio but of

interpersonal communication in West Africa. Across the continent
on the other hand, a USIA survey in Kenya found that radio did not
hold as much of an edge over the print media in East Africa.[15]

A cross section of 175 adult Africans in Nairobi was asked how
they usually found out what was going on in the world and which
medium—radio or newspapers—they considered most reliable.

Results showed that even though more people listened to radio
at least once a week than read a newspaper regularly (70 percent to
54 percent), more said they got world news from newspapers (42
percent vs 34 percent via radio) as well as news in general (41 percent to 38 percent). However, 46 percent felt radio was the most
reliable source for news as against 34 percent for newspapers. Only
one in five in Nairobi owned his own radio; more than half listened
in circumstances where programs were selected by others.

The importance of radio is underlined by the role it often plays
in political crises. In almost all coups d'état—successful and unsuccessful—seizure of the radio transmitters is one of, if not the, primary goal. President Kasavubu of the Congo was able to win his
struggle with Premier Patrice Lumumba because at a critical moment
the United Nations forces denied Lumumba access to Radio Leopoldville. However Kasavubu's fellow Bakongo and personal friend, Abbé
Youlou, then leader of Congo (Brazzaville), allowed Kasavubu to use
the high-powered, French-built transmitter located in Brazzaville
across the Congo River from Leopoldville.[16]

When rebellious army troops seized power in Dahomey in December 1969 (the fifth coup there in nine years of independence)
the insurgents captured the radio station *before* they stormed the
presidential palace. An attempted coup in the Congo (Brazzaville)
in March 1970 was crushed when loyalist troops and tanks surrounded
the radio station held by a group of 30 rebel soldiers who had seized
the transmitter and announced the ouster of President Marien
Ngoubai.

In visits to Radio Ghana in Accra and Radio Nigeria in Lagos,
I was struck by the fact that both broadcasting installations, fenced
with barbed wire, were heavily guarded by armed soldiers behind
sandbagged barricades. This is indeed a tribute to the political importance of radio.

A number of conditions, then, have favored the development of
radio as the leading mass medium. Indeed, it may be said that radio is
the only news medium reaching a broad public. Newspapers, television
cinema, magazines, and books do not reach large audiences and tend
to be elite or specialized media. But under some circumstances, it may
be more desirable to reach and influence the educated few rather than
the illiterate many.

NEWSPAPERS

In various cities throughout the continent, there have been daily newspapers for all of the twentieth and part of the nineteenth century. Yet today the daily press is still pitifully small, weak, and inadequate. Of the 6,861 daily newspapers in the world in 1968–69, only 179 were in Africa.[17] None of the great newspapers of the world is there, although *Al Ahram* of Cairo has much influence in the Arab world and the *Rand Daily Mail* of Johannesburg has won a worldwide reputation for its opposition to South Africa's racial policies.

The circulation level of dailies in Africa (one copy per 100 population) was the lowest in the world. Total copies of *all* daily papers (2.7 million) was about half that of the tabloid *Daily Mirror* of London. Moreover, in the years since independence, the number of daily newspapers has not increased. (In absolute numbers there are certainly fewer dailies of any kind. Arno Huth in *Communications Media in Tropical Africa* said that Africa in 1960 had 220 to 250 daily newspapers. In late 1969, while compiling a table on world daily newspapers for the *Britannica Book of the Year 1970*, I found only 179 dailies.)

The variety and quality of the daily press reflect the diversity and inequities of Africa itself. Dailies are unequally concentrated in a few cities around the fringes of the continent. The largest and most modern newspapers, twenty-one dailies, are published in South Africa; Nigeria has had the liveliest and most diverse daily press in tropical Africa with about eighteen; and United Arab Republic has eight dailies. Two island nations off the East coast, the Malagasy Republic and Mauritius, had six and fourteen dailies, respectively. There are, however, vast expanses within the continental land mass where daily newspapers are never seen. Malawi, Botswana, Burundi, Rwanda, Lesotho, and Swaziland have no daily newspapers whatever. . . .

Since the press followed the Europeans into Africa, the earliest papers served the white settlers. By the 1880s South Africa had a variety of newspapers in English and Afrikaans. Salisbury, Rhodesia, has had a newspaper (the Rhodesia *Herald*) since 1891. Kampala, Uganda, and Mombasa, Kenya, had newspapers before World War I and Nairobi residents have been reading the *East African Standard* since 1914. *Paris-Dakar*, later *Dakar-Matin*, first appeared in Dakar, Senegal, the administrative center of French West Africa, in 1935.

Today European influences are immediately apparent in the format and style of African newspapers. In fact, one looks almost in vain for what might be an indigenous African influence.

The European-oriented *East African Standard* group, with

papers in Kampala and Nairobi, and until recently, Mombasa and
Dar es Salaam, has long dominated the journalism of East Africa.
The press of Kenya is completely British in appearance and format
because the editors and publishers have long been British journalists;
only in the past several years have Africans been added to editorial
staffs. The *East African Standard* in its typography, makeup, and
writing style is similar to that of a conservative provincial paper in
Britain. It is a newspaper with which the white settlers have long
felt comfortable.

While East Africa reflects the stodgier side of British journalistic
influences, West Africa's press is a direct descendent of Britain's
lively tabloid tradition. The technically best newspapers of West
Africa were financed by the London *Daily Mirror* group (but edited
by Africans) and included Sierra Leone's *Daily Mail*, Ghana's *Daily
Graphic*, and Nigeria's *Daily Times*, whose circulation of 120,000
was the largest in black Africa.

Not only the *Times* but most of the rest of Nigeria's lively and
at times impudent press was still British influenced; however, much
of the vigorous and colorful language of urban Nigerians showed in
its writing. The *Daily Times* closely resembled its British cousin, the
Daily Mirror, London's biggest daily. Unlike other African examples,
the Nigerian press came close to being a popular press that looked
beyond the Europeans and the African elites. But the journalism
was unmistakably out of Fleet Street—breezy, light, heavy on crime
and court news, plenty of tightly cropped pictures, bright and often
irreverent headlines, and flamboyantly written.

The press in Senegal and Ivory Coast, both daily and periodical,
is completely French in appearance, style, and makeup. The Ivoirien
government daily, *Fraternité Matin*, could easily pass for a French
provincial daily, so completely Gallicized is it, as could the weekly
party newspaper, *Fraternité*. Comics, syndicated features, and "boil-
erplate" are straight from France.

Probably the three best newspapers on the continent are published in Johannesburg, South Africa, and their British roots are
obvious. They are the vigorous and outspoken *Rand Daily Mail; Star,*
the largest daily in both number of pages and circulation (179,000)
in all of Africa; and the biggest weekly paper, the *Sunday Times*
(circulation 400,000).

Such European-owned papers, edited for resident Europeans,
have been better able to cope with the vexing obstacles that still
inhibit the development of African daily journalism:

• High illiteracy and poverty which greatly restrict potential
readership;

- Lack of local capital to support newspaper enterprises;
- High cost of printing and newsprint because the presses, type-setting equipment, and newsprint must be imported from abroad;
- Difficulties of distribution because of inadequate roads and lack of transport facilities;
- Continuing shortage of both technical staff and maintenance of equipment, to say nothing of trained journalists—a major problem in itself.

But despite the obstacles, newspapers have been published—and published by Africans—for a long time. British West Africa (Nigeria, Ghana, and Sierra Leone) has had a long and honorable newspaper tradition, extending back into the early years of the nineteenth century. In Nigeria alone, nearly 100 newspapers or periodicals have been published by Africans since the British intrusion and before independence. James S. Coleman said the *African-owned* nationalist press was the most potent instrument used in the propagation of nationalist ideas and racial consciousness.[18] In North Africa, an opposition press, often clandestine and in Arabic, played much the same role.

The whole nationalist political movement in tropical Africa, especially in West Africa but elsewhere as well, was ignited and nurtured by small political papers in English, French, and the vernaculars. Polemical, irresponsible, and lacking in hard news, these small sheets played a major role in wresting political control from the colonial governments.

Since independence, these partisan papers, often subsidized by political parties, have given way to government-owned newspapers as the nationalist leaders—the Nkrumahs, the Azikiwes, the Bourguibas, the Nyereres, the Kenyattas, and the Kaundas—moved into the government offices.

In addition to the European-owned papers, the remaining party-subsidized press, and the new government papers, there are some small independent or semi-independent journals which pursue a precarious and often ephemeral existence. In the provincial areas, government subsidies often help support monthlies and biweeklies in the vernaculars, but their technical quality is generally low. Mission and church-affiliated papers are found in most countries, ranging from the sophisticated and authoritative news weekly, *Afrique Nouvelle*, of Dakar, to small mimeographed sheets in the hinterlands.[19]

Regardless of the variety of papers, the striking fact remains that there were three times as many radio sets as copies of daily newspapers in Africa (12.5 million to 2.7 million, respectively). That statistic is vivid testimony to the fact that daily newspapers have been particularly vulnerable to the enormous barriers to media development—great distances, language diversity, poverty, illiteracy, etc.—and as a result are thin publications, lacking in most cases any firm economic base. (The 21 dailies of South Africa are a notable exception because they are essentially "European" publications, well-financed and directed at an affluent European public.)

The continent generally lacks adequate modern newspaper printing facilities—even Dr. Nnamdi Azikiwe's historically important and influential *West African Pilot* was published by handset type on a flatbed press. Printing machinery and newsprint must be imported and are costly.

Transport problems and slow mail delivery inhibit the circulation of daily newspapers in rural areas, although daily papers are often flown from one city to another. Newspaper sales tend to be confined to the city of publication, where street sales rather than home delivery is the rule.

The *Daily Times* of Lagos reached its comparatively high circulation not so much because it was undeniably a good newspaper but because it had dependable production facilities and a very efficient distribution system. The *Daily Times* was carried by plane, "mammy wagon" (the petty traders' buses), boat, and by the company's own trucks to all regions of Nigeria, usually arriving a day ahead of its competitors, who lacked the resources of this British-owned enterprise. As a result it has been one of the few national papers in Africa —"national" in that it could be purchased in most larger cities of Nigeria.

Many newspapers come and go; some quietly disappear and then without notice resume publishing. Press runs vary greatly and sales can be drastically affected by weather (a heavy rain may shrink sales sharply), political factors, and whether there is a good lead story with high reader interest. Abidjan in the Ivory Coast has had 40 papers in 25 years, but only one real daily during the 1960s.

The total circulation of daily newspapers for all of Africa in 1960 amounted to only 1 percent of the world's total, as compared to 4 percent for Latin America and 22 percent for Asia, and the African percentage has not improved significantly. However, newspapers reach more people than circulation figures indicate. Papers are passed from hand to hand or posted in public places. Often they are read aloud to illiterates on the streets or in public establishments.

It is difficult to determine how many persons read each copy of a newspaper. Readership varies, but is probably more than the 2.5 persons estimated to read each copy of a daily newspaper in America. A study conducted by the Kenya Information Department in 1958 indicated that 5 to 6 persons read each copy of a vernacular newspaper.[20]

A market survey in French West Africa by Parisian advertisers found that a single copy of a newspaper was often read to a hundred illiterates and that the African public was regularly informed as to the news in the local press.[21] This estimate certainly seems high. Illiteracy, of course, restricts the potential number of readers for dailies, but according to one USIA study, this is not the whole story. It was found that those reached by newspapers, magazines, and books are most likely to be in positions of influence in their communities, and who thus can effectively channel the content and messages of the news media to the illiterates.[22] Much depends on how well newspaper readers are linked to interpersonal channels.

TELEVISION

Television, that newest and most versatile medium of mass communications (it has been called the "complete medium"), burst over post-independence Africa like a skyrocket, and like a skyrocket is already leveling off if not coming down. Unlike radio and press, television in Africa is almost entirely a product of the years since political independence; in some places television is regarded as a national status symbol comparable to an airline or a presidential palace.

A regular television service was established in Morocco in 1954 (for just two years), and in the Western Region of Nigeria in 1959, but the rest of the continent remained almost untouched until 1962. Then a number of new nations hurriedly established transmitting facilities, usually at great cost. Some 23 nations were soon transmitting to an estimated 428,000 receivers plus another 422,000 sets if the UAR was included. The biggest increases in the purchases of TV sets came in 1962–63 and the number of sets has not increased markedly since. Africa's total number of television sets accounted for less than half of 1 percent of all sets outside the United States and Canada. . . .

So far, television has proved to be an expensive and ineffective medium. The Sierra Leone Television Service, for example, was established in April 1963. Scottish Television was the original contractor but it was later operated by Thomson Television International. Cost of the studio and transmitter buildings, including equipment and staff expenses for the first year, came to about £150,000. Yet the transmitter at Aberdeen Hill covered only the city of Freetown (population 130,000) and an area with a radius of fifteen miles. The number of sets in use seven years later was optimistically estimated at only 1,500. Thus the *installation* of television broadcasting, not counting the cost of individual receivers, was about £1,000 or $2,800 for each television set.

Television in Africa was affected by a special set of circumstances, which the current slowdown in the medium's growth reflects. Foremost was the high initial price of receiving sets plus expensive maintenance costs and the necessity of electricity as a power source. (A low-cost, dependable transistor television receiver is not yet available.)

As recently as 1965 receivers in use were still quite low, particularly for the following countries: Congo (Kinshasa), 500; Gabon, 400; and Upper Volta, 100.[23] (How many are in working order at any given time is impossible to determine.) Among Kenya's 9,900 sets that year, less than 500 were reported to me as being in the hands of Africans; the others were all owned by Europeans and Asians.

The expense and complexity of producing programs further impede television growth. This is reflected in the hours-per-week of TV programming in 1965: Congo (Kinshasa) was on the air 10½ hours a week; Gabon, 10; Malagasy Republic, 15; Niger, 8.[24]

Television seems to be having a particularly difficult time getting underway in francophonic Africa. The experience of the Republic of the Congo (Brazzaville) has been typical. There, television was on the air 16 hours a week, but after a year of operation, only some 400 sets were in use, and the National Assembly recommended the abolition of television.[25]

Because of the desperate shortage of trained personnel to produce television programs, many African systems relied heavily on "canned" programming produced in the United States, France, and Britain.

Local television news programs, particularly, were few in number, unprofessionally produced, and lacking in substance. In African countries with both radio and television, the news was more effectively presented on radio. Foreign news film was often supplied by Visnews, an organization partly owned by BBC and Reuters. An African television station, typically on the air for four or five hours a night, included only about thirty minutes of news, with possibly some of it local news film. Unfortunately, most of the rest of the other time was filled with imported syndicated series such as "The Lucy Show," "Bewitched," "Perry Mason," "Bonanza," "The Nurses," "The Saint," etc., ad nauseum. At one time the most popular show on Nigerian television was "Wrestling from Chicago." Until Africans can produce the bulk of their own programming, including news and public affairs shows, the promise of television will remain unfulfilled.

In 1968, of the countries I visited, only South Africa and Senegal had yet no television. South Africa was moving into closed-circuit television for educational and special purposes and may soon have general television. Senegal has sensibly been conducting a five-year pilot television project to test its local feasibility.

In the countries where television has arrived, however, it has proved a costly and frustrating medium. African nations lack the economic base to support television as a *mass* medium. An overwhelming majority of Africans are not in any position to become television viewers, and broadcasters lack the capability and resources to provide meaningful and relevant programming. What development of television there has been has resulted from foreign technical assistance (BBC, NBC, Scottish television, France's OCORA, and others have set up the transmission systems) and from large injections of government funds which the African economies can ill afford. Consequently, television in Africa was just limping along and was viewed by a comparative handful of people, often mostly Europeans and Asians who lived within a few miles of the transmitter.

Although some argue that the money spent on television would have been better invested in extending radio broadcasting, few would deny the long-range potential of television in mass education, public information, entertainment, and as an aid to government efforts to speed national integration. Thus far, however, African television has taken only a few halting steps toward realizing its possibilities. . . .

EXTERNAL MEDIA

Any overview of news media must note the importance of both foreign media and the media content produced abroad but carried in local media.

Every African nation has a modern sector, however small it may be, and those who operate in this sector use news and information in much the same way as do their opposite numbers in industrialized countries. Because their own communication network is less developed, however, they pay relatively more attention to communications originating abroad.[26] The extent to which urban, educated minorities in Africa attend to news and information from foreign sources is impressive indeed.

Some of this media fare is commercial in origin; some is from foreign government sources and hence is political communication, that is, propaganda.

As mentioned, most motion pictures and television programs viewed by Africans are produced in the United States or Western Europe. In addition to hearing *locally* broadcast (or relayed) programs from abroad, many Africans listen to news and entertainment directly from the BBC from London, the Voice of America (relayed from Monrovia, Liberia), Radio Moscow, Radio Cairo, Radio South Africa, and other foreign senders.

Throughout francophonic Africa, newspapers and magazines of France are widely read by *évolués*. *Le Monde, France-Soir, Figaro,* and other Parisian dailies are on the newsstands of Rabat, Dakar, and Abidjan within twenty-four hours of publication. A broad range of British newspapers and magazines has an extensive readership in East and West Africa. *West Africa,* an informed and intelligent journal of news and opinion, is published weekly in London and is read by the African elites. The overwhelming majority of the books sold in African bookstores are published abroad. The *International Herald-Tribune,* printed in Paris, is widely available in Africa, as are *Time, Newsweek,* and *Life.*

Another genre of influential publications is the handful of intellectual magazines published both in Europe and Africa. The best examples are *Afrique Nouvelle* (Dakar), *Transition* (Kampala), *Jeune Afrique* (formerly published in Tunis but more recently in Paris), and the *Legon Observer* (Accra). Place of publication, however, is not especially important, for the bulk of readership is usually in other African countries or in Europe and the United States. Aimed directly at the intellectual elites, these publications have a disproportionately great influence because the intellectual class represents a large segment of the "effective" new Africans—those able to read, buy things and in a position to influence events. The quality of writing, the seriousness and controversial nature of the content, and general overall editorial excellence of these magazines are well above that of the more provincial daily and weekly news publications.

This flood of foreign media fare is extremely significant. In one sense it denotes the new African nations' increasing enmeshment in the international network of mass communications, as part and parcel of their involvement in the modern world. In another sense it may be another indication of the lingering "neo-colonialist" relationship between African and Western nations as well as proof of the inadequacy of their own media.

NOTES

1. For an example, see Leonard Doob, *Communication in Africa: A Search for Boundaries* New Haven, Conn.: Yale University Press, 1961.

2. U.S. Information Agency, *Communications Data Book for Africa,* Washington D.C.: Government Printing Office, 1960, p. 1.

3. Unesco, *Mass Media in the Developing Countries* (Reports and Papers on Mass Communication No. 33), p. 16.

4. USIA, *op. cit.*

5. Rosalynde Ainslie, *The Press in Africa*, Rev. ed., New York: Walker & Co., 1968, p. 154.

6. Lord Hailey, *An African Survey*, Rev. ed., London: Oxford University Press, 1956, p. 1246.

7. Unesco, *World Communications*, New York: Unesco, 1964, p. 28.

8. Robert Hartland, "Press and Radio in Post Independence Africa," in U.S. National Commission for Unesco, *Africa and the United States: Images and Realities* (Eighth Annual Conference, Boston, Mass., Oct. 22-26, 1961), p. 194.

9. Tom Hopkinson, "Newspapers Must Wait in Priority Queue," *IPI Report* 16:2, June 1967, p. 18.

10. Griffith J. Davis, "Sector Analysis—Communications Media" (AID paper, June 1962), p. 3.

11. U.S. Information Agency, "Radio Listening in Four West African Cities," Pubn. PMS-43 (December 1960), p. 11.

12. USIA, "Mass Media Habits in West Africa," Pubn. R-64-66 (March 1966), p. 1.

13. *Ibid.*

14. U.S. Information Agency, "Basic Attitudes and General Communication Habits in Four West African Capitals," Pubn. PMS-51 (July 1961), p. 12.

15. U.S. Information Agency, "Media Use Among Africans in Nairobi, Kenya," Pubn. R-91-63 (May 1963), p. 12.

16. Victor C. Ferkiss, *Africa's Search for Identity*, New York: George Braziller, 1966, p. 163.

17. "World Daily Newspapers and Circulations, 1968-69," *Britannica Book of the Year 1970*, Chicago: Encyclopaedia Britannica, 1970, p. 650.

18. William John Hanna (ed.), *Independent Black Africa*, Skokie, Ill.: Rand McNally, 1964, p. 244.

19. Hartland, *op. cit.*

20. U.S. Information Agency, *Kenya: A Communications Fact Book* (Dec. 12, 1961), p. 15.

21. "La Presse en Afrique Noire," *Vente et Publicite* (Paris), July-Aug. 1954, p. 116.

22. USIA, "Mass Media Habits," p. 39.

23. U.S. Information Agency, "Overseas Television Growth in 1965," Pubn. R-111-66 (June 1966), p. 8.

24. U.S. Information Agency, *Communications Data Book for Africa*, p. 62.

25. U.S. Information Agency, "Overseas Television," p. 21.

26. W. Phillips Davison, *International Political Communication*, New York: Fredrick A. Praeger, 1965, p. 152.

A Reluctant Revolution Among Asian Newspapers *

JOHN A. LENT

JOHN A. LENT has taught journalism and English in four United States universities and colleges, worked part time for two newspapers, edited an underground paper, and been a director of public relations and information. He has published many articles for professional journals and several books dealing with the foreign press. He is editor of The Asian Newspapers' Reluctant Revolution.

sia, according to Amitabha Chowdhury, director of the Press Foundation of Asia, is perched on the edge of a communications revolution, unable to "help the revolution break in its full intensity, sweep newspapers into a new world of mass circulation . . . and embrace with delight the technological advances of the mid-twentieth century."

Chowdhury feels this is so because Asian media lack a few powerful catalysts present when media of the West were revolutionized. Among them are: the lowering of the price of newspapers, identification of a market and designing media accordingly, advent of modern technology for mass media and the appearance of media

* Reprinted from *Gazette*, 18, 1 (1972), pp. 1–23. Used by permission of the publisher and the author. Data for portions of this article was excerpted from *The Asian Newspapers' Reluctant Revolution*, edited by John A. Lent and published in 1971 by Iowa State University, Ames, Iowa.

managers who combine the skills of an imaginative editor with those of a ruthlessly ambitious businessman.

Still other necessities to a modern media system that do not exist in abundance in Asia are governments tolerant of free expression, raw materials to sustain media comfortably and literacy and education levels to assure adequate readership for printed media.

PRESS FREEDOM

Basic to an understanding of the Asian newspaper's problems is the relationship between government and the press. It is true that most Asian nations guarantee freedom of the press in their constitutions. Also true, however, is that numerous constitutions have been suspended or dispensed with on the grounds of emergency conditions, thus making press freedom in such countries only what the governments say it is. Reasons for government control range from actual war justifying censorship, as in Indo-China, to a shortage of foreign exchange for the purchase of newsprint, as in India.

When one speaks of a lack of press freedom in Asia, it is almost natural to think of *Communist China* first. Communist Chinese newspapers, required to operate as dependent institutions in support of the Communist Party, are carefully organized both structurally and functionally. Structurally, the press of China consists of a national news agency, a national, regional and lower press, while functionally, newspapers are organized into those published by political organizations (meaning the Communist Party), the so-called mass organizations and the public institutions. At each level, a strict control is maintained.

Other areas of Asia have presses almost as stringently controlled as that of Communist China. For example, Laos, Cambodia, and Vietnam have never experienced the advantages of a free press, mainly because between fighting the Japanese occupation, colonialism and civil strife, the governments have not had time to establish free presses. Censorship laws in *Laos* have been enforced by the police;[1] in *Cambodia*, a censorship division has existed within the Ministry of Information.[2] All *Vietnamese governments* since World War II have paid lip service to press freedom with sugar-coated euphemisms designed to make them look better in Western eyes.[3] The situation in reality is quite different, however. Newspapers are suspended regularly;[4] editors are jailed. Within less than a year after a new constitution was promulgated in the late sixties, over three dozen newspapers were suspended. One of the guarantees of that constitution was freedom of the press.

Nguyen Thai, a former assistant minister of information and newspaper editor in South Vietnam, feels the newspapers of South Vietnam have been hampered by at least two major problems:

As in other underdeveloped countries, the situation of underdeveloped press in South Vietnam is due mainly to two sets of factors: technical and socio-political. First, on the technical side, the equipment for newspapers production in South Vietnam is obsolete and backward. . . Secondly, on the socio-political side, the lack of freedom of the press is still too obvious despite the complicated and changing press regulations which try to pay lip service to press freedom. This situation of course discourages honest and competent journalists from getting involved while it maintains an abundance of dishonest and irresponsible journalists who survive by trying as the Vietnamese popular saying goes, "to use lies to make money." The real problem of the South Vietnamese press lies in the socio-political conditions which encourage its excessive fragmentation. The 158 dailies and periodicals of South Vietnam are only journalistic reflections of the fragmented politics of South Vietnamese society. These ineffective and ephemeral newspapers are very similar and related to the numerous small and powerless political parties and groups in South Vietnam. By dividing itself to the point of inefficiency and impotency, the South Vietnamese press, like the political elite, has no real impact on the life of the people. Its influence on society is marginal and its very existence is constantly affected by each political change or turmoil in the country.

Burma is another country where press subjugation is nearly complete. Traditionally the press there has relied heavily on government advertising since consumer goods outlets and demands have been scanty. News services have been dependent upon government subscription and circulation and broadcasting from the outset has been a government monopoly. Any printed medium is subject to closure by executive order if it does not serve the needs of the state. By 1968, all newspapers were nationalized, except *Rangoon Daily*, it serving the illusion of a free press although in reality the paper is a government puppet. Since 1962 when the military government dictated that newspapers should serve national goals, four Chinese, five Indian, ten Burmese and English language papers were forced to close. Some Burmese editors have rebelled; one, U Sein Win of the Guardian, fought the government strenuously during the early sixties, even refusing vital government advertising. Because of his violation of the press acts, U Sein Win was in and out of courts and prisons regularly.

According to a 1970 International Press Institute report, U Sein Win would be considered fortunate compared to other editors, who, after breaking press laws, were likely to run into something like this:

More than five years ago, a reporter named Maung Maung was arrested in Burma and then spent 15 months in prison prior to facing trial before a special court headed by an Air Force major. After the prosecution had presented its case, the major went on a nine months study trip abroad so the case was postponed pending his return. When he came back he was posted by his unit to attend another course and the case had to wait yet again. A year later (in 1969), after four years of imprisonment, the case had not been completed and so far as is known it still drags on.[5]

The press of *Ceylon* could follow the nationalization precedence set in Burma if the prime minister, Mrs. Sirimavo Bandaranaike, has her way. Using the guise of too much chain ownership among the newspapers, Mrs. Bandaranaike, in 1963, set up a commission to investigate newspaper ownership. Her commission recommended that Lake House chain, the largest media concern of Ceylon, be handed over to the government. This nationalization attempt became a vital issue in the 1965 election in which she was defeated. Campaigning for the prime minister post again in 1970, Mrs. Bandaranaike promised the people freedom of the press; after her election, she proceeded to guarantee this freedom in an unusual manner—by withholding all government and public corporation advertising from Lake House, which incidentally had not supported her 1970 election bid. A ministerial committee was appointed in 1970 to study the feasibility of a press council for Ceylon, but more importantly, the committee's purpose was to find ways to obliterate what it called "domination of the daily press by capitalist monopolies."

Press freedom in *Thailand* has been an up and down proposition, depending on the government in power. The trend today must be considered as more restrictive.[6] No new publications can be established without licensing, no press abuses can be directed against the royal family, the State, government departments, public morals or national morale. As the 1970s approached, bills to shackle the press of Thailand were introduced that would intimidate the media in terms matched only in Eastern Europe and Latin America. Some of the proposed bills have since been defeated.

Newspapers in *Indonesia*, since General Soeharto took control in March 1966, discuss affairs of government as if they expected to influence decisions. Newsprint subsidies, since 1967, have been ended to free the newspapers from dependence on the government. But licensing by the government still regulates newsprint supplies, advertising rates and other aspects of newspaper operation in Indonesia. A Basic Press Law of 1966, guaranteeing against censorship and suspension of newspapers, has been a giant step forward for the Indonesian journalists, who suffered many setbacks during the tenure of Sukarno. Just before his ouster, for instance, Sukarno had suspended all Chinese-language newspapers in Indonesia; at other times, his government either suspended papers or house arrested editors. An editor who must hold some sort of record for being held under house arrest was Mochtar Lubis of *Indonesia Raya.* In 1956, Lubis had been tried on libel charges stemming from exposes he had written about military and government officials, including Sukarno. He was arrested later acquitted and then held under house arrest without further charges until 1966.

The *Philippines* and *Taiwan*, both fond of boasting of their respect for democratic principles, came in for sharp criticism in 1970 as a result of the internationally-famous Yuyitung case. Rizal and Quintin Yuyitung were editor and publisher of the *Chinese Commercial News* in Manila, a newspaper that has been accused of being everything from pro-loyalist to pro-Japanese during World War II to pro-Communist more recently. In 1970 the Yuyitungs were deported from the Philippines, the Philippine immigration commissioner handling the case personally. They were charged with publishing pro-Communist news. The evidence was sparse; they were said to have published New China News Agency dispatches and used "Mao Tsetung" as the name of Communist China's leader, rather than "Bandit Mao," the name other Nationalist Chinese papers normally use. The Yuyitungs were shipped off to Taiwan where, through the intercession of the International Press Institute, their lives were spared, even though their prison sentences were not. This action was especially damaging to the Philippine press which considers itself the freest in Asia, if not the world. However, other threats to Philippine press freedom have been on the rise during the Marcos administration. Eduardo Sanchez of the Philippine Press Institute lists these dangers:

Legitimate newsmen (in the Philippines) are beginning to feel a threat to their press freedom. The sources of this fear are the constant government references to newsmen as whiners, gripers and time wasters. The subtle entry of administration friends into mass media and the government publication of its own newspaper and an attempt to establish a government owned news agency also pose as threats.[7]

Restrictions of press freedom on *Taiwan* are not so subtle. There, a Publication Law of 1958 is still on the books, giving the government, by administrative action, the right to revoke a paper's license to publish.[8] Another reason critics doubt the press freedom of Taiwan is that the government still subsidizes 80 percent of the chief news agency's operations. Chinese on Taiwan reply that the island must maintain some press laws because of the semi-state of war that exists with Communist China.

Former British colonies, *Pakistan, India, Malaysia* and *Singapore* and *Hong Kong* all have stipulations that give the governments more than the usual amount of media control. All five territories work under licensing or registration systems; in Hong Kong, an annual registration fee and an initial security deposit are necessary. The deposit is automatically forfeited if a paper fails to comply with laws governing publication. Both a printing permit and government licensing are required in *Malaysia* and *Singapore*. The licenses are used to suppress agitation for insurrection. Editors must renew the licenses yearly. All five governments have put aside constitutional guarantees during different emergency situations in recent years. For example, in *Hong Kong*, six of the number of Communist newspapers that publish there were suspended in 1967, some of their editors imprisoned on sedition charges. This action led to protest marches in Peking and the burning of the British Embassy there. In July 1967, Hong Kong passed an emergency ordinance providing for search and arrest of editors who endangered public safety. Nearly three years later when Hong Kong released the Communist editors, China responded by setting free Antony Grey, a Reuters correspondent who had been imprisoned in retaliation for Hong Kong's action.

Malaysian newspapers worked under emergency regulations during the 1950s threat of Communist infiltration. More recently, since the May 1969 disturbances in *Malaysia*, the government has tightened its media controls—barring any racial or religious news.[9] Defense of India Laws were put into effect when *India* ran into conflict with China during the sixties. They have since been rescinded.[10] The martial law existent in *Pakistan* has handicapped media for years. Although there are no censorship laws now, the publication ordinance in effect is enforced to check on unhealthy practices in journalism. An assessment of the Pakistani press in 1965 by Tarzie Vittachi, a director of the Press Foundation of Asia, holds today as well:

A major result of publishing newspapers under a prolonged period of martial law was the psychological enslavement of some of the publishers and editors, who, in order to save their investment, their livelihood, or power-status produced fawning newspapers which day in and day out, sought to give the impression that all was well in the best of all possible Pakistan.[11]

Because the printed media of Pakistan and India must depend on large appropriations of government advertising and because Hong Kong, Malaysian and Singaporean newspapers must get the major part of their news from government information agencies,[12] some Asian media-watchers feel freedom of the press is no longer based on British press principles in these former British colonies.

In *Afghanistan,* all provision newspapers with the exception of three, which have independent editors, are government owned and controlled. Their editors are appointed by the government.

Suppression has been the standard in regards to the press of

Korea.[13] The one occasion when media were truly free, irresponsible journalism predominated. That occasion was the 1960 April uprising. Because mass media had helped topple the Rhee government at that time, the Koreans placed an implicit trust in newspapermen after 1960. Noting the favors granted to newsmen, everyone wanted to become a newsman. It was said that one could become "publisher" of a newspaper for only 2000 won (about $1.50 United States), 1000 won to register with the authorities, another 1000 to have personal name cards printed. On the strength of such identification papers and name cards, all self-furnished, so-called "publishers" showed up at the Ministry of Transportation and demanded first class train tickets as a token of respect due a "publisher." Or, from the Ministry of Communications, free installations of telephones were demanded. Most of these "publishers" did not even bother to issue a fly-by-night sheet. Fortunately, self-purification on the part of the conscientious element of the media cleaned up the corruption and a Press Ethics Commission was set up within a year. In addition to the ethics commission, a press institute was developed in Korea.

Press institutes in seven Asian nations, in addition to press councils, courts of honour or press ethics commissions in India, Philippine Pakistan and Korea—plus talk of councils in other nations as well— are all encouraging signs for the promotion of a free and responsible press in Asia. The Press Foundation of Asia, headquartered in Manila, acts as a unifying agent for these institutes and councils.

ECONOMIC PROBLEMS

After freedom of the press, probably the most lingering problems of Asian media are those lumped under the category of economics. More basically, it's a matter of not enough money available for newspapers to purchase their own plants, newsprint and modern equipment. Additionally, a lack of purchasing power among the people affects circulations and advertising.

It is a paradox that Asian newspapers are handicapped by insufficient and outmoded printing equipment for it was in China that Pi Sheng invented movable type as early as 1041–1048 A.D. Also paradoxical is the fact that the part of the world that produced paper as early as the time of Christ suffers from a severe want of newsprint today.

Even to own a crude, antiquated press that would not be much of an improvement over Pi Sheng's invention, is a luxury not in the reach of many Asian newspapers. For example, of 36 Chinese language papers of Hong Kong surveyed in 1966, only nine had their own plants. In Indonesia, to offset the tremendous investment needed to start newspapers, the government in 1949 imported large quantities of printing machinery and set up printing units in major cities where Indonesian language newspapers could be printed at controlled prices. Shortages of foreign capital have limited the amount of printing equipment brought into other countries as well—such as India, Pakistan and the Philippines. In Malaysia, no rotary press exists either in Sabah or Sarawak, for instance; most newspapers use flatbed Heidelbergs.

In other countries, technology to handle unique scripts has been invented but few newspapers can afford the machinery. Monotype machines in Korean, Burmese and Thai are available as are typewriters in Burmese and Korean, but in these countries, most type is still set manually, most copy handwritten.

Taiwan has been manufacturing modern rotary presses that cannot find Asian markets. On Taiwan itself, *United Daily News* and *Central Daily News,* two of the largest dailies, are the only plants sporting new Taiwanese presses.

In contrast, Japan not only produces but also utilizes some of the most sophisticated communications technology in the world. For example, as early as 1959, Japan became the first country to transmit entire newspaper pages by facsimile, connecting the Tokyo and Sapporo offices of *Asahi* by microwaves. When *Asahi* was having trouble getting its delivery vans through Tokyo traffic, the paper decided to send news into Japanese homes via signals. Thus, home facsimile, or homefax, appeared on the market. In Japan, computerization of production, technical and editorial tasks of media is possible, equipment being available for classifying, compiling and retrieving information.

But, unstable economies, lack of foreign exchange and increasing production costs all mitigate against most Asian newspapers having equipment similar to that of Japan.

In other cases, equipment is not available to handle the languages in use. For example, try finding a typewriter capable of handling thousands of Chinese characters or a linotype or monotype that can do the same thing. The Thai language—with its 44 consonants for the syllabic alphabet, 14 forms for the nine vowels with combinations of stops, and vowel and tonal marks both above and below the line—does not allow for the development of mechanical typesetters. Korean newspapers have the benefit of Korean-language typewriters but cannot use them because the papers are set in both Chinese and Korean. Even though Seoul dailies have 7,000 Chinese characters in each font, it is still necessary to keep a man in the composing room ready to carve on a piece of wood the rarely-used Chinese characters that one finds in proper names. Technical problems have become so acute in Korea that the Korean Newspaper Publishers Association in 1967 resolved to limit the number of Chinese characters for use in dailies to 2,000. Scores of Chinese-language newspapers throughout Asia face similar problems, including the one of finding pieces of type in typecases that are oftentimes 60 to 80 feet long.

Multiplicity of languages is a problem in many Asian nations—in India, where Bombay alone has 222 mother tongues with none a majority language, in the Philippines, Malaysia, China and Pakistan, to cite a few cases. Thus, a one-language medium cannot expect to reach the entire population in such states. In India the problem becomes even more complicated by the fact that a single language such as Hindi will differ from one city to another. Dr. K. E. Eapen told of the toils of a reporter under those conditions:

A correspondent of an English daily in Bombay City acting as a stringer to a Gujarati paper, has to do somersaults while reporting court or legislative proceedings of the state in Marathi.

Traditionally, some countries had substituted English or Chinese for a native language, and the media were produced in those scripts. Since independence, however, the English and Chinese presses of some Asian nations have been in trouble. For instance, in India, Hindi has replaced English as the top newspaper language.

In both East and West Pakistan, English-language dailies account for only 150,000 of the estimated 800,000 circulation, native-language papers outselling them at least four to one. The same is true in Ceylon where the largest circulated newspapers today are those in Sinhalese, not English.

During the past decade, there have been concentrated efforts to promote national tongues in at least the Philippines, Malaysia and Indonesia. But in the former two states, the development of a national language has not been mirrored in the newspapers. English will still predominate for the next decade or so. In the Philippines, a transitional-type newspaper was issued during the 1960s to make English-speaking residents fluent in Tagalog. The paper mixes English and Tagalog (called Taglish) within the text of stories, thus a reader might start reading a sentence in English and by the time he reaches the period, find himself reading Tagalog. Malaysia and Singapore have newspapers in languages other than English also (for example, Tamil, Jawi, Romanized Malay and Chinese) but the circulation leaders are mainly English-language dailies. In Sabah the two English-language newspapers each carry a two-page insert of news in Bahasa Malaysia, giving some emphasis to the local tongue.

Linked with the language problem is that of literacy, a modernization factor that on paper, at least, is relatively developed in many parts of Asia. The figures are deceiving. Because of a lack of reading materials in many regions, large numbers of people lapse in their reading skills, leading to a high degree of functional illiteracy. Indonesia can claim a literacy rate of 80 per cent, the Philippines 70 per cent, Burma 65 per cent and North Vietnam 95 per cent, but the figures mean nothing if through disuse the people cannot read much more than their own names. The North Vietnamese, in making their claim of 95 per cent literacy, attribute the high rate to an intensive campaign that placed the alphabet before the people at all times—on rocks, trees and even animals. There is no doubt the Communist world of Asia worked diligently on the illiteracy problem. Communist China has done wonders although literacy rates there are still lagging. The so-called lower press—usually rural editions of provincial papers or more usually wall newspapers—has been very important to the literacy campaign of China. Before 1956, the growth of newspapers in China was mainly in urban centers; since then, press development has deliberately been focused in the countryside.

Just because newspapers are available does not presume they will be bought or read. For example, in areas of Southeast Asia, it has been found that people who feel they can afford sewing machines, radios and wristwatches, do not purchase newspapers. The newspaper reading habit has not invaded all parts of Asia yet.

Particularly because of poor transportation facilities, media distribution has been hampered in Asia for years. Even in a compact city such as Hong Kong, dailies find it necessary to add a surcharge for home delivery. In Pakistan, despite recent revolutionary improvements in transportation, it is still impossible for a Dacca daily to reach every East Pakistan city the same day of publication. The problem is compounded in the island republics of Malaysia, Indonesia and the Philippines where circulation managers would succumb to perforated ulcers if they tried to reach all of the thousands of islands. In East Malaysia, for example, newspapers are left behind by airlines in cases of overloading, sometimes never to be picked up and delivered. Another type of problem plagues South Vietnamese publishers. There, distribution depends on the good-will of distributors, the "Big Four" of whom operate "on rather the same lines as the gang leaders of the Chicago of the 1920s, dividing up the city into strictly defined quarters, beyond which none of their agents dare trespass."[14] Japanese publishers are faced with a shortage of newsboys to deliver newspapers. This scarcity of boypower has made for an increase in newsstand sales in Japan.

If one accepted newspaper distribution methods of Quemoy, neither newsboys nor newsstands would be necessary. On Quemoy, they shoot newspapers to their destinations by guns. Wang Ping-Chua director of Quemoy's two papers, claims his products are loaded into artillery shells that are then fired toward China. The shells explode in the air over China, showering newspapers over the Chinese country-side and in the process, acting as a psychological warfare medium.[15]

Asia has cities full of newspapers while outlying areas are devoic of the medium. Hong Kong, for example, has 55 dailies and 26 week-lies and a ratio of 32 newspaper copies per 100 population.[16] This ratio does not reflect actual readership for in Hong Kong teahouses, a customer may buy one paper and then exchange it for still another after having read the first. Of the 40 dailies in Korea, 18 are in Seoul of the 31 in Taiwan, 16 are in Taipei; practically all of the 40 dailies and 119 periodicals of South Vietnam are published in Saigon. This concentration of newspapers in the capital cities certainly holds true in the Philippines, Burma, Thailand, Ceylon, and of course, the city-state of Singapore. In Southeast Asia, only Indonesia and Malaysia have a substantial number of papers in outlying regions. India and Pakistan have numerous press centers, as does Japan. Because of this centralization trend, provincial newspapers have usually suffered in Asia. For instance, until very recently, Thailand and the Philippines did not have dailies outside their capital cities. Provincial newspapers that did develop in the Philippines were plagued by insufficient ad-vertising, equipment, newsprint and reader interest.

Besides hindering the growth of a provincial press, centralizatio of media in capital cities also has the effect of spreading profits too thinly. For example, only one of the 18 dailies in Seoul is making a profit from its circulation and advertising; the rest survive by devisin money-making projects, such as sponsoring concerts, sports events or dealing in real estate. In Manila, jealousy among publishers and broac casters does not allow for profitable consolidations and therefore the city is oversaturated with dailies and broadcasting stations. Many of the Manila media only have one reason for being—to serve as weapoi for financial and political conglomerates. Ceylon dailies, concentrate in Colombo, survive because many are parts of chain ownerships, the stronger members of which make up financial losses.

An exception to the centralization syndrome is Japan, which has spread its media over the islands. Besides a highly-developed pro-vincial press system, Japan has benefitted also from the efforts of th Big Three newspapers to maintain editions in as many regions as pos-sible. The enormity and far-reaching aspects of the Japanese press ca be gauged by looking at some figures. First of all, total circulation of 117 dailies affiliated with Nihon Shinbun Kyokai at the end of 1969 was 35 million, making Japan second in the world in copies circulated per population. One paper alone, *Asahi,* has a daily circulation of 5.5 million for morning and 3.5 million for the evening edition, published from five major publishing centers in Tokyo, Osaka, Nagoya, Kokura and Sapporo. *Asahi,* with a staff of 7,900 employees, maintains 295 domestic bureaus and publishes 42 daily editions and 124 sub-editions. In other words, the 42 morning and evening papers are further subdivided into zoned editions for various regions of Japan.

Newsprint shortages obviously stultify circulation and growth of Asian printed media. In Korea, newspapers by joint agreement, limit the size of daily editions to eight pages. Newsprint shortages in Indonesia have caused newspapers to reduce press runs, suspend street sales or just skip a day of publication. South Vietnamese newspapers have been known to exaggerate circulation figures in order to get a larger allocation of newsprint at official prices. In India, the government checks chain ownership patterns by denying newsprint quotas to papers brought out by chains. Taiwanese editors, in an effort to conserve newsprint, use a smaller type face than normal so that today a page of a Chinese-language paper contains two and one-half times the wordage of a United States counterpart. The Taiwan government has limited the number of newspapers in addition to the number of pages in existing newspapers. This law has been relaxed somewhat now that Taiwan produces virtually all of its own newsprint. Other nations hope to produce newsprint as well; groups in the Philippines, for example, have been experimenting with indigenous materials such as straw, rice and bamboo as raw materials for newsprint. The Press Foundation of Asia has been working on projects to develop regional newsprint mills. But despite these efforts, most of the newsprint for Asia still came from the outside at almost double the prices paid by United States newspapers. In 1969, 11 Asian nations imported 435,858 metric tons of newsprint, most of it from Scandinavia and Canada.[17]

In most of Asia, the penny press has not yet arrived and newspapers therefore are still out of the price range of the average man. The price of a daily in Calcutta, Kuala Lumpur, Bangkok or Manila is six times higher than prices of New York dailies relative to income. The average Filipino or Thai would have to fork over 20 to 22 days of wages to subscribe to a daily year round. Even a Japanese industrial laborer must give up four days of wages to buy a set of papers (morning and evening editions) for one year. But to bring the price of newspapers down, low cost production methods are needed and these are not yet on the horizon. Because of their prices, newspapers in Asia are cherished and kept around a little longer than in the Western world. Saigon newspapers pass from hand to hand a number of times through a unique renting system.

It is common practice to rent your daily for a few hours, then return it to the newsstand where the process is repeated throughout the day. As if this were not bad enough from the publisher's point of view, the newsboys are not above returning the whole bunch of many-rented papers to the publisher claiming they were unsold.[18]

Of course, we have already mentioned the exchange of newspapers that occurs in Hong Kong teahouses. In other parts of Asia, the common man is able to read a newspaper through display case editions placed somewhere prominently in town or through tatzepao (wall papers) as in China.

Professionalization and training of Asian media personnel have been given a couple shots in the arm recently through press institute seminars and the creation of journalism schools. However, a dire need for trained journalists still haunts most of Asia. For example, of Malaysia's 500 journalists (in a population of 9 million), only 150 have any training at all. Burma does not have anywhere near that number of trained personnel and without any journalism training programs is unlikely to improve its situation in the near future. India has had journalism training for over four decades but still is not as advanced in that respect as developing nations of Latin America. There are bright spots, of course. Taiwan journalism education, now over 50 years old, has the benefit of six university journalism programs, Korea nine, Philippines five, Hong Kong and Pakistan at least two each. In 1968 the Chinese Language Press Institute was established in Hong Kong for the purposes of offering in-service training courses and seminars, experimenting in the mechanization of the Chinese language and standardizing translated terminology. A southeast Asia Press Centre, established in Kuala Lumpur in the late sixties, has trained more journalists within two years than had been trained in the entire history of Malaysia. Also, in recent years, Japan, realizing her superiority in technological know-how, has been operating training schemes in photography and printing for the benefit of other Asians.

Many Asian journalists have not needed much training to carry out their reportorial assignments, relying on formula writing of subjects such as sex and politics. For example, the most prosperous Thai papers have been the least responsible and most sensational. Three of the largest dailies in Bangkok dress themselves in four-color illustrated wrappers every Saturday, the wrappers usually featuring pictures of actresses and models in scanty attire. To make itself distinctive, each Thai daily is identified by a trademark color which it sports in daily banner headlines. Also unique to Thai journalism is the verse editorial, a combination of illustrative cartoon and satirical verse, aimed at public officials and issues.

In Saigon, when newspaper readers weary of politics, they are given the next best thing—sex. One paper has kept reader interest high because of its series on the sex exploits performed by a fictional character called Cau Cho, which translates to something like "Sexy Cat." Pornography and gambling make up the news interest formula of many Hong Kong dailies—especially the Communist and pro-Communist organs which are edited with the low income and less literate reader in mind. Hong Kong newspaper readers have been treated to pictures of nudes, along with features on how to plan a seduction. The sex-libel news content of so-called "mosquito" papers of Malaysia and Singapore became so brazen that the governments of those territories decided to close all such fly-by-night sheets. Not all Asian newspapers concentrate on sex-crime-politics, however, and some papers which have traditionally done so are changing their ways. For example, sex and crime are being de-emphasized in a couple of major Philippine dailies, being substituted by more investigative and interpretive reporting.

In Communist Asia, very little choice exists as to the contents of newspapers. Press content in China, for example, must be in close coordination with the main political and economic tasks at each stage of national development, planned and directed by the Communist Party. Three factors which have determined functions and contents of Chinese newspapers since 1949 are 1) Marxist-Leninist ideology, 2) structural characteristics of each newspaper and 3) developmental traits of each stage of China's modernization.

Generally, most of Asia's newspapers suffer from a lack of international, investigative and background news. Indonesia, where only 15 per cent of the news budget is allocated to foreign news, typifies the situation in most other regions of Asia as well. Also absent has been reporting of regional news, Asian newspapers not being interested in their next door neighbors. Plans are being completed at this time for a regional news agency for Asian newspapers which could change the situation.

THE BEGINNINGS

Precursors of modern mass media in Asia usually took one of two paths: they either shared information with the masses through ballads, songs or the theater, or they greedily gathered information for the sole benefit of the royal courts. In China, scholar-officials were hired to collect and write the news, often in the form of poetry, and then relay it directly and only to the emperor.

Newsletters in other parts of Asia also had their origins in official surroundings. In Korea, *The Royal Court Report,* published during the 16th century, had many of the features of a newspaper but its audience, like the Chinese newsletters, was quite narrow.[19] In Thailand, Burma, India and Pakistan, most of the first newsletters and newspapers were under royal patronage. In fact, King Mongkut himself was editor of one royal newsletter in Thailand and a number of his successors on the throne were editors or contributors to newspapers. On the Indo-Pakistan subcontinent, Muslim rulers for centuries had an efficient newsgathering system made up of writers in various provinces who, through state newsletters, kept rulers fully informed. Read aloud in royal courts, the newsletters included orders issued for the redress of wrongs perpetuated by unsatisfactory officials.

Contrary to this "only the emperor shall know" philosophy was the yomiuri Kawaraban, circulated widely among the Japanese from 1610 to 1867. A kawaraban was an engraved clay or wooden plate used to disseminate information to the population on social events and natural disasters, sensual matters and double suicides.

Ironically, European colonists and missionaries brought the art of printing to most of Asia, even though next door, China had possessed the art of printing since at least 1000 A.D. By the end of the 19th century, the Westerners had initiated magazines and newspapers in most of what is now Asia.

Spanish friars brought the first printing presses to the Philippines in 1593, and there, published newsletters as early as 1637. Thomas Pinpin published the newsletter, *Succesos Felices,* in 1637 and the sheet was so successful that a second issue appeared two years later. In Thailand, members of the French Catholic Mission introduced printing as early as 1622. Protestant missionaries got into the act also and by the 1830s, one of them—a Dr. Dan Beach Bradley—had published Thailand's first newspaper, *Bangkok Recorder.*

Elsewhere in Southeast Asia, French colonial authorities published the first newsletters of Indo-China in the mid-19th century. Long before that, in 1615 to be exact, a bulletin was issued in what is now Indonesia for the employees of the Dutch East India Company. A number of the first newspapers of Malaya and Singapore were established by British Christians, as was the first non-English newspaper of India. But missionary publications, although among the first in Asia, did not always gain the momentum needed for long life.

As mentioned before, newsletters in pre-Westernized Asia were designed with only the royalty in mind. Once the colonists arrived, the first newspapers became their private presses. The first newspaper of the Philippines, *Del Superior Gobierno*, was issued to satisfy Spanish colonists' desire for information about Europe. Whenever a ship arrived in Manila carrying information about Europe, the governor-general of the islands would rush to his press and issue another *Del Superior Gobierno*. The early newspapers in what is now Pakistan were meant to maintain liaison among the British colonists. In Ceylon, no record of newspapers exists before the British arrived. The second paper on that island, the *Colombo Journal*, appeared in 1832 partly through the encouragement of the governor of Ceylon. British authorities had something to do with the creation of the first newspapers in Burma as well.

In Japan, a nation that resisted the colonization pattern, the first newspaper was not devoid of Western influences. *Batavia Shimbun* was a duplicate in Japanese of an official Dutch journal published in Batavia, or what is now Djakarta. A number of the early Hong Kong newspapers were merely translations of English language journals.

The modern press of India was initiated as a weapon against the colonists rather than for them. It was in 1780 when James Augustus Hicky brought out the *Bengal Gazette or Calcutta General Advertiser* as a scandal sheet to strike out at members of the East India Company, the governor-general and his staff.

As if triggered by a push of a button, nationalistic, revolutionary and independence movements seemed to emerge at about the same time in many parts of Asia. In at least China, Philippines, Burma, Indonesia, Singapore and Malaysia, the people became restless at the dawning of the 20th century—restless because of foreign rule or traditional monarchies of their own making. In Ceylon, India, Pakistan and Indo-China, the restlessness was more acute between the world wars. Revolutionary desires and hopes were the impetus for the creation of nationalist presses bent on arousing the people from their long slumber. During the late Manchu Dynasty of China, when sentiment ran high for political reform, scholar-reformers, including Kang Yu-Wei and Liang Chi-Chao, published newspapers in Shanghai and Peking advocating political change.

Little doubt exists about Philippine journalists' role in that nation's revolutionary process. Many national heroes of the Philippines were journalists who led the country from under Spanish rule in the 1890s, chief among them being Jose Rizal, Marcelo del Pilar and Graciano Lopez-Jaena, all prominently identified with the revolutionary journal, *La Solidaridad*. In Singapore and what is now Malaysia, a revolutionary press appeared as early as 1904, with the publications of Teo Eng Hock and Tan Chór Lam. The battle Teo and Tan fought was that of all overseas Chinese—whether China could be saved by reform or by revolution.[20]

Korea's first modern newspaper, *The Independent* (or *Tongnip Sinmun*), displayed its nationalistic tendencies in ways other than its name alone. The paper listed among its goals the exclusion of foreign dependence, protection of national sovereignty, elimination of class distinction and expansion of civil rights. Another newspaper which established itself as the mouthpiece of the Korean people was *Dong-a Ilbo* which raised the ire of the Japanese during the nearly four decades of occupation. The paper reported on the independence movements that were breaking out all over Korea.

One journalist, D. R. Wijewardene, is credited with initiating and sustaining the nationalist movement in Ceylon during the 1920s and 1930s. His *Ceylon Daily News,* during the inter-World Wars era, was used to promote the aims of the Ceylon National Association and Ceylon Reform League, both nationalistic groups organized by Wijewardene. Elsewhere in South Asia, journalists displayed a fierce nationalism that called for the separation of India from Great Britain and the subsequent state of Pakistan. Describing the nationalist press, K. E. Eapen has said:

The nationalist press functioned as the spearhead of the freedom movement. This has left an indelible mark on the profession as a whole. When freedom arrived in August, 1947, there were enough journals owned by Indians and enough Indians exposed to good journalism so that there was little of a vacuum as the remaining British-owned papers passed into Indian hands.

Among Indian journalists who persistently advocated a break with Great Britain were B. G. Horniman, Mrs. Annie Besant and Mohandas K. Gandhi.

In Pakistan, Muslim newspapers of the 20th century had a great deal to do with the formation of a separate Muslim nation. One of the most significant of these was *Zamindar,* frequently persecuted for its valiant stand for freedom of expression. During the early decades of this century, *Zamindar* was required, on a regular basis, to deposit large monetary sums to the government as security. When these funds were forfeited, as they invariably were, the paper was asked to deposit even larger amounts. Nearly every time, readers, appreciative of the efforts of *Zamindar,* donated the security money.

Elsewhere, national liberation movements, abetted by the press, developed in Burma after 1906, in Indonesia in 1908. During the 1920s and 1930s, the press of Indo-China became very nationalistic and anti-French.

A natural progression seemed to develop from newspapers used as opinion leaders and spearheads of political causes to newspapers thought of as commercial entities. It was in Japan that this trend was most pronounced, especially after the populace tired of the political sheets of the 1890s. Two giants among the commercially-oriented press of Japan were established during the latter quarter of the century, *Asahi* and *Mainichi*. The third of the contemporary Big Three in Japanese newspaper publishing, *Yomiuri*, began its surge to prominence in the 1920s.

Initially, Chinese editors in Asia did not perceive their newspapers as profitable businesses either. Westerners introduced the profit motive to them. *Sheng Pao* and *Hsin Wen Pao* were commercially successful newspapers that resulted. In Singapore and Malaysia as well, Chinese newspapers of the latter 19th century began to see the advantages of advertising and circulation practices. Notable among such papers was *Sing Po*. The first Chinese-language newspapers of Hong Kong were commercial enterprises from the start, emphasizing shipping and market news.

As big business practices entered the journalism profession, mergers, consolidations and multiple ownerships were the results, but certainly not to the extent that they were in nations such as the United States and Great Britain. Multiple ownerships among media have become subjects of controversies in a few Asian states, especially in the Philippines, India and Ceylon. It was Alejandro Roces, Sr., who in the 1920s established the TVT media chain in the Philippines. Since that time, most media in the Philippines have become parts of cross-channel, multi-business ownerships. If one looks at the *Manila Chronicle*, to cite one example, he finds it is owned by the Lopez family (one of the heads of which is vice president of the Philippines) which also controls a network of about two dozen radio stations, TV channels, magazines and large sugar interests.

A cross-national newspaper chain was started by the Aw family of Tiger Balm ointment and Tiger Balm Gardens fame. The chain includes the *Standard* of Hong Kong, *Sin Chew Jit Poh* and *Sing Pin Jit Pao* in Malaysia as well as newspapers in Singapore and Bangkok.

Besides the national independence movements, World War II, in a left handed fashion, was another stimulator of modern Asian newspapers. After four years of Japanese occupation, news-hungry nations developed hundreds of newspapers during the post-war period. For example, in Burma 56 new papers sprang up in 1945-6; in Indonesia, 124 dailies by 1948, and the same elsewhere in liberated Asia.

But the Japanese occupation itself was another story—a story filled with suppression, brutality and suspicion. For example, by 1941 most Chinese newspapers in Hong Kong and Shanghai had been closed by the Japanese; other papers of China became mobile units

either following the frontline or receding from it. In Korea, occupied
by Japan since 1910, an all-out effort was made in the 1930s to des-
troy the language, alphabet and press agencies of the nation and
replace them with Japanese equivalents. As early as 1939, *Dong-a
Ilbo* and *Choson Ilbo* were ordered to suspend "voluntarily," and
shortly after, Korea was left without an independent Korean-language paper.

As Japan became more imperialistic in the thirties, its own press
was vehemently in opposition to such expansionism. Local papers
especially were critical of government war aims. *Fukuoka Nichi-
nichi,* for instance, had angered the army to such a degree that local
military divisions demonstrated air raid maneuvers, using the news-
paper.building as a target. They did not drop bombs but kept up a
continuous harassment campaign instead. Other Japanese newspaper
offices were raided when they criticized war efforts. As the war intensified and supplies dwindled, Japanese authorities reduced the
number of pages in dailies at first, and later reduced the number of
newspapers themselves. Between 1937 and 1940, the number of
Japanese dailies dropped from 1,200 to 104, and by 1942, the figure
was down to 52.

In most of Southeast Asia, the story was similar to that of the
Philippines where within two weeks of the occupation, most editors
were interned or chased into the hills and all publications, except a
handful used specifically by the Japanese, were disbanded. In Burma,
only two pre-war Rangoon papers continued during the occupation.

Residents of these occupied states sought their information
from the number of cleverly devised underground papers that flourished. Among such guerrilla papers in the Philippines, for example,
was one which issued only one copy per edition. That copy was circulated to a select list of 500 people, and it was the responsibility of
the last individual on the list to make sure the paper was returned to
the editor, who promptly destroyed it. In Indonesia, the entire press
was taken over and reorganized as part of the Japanese propaganda
apparatus. In Indo-China, the media during the war (and immediately
after) was marked by a political instability that saw the wavering
press successively under Vichy French regime, Japanese occupation
and finally Ho Chi Minh's Communist government. Thailand, on the
other hand, was officially an ally of Japan. The Chinese-language
press supposedly printed clandestinely in Thailand during the war,
opposing Japan in the process. One wonders how clandestine the
operation was, seeing that at least in one instance even the Thai prime
minister knew all the details of one underground paper and did not
act against it.

The end of the war truly made peoples of Asia politically free.

For the first time in decades and even centuries, peoples of the Philippines, Korea, Taiwan, Pakistan, India, Indonesia and Ceylon were free to govern themselves. They were free to speak out and free to issue newspapers. As a result, hundreds of papers sprang up everywhere in Asia. To give an idea of the post-war newspaper development, in Hong Kong, only 10 of the 55 dailies and 26 weeklies published today were in operation when the Japanese attacked that city. The rest have been launched since the war. In Indonesia, 75 dailies—45 of them in the national language—were developed by 1949. Because of governmental favors, mass media in post-war China were revitalized much earlier than other cultural institutions, thus setting off an explosion of new media. Liberation also restored life to Korea's press but the political confusion of the period, plus the outbreak of the Korean War, hampered rapid growth.

At the time of surrender, Japanese media were barely breathing. After the war, the press, as all Japanese institutions, was placed under the office of General Douglas MacArthur, Supreme Commander of the Allied Powers. Contrary to policies laid down by the Allies in Italy and Germany, SCAP's press policy in Japan did not disband the existing media, although a number of people who had served the imperialist government were barred from newspaper work.

SUMMARY

With his permission, another man's summary of the problems and status of the Asian press will serve here:

In summary, it may be said that the problems of the Asian press are many times more urgent and complex than their counterparts in the West where press freedom is axiomatic, where communication and distribution of the information are practically instantaneous and universal, where the press is heavily supported by advertising, where newsprint, modern equipment and trained personnel are abundant. However, the Asian press continues to try. It is beginning to realize the duty of the press now extends way beyond the traditional concept of serving as a mirror of the times. It is beginning to reject the notion that the good of the country is the job of the government and the newspapers must only report. The Asian press is beginning to realize that if it were to serve its function in underdeveloped Asia it must be a participant in this development not only giving and interpreting the facts of social and economic life but promoting them and bringing them home to the readers. It knows only too well that its readers, the whole of Asia, must realize how serious the development problem is. It must think about the problem, must open the people's eyes to the possible solutions. The Asian press cannot succeed with anything less.[21]

NOTES

1.   Another source said of press freedom in Laos: "In Laos there is no prior censorship but self censorship is strictly observed. They even have laws and regulations which would be used if a newspaper would violate its self censorship. In addition, four major private newspapers are owned by aristocrats of high military offices." (Eduardo Sanchez, "State of the press in Asia," Paper presented at I Asian Assembly 1970. Mr. Sanchez sent author copy of tape of his reading of the speech.)

2.   In early 1971, a decree was issued suspending that part of the constitution guaranteeing freedom of expression. A censorship committee was also formed. In addition, all media in Cambodia are government owned and controlled. (*IPI Report,* 19:10 February 1971, p. 6.)

3.   At the beginning of the seventies a new press law was promulgated in South Vietnam guaranteeing press freedom. Soon after, however, Saigon newspapers were being seized en masse.

4.   To point out how regular this suspension and confiscation of newspapers is in South Vietnam, one editor, Ngo Cong Duc of *Tin Sang,* wrote IPI in the spring of 1971 reporting that his paper had been confiscated 103 times while others have been stopped by the government as many as 30 to 35 times each. He added: "I think that with such figures, the Vietnamese press is undoubtedly the most persecuted press in the world." (Anon. "A Saigon publisher accuses: 'Our press is the most persecuted in the world,' " *IPI Report,* 19:12 April 1971, p. 5.)

5.   Anon. "Grim times for the press of Burma," *IPI Report,* 19:5 (September 1970), p. 12.

6.   A May 27, 1971, press service dispatch from Bangkok reported: "The Thai government is again cracking down on the local press. At the end of March, General Prapass Gharusathira, concurrently Deputy Prime Minister, Commander-in-Chief of the armed forces, and Interior Minister, announced that the general instability in Thailand required stronger government press laws. . . . Last year the government introduced a new press bill which would allow it to close newspapers for anti-government statements without recourse to law. The timing of the bill turned out to be quite an embarrassment for the Thai government since it coincided with the visit of Vice-President Spiro Agnew to Bangkok in January. Instead of knuckling under to the bill, the local papers banded together to fight the issue. To call attention to the repressive law, all the papers agreed to a news boycott of the entire visit, substituting editorials on freedom of the press instead. The news boycott left Thai officials redfaced. . . . Since then, the government has made repeated warnings to the press, mostly concerning coverage of the suppression of an insurrection in southern Thailand. Although the Thai press is forbidden by law to criticize the government, its leaders or policies, the activities in the south became a vehicle through which the papers were able to focus on corruption, mismanagement and discrimination, merely by reporting events in the three southern provinces. . . . General Prapass hinted to newsmen that since the reportage of events in the south was unfavorable to the government, it might be necessary to ban the reporting on subjects which were not officially released."

7.   Sanchez, *op. cit.*

8.   Arrests of editors accused of being Communists occur occasionally on this island republic. In December 1970, nine prominent Chinese journalists were arrested on that charge, two of whom committed suicide. (Anon. "Chiang's China strikes again," *IPI Report,* 19:9 January 1971, p. 11.)

9. In May 1971, Singapore faced a press freedom crisis, reported here in a letter sent to all International Press Institute members by Director Ernest Meyer:

"Altogether three newspapers have, in one way or another, been affected by Government action in Singapore during this last month.

"In one case, that of the English language Eastern Sun, it would not appear prima facie that this is a matter calling for intervention by the Institute. The paper closed following a Government statement that its proprietor had received US dollars 1.2 million 'from a communist intelligence service.' The proprietors have not commented on this allegation but the key journalists on the paper resigned saying that they could not be associated with such a matter and in consequence the management closed the paper. There has been no appeal to the Institute.

"In the second case the Government has detained under internal security act four senior executives of the Nanyang Siang Pau, a Chinese language newspaper. Government statements allege that they were deliberately using the newspaper to foment racial discord. A writ of habeas corpus has been filed and is due to be heard on May 26. In this case an appeal has been made to the IPI. I have arranged in agreement with the Chairman of the Executive Committee for a Singapore lawyer to hold a watching brief for the Institute at the hearing and to report to me so that when we meet in Helsinki we shall have the latest information.

"The third case concerns the English language Singapore Herald. In its brief 10 months life, although it has declared it has no intention of opposing the Government except when fair comment is called for, the paper has nevertheless incurred Mr. Lee's severe displeasure. As a result, all Government advertising and access to official information were denied to this paper.

"Despite this, the paper continued publication but in the process its initial capital had been exhausted. Following his action against the Nanyang Siang Pau and the Eastern Sun, the Government began, in public statements, to associate the Singapore Herald with these black operations.' In particular the Government claimed, without being specific, that the original investment in the Herald, which was from Singapore citizens and a group of Malaysian businessmen, was not for normal commercial purposes, but was politically motivated. Insinuations were even made against Miss Aw who had come to the rescue of the paper with a personal investment and with a proposal to persuade some other newspaper publishers, almost all IPI members, to join her in the undertaking. A series of Government statements casting doubt on the sources and the motives of those investments culminated in a visit by Miss Aw to Singapore at the request of the Prime Minister for a discussion on the reasons of her investment.

"Despite all assurances and the offer of every facility to check these matters, Mr. Lee professed to be unconvinced. He concluded his second meeting with Miss Aw, which lasted 5½ hours by bringing into his room local officers of the Chase Manhattan Bank to whom the Singapore Herald was by now heavily indebted. The Prime Minister demanded that the bank officials confirm the amount of the debt and then state that, Miss Aw having reached the limit of her own personal commitment, they would now foreclose on the paper. On the following day the Chase Manhattan Bank officers appeared with the Prime Minister at a press conference during which they publicly reiterated their decision to foreclose.

"The staff of the Singapore Herald, apart from appealing to the International Press Institute for help, have made courageous efforts to keep their own paper going. Not only have they agreed to forgo their salaries but the reporters, proofreaders, typists and staff of all grades have gone on the streets to sell the paper. On the first day they raised the circulation from a normal figure of just under 14,000 a day to 29,500 and it is now well over 40,000."

At the IPI General Assembly in Helsinki in June 1971, the Prime Minister said he suspected the United States government and Chase Manhattan Bank of involvement in undercover financing of the Herald. In a BBC radio interview, he said two Singapore editors would be tried for allegedly spreading lies about him. All of this added up to a situation described here by a former editor who remains anonymous for obvious reasons: "There are no prospects for budding journalists or those who aspire to join the Fourth Estate. In the face of allegations and counter allegations, the Straits Times, Malay Mail, Sunday Times and Sunday Mail, reign supreme. No local financiers would invest in an English daily now. Very sad and unfortunate. Local financiers prefer real estate business, or, invest in Fixed Deposit wherein they are sure of a good profit at the end of each trading year. Any one who wants to start an English newspaper now could be described as crazy or an agent." (Correspondence to author, June 7, 1971.)

See John Gale, "IPI in turbulent assembly calls for Singapore probe," *Editor & Publisher*, June 19, 1971, pp. 14-5, 21; "Lee cracks down," *Newsweek*, June 7, 1971, p. 49.

10. However, the instability of the ruling Congress Party has been reflected recently in government attitudes toward media. In 1970, the BBC office in Delhi was closed, for example, but as the IPI reported, "although distasteful, this incident should not be allowed to harm the image of a great section of the Indian press which has a record of freedom which one hopes will require more than the instability of the Congress Party to mar." (Ernest Meyer, "Press freedom in 1970," *IPI Report*, 19:9 January 1971, p. 8.)

11. Tarzie Vittachi, "State of the Asian Press," *The Asia Magazine*, March 14, 1965, p. 14.

12. A 1970 source indicated that the use of government information handouts gets more serious yearly in Malaysia. "The main problem is that the newspapers. . . have come to rely on the Press Division as their *only* source of news. The Press Division handout is the staple diet of the local reporter—to such an extent that events often go unreported unless they are issued from the information service. . . In both states (Malaysia and Singapore?) there are great areas of doubt about what they are allowed to print so that if any item comes through the Press Division it is seen by the papers as 'official' and therefore safe to use." (Jack Glattbach, "The state of the press in East Malaysia," mimeographed report written for South East Asia Press Centre, Kuala Lumpur, August, 1970.)

13. During the 1971 elections, one of the presidential candidates, Kim Dac-Jung, made the lack of press freedom in Korea one of his key issues. He feared a rigged election as the "press is under the complete control of the South Korean Central Intelligence Agency," he said. He pointed out that the press could never criticize President Park or the CIA. (*IPI Report*, 19:11 March 1971, p. 2.)

14. Nghiem Xuan Thien, "Where the newsboys' cry is 'Rent all about it!' " *IPI Report*, March 1971, pp. 8-9.

15. Steve Hsu, "Paperboys with cannon," UPI dispatch in *Rocky Mountain News*, August 3, 1969.

16. Whereas there are 102 copies of newspapers per 1000 persons on a worldwide basis, the average in Asia is 14 per 1000. Japan has 487 copies of papers available per 1000 people and Singapore 268; Laos, Burma, Indonesia, India, Afghanistan and Nepal have average daily circulations of less than 10 copies per 1000 population. Malaysia, Taiwan, Korea and South Vietnam have an average of little more than 50 per 1000 while Pakistan, Philippines, Cambodia, Ceylon and Thailand, from 10 to 45 per 1000 persons.

17. Sanchez, *op. cit.*

18. Thien, *op. cit.*

19. Won Ho Chang, *Freedom of the press in Korea: A study of its historical development*, Masters thesis, University of Southern California, 1970.

20. Chen Mong Hock, *The early Chinese newspapers of Singapore 1881-1912*, Singapore University of Malaya Press, 1967, p. 97.

21. Sanchez, *op. cit.*

Government Control
of the Press in the
United Arab Republic*

ADNAN ALMANEY

ADNAN ALMANEY is Associate Professor of Communication and Management at De Paul University, Chicago.

The purpose of this study is to explore press-government relationships under Gamal Abdul Nasser's regime from 1952 to 1970 in the United Arab Republic. The study will focus on (1) how the press was brought under complete government control, and (2) the rationale behind this control and its effect on the press. To place the discussion in proper perspective, a brief historical review of the press-government relationships before 1952 is necessary.

THE PRESS BEFORE 1952

The history of the Egyptian press dates from 1789 when Napoleon invaded Egypt; one year later, he published the first Arabic newspaper, *Al-Hawadith al-Yawmiyah* (The Daily Events).[1] This paper ceased publication in 1801 when the Ottomans expelled the French from Egypt, and no newspaper was published until Mohammad Ali was appointed governor of Egypt in 1805 by the Ottoman Sultan.

*Reprinted from *Journalism Quarterly*, Summer 1972, pp. 340–48. Used by permission.

As part of his program to modernize Egypt, Mohammad Ali established the Bulaq Press which printed, among other publications, *Al-Waqa'i al-Misriyah* (The Official Gazette). The governor took a personal interest in the paper and exercised direct control of its content; nothing could be published without his approval.[2] Even before this paper was published, in fact, Mohammad Ali had issued in 1824, a decree prohibiting the use of the Bulaq Press for printing any publication without his permission.[3] This decree marked the first official press control in Egypt.

Khedive Ismail (1863–1879), an admirer of Europe, encouraged publication of privately owned papers and thus may be credited with the rise of the Egyptian popular press. Ismail's liberal policies attracted many Lebanese and Syrian intellectuals who started their own papers, one of which, *Al-Ahram* (The Pyramids), was published in 1876. Although granting more freedom to the press than his predecessors, Ismail kept a watchful eye on publications and suppressed any critical voice.[4]

Ismail's extravagant schemes to Europeanize Egypt led to national bankruptcy and foreign intervention which later sparked the 1881 Egyptian army revolt. The revolt was crushed by the British, who now emerged as the real power in Egypt, although theoretically the country remained an Ottoman province.

One consequence of British occupation was the emergence of the party press. Initially privately owned, this press was created by Western educated, upper-middle class intellectuals who, unable to challenge the British militarily, began forming political parties, using the press as their chief medium of political agitation. In 1907, for instance, Mustafa Kamil founded the Nationalist Party and used its paper, *Al-Liwa'* (The Standard), to create in the Egyptians a sense of identity as a nation. After World War I, Sa'ad Zaghlul founded *Al-Wafd* Party (The Delegation) whose paper *Al-Balagh* (The Message, later known as *Al-Misri* or The Egyptian) was used to mobilize the Egyptians behind such slogans as independence and constitutionalism. In its uncompromising stand against the British, this paper symbolized the strongest expression of national sentiment, and its message was disseminated to the largely illiterate public through word-of-mouth by small but highly motivated literate groups.

This political agitation culminated in the 1919 popular revolt. It also prompted members of the aristocracy, who now sensed the menace to their interests, to organize the Liberal Constitutional Party and propagate their own views in *Al-Siyasah* (Politics). In 1922 they convinced the British to grant Egypt limited independence; thus the country became a monarchy with a parliament and multi-party system, and Ahmed Fuad (whom Farouq succeeded in 1937) became its first king. When elections were held under the 1923 constitution, the Wafd Party won overwhelmingly; but British pressure forced the Wafd out of power, and a new pro-British government was instituted.

Just as free elections proved to be a farce, press freedom as a constitutional provision received only lip service. Section two of Article 15, for instance, declared that "the press is free within the law," that no censorship would be imposed, and that government would not confiscate newspapers by mere administrative acts.[5] Such provisions, however, proved meaningless, since the same article declared that such measures might be invoked "in the interest of the social system."[6]

In 1936 a new constitution was drafted and remained effective until 1952. This constitution lifted many press restrictions: press criticism of the king, for instance, was treated as a political and not a criminal offense, and the government was deprived of its power to suspend papers through administrative acts.[7] The clause, "The press is free within the law," however, remained unaltered, thus providing the party in power with considerable latitude in suppressing the opposition voices.

Despite the frequent repressive measures, the press between 1936 and 1952 enjoyed a certain amount of freedom, ranging from criticising the government's public policies to publicising official corruption. Such freedom was made possible largely by the peculiar political, economic, and social structure of the country. Egyptian politics consisted of a triangle of forces: the palace with its political parties, the Wafd Party, and the British who exerted their power alternatively on the other two forces. Although struggling among themselves for maximum power, "the various parties in fact presented a common front against the unprivileged groups. . ."[8] who were kept removed from the political process.

Press freedom, therefore, could not seriously threaten the political structure, nor could it have a serious impact on the predominantly illiterate lower classes. The gap between the privileged and the unprivileged groups was too vast, and the middle class was simply too small and too weak to effect any change in the structure. Owners of independent papers, with the exception of *Al-Ahram* and a few others, were forced by the low literacy rate and insufficient advertising to solicit funds from various political groups in return for favorable editorial treatment.

Despite the mounting social ills, the landowners failed to initiate any serious reform programs. Thus the population increase went unchecked, farmers left their land to overcrowd the cities, unemployment rose, and inflation spiraled; and the Egyptian intellectuals, in their search for new political direction, turned to such radical groups as the Muslim Brotherhood and the Communist Party.

THE 1952 REVOLUTION

The foregoing factors, in addition to the 1948 Palestine fiasco, prompted a group of middle-class army officers led by Gamal Abdul Nasser to depose King Farouq on July 23, 1952 and to establish a republican regime. Shortly thereafter, the Revolutionary Command Council (RCC) abrogated the constitution, appointed General Naguib as the "leader of the Revolution," dissolved political parties, and imposed press censorship as criticism of the military takeover mounted.

Aware of the void caused by the abolition of political parties, the government created in January 1953 a single political organization, the Liberation Rally, with Nasser as its Secretary-General. A three-year transition period was proclaimed, and a temporary constitution was adopted to guide the country until 1956. A year later, however, a feud erupted between Nasser and Naguib over Egypt's future political structure. Naguib, backed mostly by members of the dissolved parties, favored the restoration of parliamentary rule; whereas Nasser, backed by army officers, opposed it.

After eliminating Naguib as a political rival, Nasser next moved against the press, which not only sided with Naguib but had begun to attack Nasser fiercely. This kind of criticism was possible, because the government had briefly lifted censorship in March 1954. The press exploited this freedom liberally, prompting Nasser to reimpose it one month later. The newsmen, accused of "betraying themselves by spreading suspicion and doubts against the Revolution,"[9] were given a stern warning to be either approving of the government's activities or to be noncommittal.

To control the press more effectively, the government went beyond the mere imposition of censorship and took punitive measures against anti-regime publishers. The major target of these measures was the Press Syndicate. Salah Salim, Minister of National Guidance, ordered the dissolution of the Syndicate, charging that seven members of its ruling council, as well as 14 other journalists,[10] had received bribes of up to $140,000 from the old politicians in return for favorable press treatment. Among journalists mentioned by the minister were the Syndicate's president and secretary. Each was accused of receiving $15,000 of the government's "secret" funds and therefore, both were, according to the minister, guilty of participating in the corruption and of failing to expose the evils of the old political system.

Probably no press criticism had irked the government more than that made by Mahmoud Abul Fath and his brother Hussain Abul Fath, owners and publishers of *Al-Misri* (The Egyptian), the organ of the defunct Wafd Party. *Al-Misri* first appeared in October 1936 and grew in circulation to about 100,000, thus becoming one of the three largest newspapers in Cairo. When censorship was lifted in March 1954, the two brothers launched furious attacks on Nasser not only in *Al-Misri* but also in the other newspapers and magazines controlled by their publishing empire. Among these publications were the *Egyptian Gazette,* the only Cairo English-language daily; and two French-language dailies, *Journal d'Egypte* and *La Bourse Egyptienne.* Determined to purge the press of these two outspoken critics, the government charged the Faths with committing acts against the national interest. Mahmoud was accused of fostering propaganda abroad against the regime, and Hussain was charged with attempting to obtain an arms contract from the Ministry of War and Marine for his own benefit and in disregard of the country's interests.

Describing the case as one involving the principles of a free press, Dr. Wahid Rafat of the defense counsel argued that it was no crime for a newspaper to urge the return of parliamentary life, and that the Revolutionary Command Council itself had been divided on this issue.[11] Nevertheless, Mahmoud Abul Fath, tried *in absentia* while in Switzerland, was sentenced to ten years' imprisonment and ordered to forfeit about one million dollars. His brother received a suspended sentence of 15 years' imprisonment. The RCC confirmed the sentences and revoked *Al-Misri's* license. Because the licenses of the Faths' publications were held in the names of other officers of their publishing corporation, the papers continued to appear under the control of a government custodian, and their revenues were seized to meet the confiscation order. The fate of *Al-Misri's* publishers was not lost on other journalists. Since then no journalist has openly criticized the regime or demanded the return of parliamentary rule.

After suppressing the critical voices, the government decided in 1955 to revive the Press Syndicate. Under a new administration, the Syndicate's ostensible objectives were to increase the efficiency of the press, promote a spirit of cooperation among its members, and raise their moral and material standards. To tighten its control even further, the government decreed that no Egyptian would be permitted to practice journalism until he had joined the Press Syndicate.

Now that the threat of press had been adequately neutralized, the government in May of 1955 eased press censorship slightly. This

move was probably also prompted by the fact that the transition
period (proclaimed in 1953) was scheduled to end in 1956, and the
regime sought to provide a seemingly free atmosphere for people to
discuss and vote on the officially proposed plan for future political
structure. The plan specified that no political parties would be allowed to function; instead a National Union—made up of peasants,
laborers, and professionals—would be established. In June 1956 the
plan was approved in a plebiscite. As a result, the RCC was dissolved,
Nasser proclaimed President of the Republic, and a new constitution
enacted. Certain articles in the constitution gave rise to hopes of
some democratic revival. Article 45, for instance, stated that "Freedom of the press, publication and copyright is safeguarded in the
interest of public welfare and within the limits prescribed by the
law." Article 44 proclaimed that "Freedom of thought and of scientific research is guaranteed."[12]

Despite these trappings of constitutional protection, the press
continued to function under rigid censorship. In fact, censorship did
not seem to answer the government's desire to mobilize the press in
the "service of the people." The search for a more effective control
system resulted in a number of proposals, including: 1) forcing newspaper owners to turn their publishing houses into limited liability
stock companies in which they would hold no more than 25 per cent
of shares; 2) turning over a large share of the publications to syndicates, trade unions, and professional organizations, all under government control; 3) appointing hand-picked managers in each publishing
house to supervise news content and to prevent the bribery of journalists through subsidies of advertising; and 4) promulgating new press
laws defining the restrictions to be imposed on publications.[13]

When presented to publishers at a meeting called by the Press
Syndicate, these proposals were rejected. This rejection, and perhaps
the fear of adverse regional and international publicity, caused the
postponement of any more drastic repressive measures, such as press
nationalization. Instead, the government began publishing papers of
its own such as *Al-Sha'ab* (The People) which soon failed, *Al-Gumhouriyah* (The Republic), and *Al-Misa'* (The Evening).

PRESS NATIONALIZATION

In May of 1960, however, the government suddenly issued a decree
nationalizing the press.[14] This decree was undoubtedly the most
drastic measure affecting press freedom since at least 1900. Termed
the "Press Organization Law," the decree removed the following put

lishing houses from private ownership, placing them under the National Union's control:[15]

1. Dar Al-Ahram, which publishes the morning daily *Al-Ahram* (The Pyramids) and the monthly economic review, *Al-Ahram al-Iqtisadi* (The Economist); 2. Dar Akhbar El-Yom, which publishes two dailies: *Al-Akhbar* (The News) and *Akhbar el-Yom* (Today's News); and three weeklies: *Al-Jeel* (The Generation), *Akher Sa'ah* (The Final Hour), and *Al-Mukhtar* (The Select); 3. Dar Al-Hilal, which publishes five weeklies: *Al-Mussawar* (The Pictorial), *Al-Kawakib* (The Stars), *Hawwa'* (Eve), *Al-Sindbad,* and *Sameer* (The Companion); and the monthly *Al-Hilal* (The Crescent); 4. Dar Rose El-Yousseff, which publishes the weeklies: *Rose el-Youssef, Sabah al-Khayr* (Good Morning), and *Al-Kitab al-Dahabi* The Golden Book); 5. Dar Al-Tahrir, which publishes two dailies: *Al-Gumhouriyah* (The Republic) and *Al-Missa'* (The Evening); and a number of other publications, including *Al-Ida'ah* (Broadcasting). Control of the foreign-language newspapers was vested in the National Union also.

Under the official order, owners who were put out of business were to be compensated for their properties. A special committee was formed to evaluate publishing properties and pay the owners in government bonds yielding three per cent interest over 20 years. The editors were assured of their jobs under the new system; but in the future, any Egyptian aspiring to be a journalist would have to obtain an authorization from the National Union.

As the new owner of all publications, the National Union, now known as the Arab Socialist Union, designated boards of directors to manage the publishing house.[16] The new boards, it was asserted, were not responsible to the government but to the Union which embodied "the will and the authority of the people." The Union's objectives, which the press must now promote, were the realization of "sound democracy" and "socialist revolution," and the safeguarding of the "people's rights." Its duties, which were now the press duties, were to become a "positive force behind the Revolution," to eliminate all vestiges of capitalism and feudalism, to prevent corruption, and to block the infiltration of foreign influence.[17]

An explanatory note accompanying the nationalization decree said that the "organization of the press" was necessary to prevent capitalists from controlling the press.[18] Having been restored to the people, the note said, the press would be used to serve national rather than selfish individual interests. Private ownership, according to the government, proved divisive and self-centered and was detrimental to the country's goal of attaining social and economic justice through a socialist revolution.

Nasser himself expressed annoyance that publishers devoted more space to sensational accounts of crime, divorce, and sex incidents than to government's social and economic programs. Unimpressed by editorial praise, he asked editors to offer constructive criticism and to devote more space to serious articles on rural problems than to sex stories.[19] Nasser was also apprehensive about foreign embassies' efforts to influence the press through advertising. In 1959, for instance, the Communist countries spent $500,000 on advertising in the Egyptian press, and the Western countries inserted advertisements costing $100,000.[20]

IMPACT OF NATIONALIZATION

Initially, press nationalization brought little change in the editing and management of the Egyptian press. The committee formed to run newspapers in the National Union's name consisted largely of former editors and owners of the nationalized press. In 1964, however, a number of Marxists and Socialists, among them Khalid Mohied din and Ahmed Fuad, were given important editorial and managerial positions. This not only balanced the moderate and somewhat conservative views of other journalists, but also greatly minimized the dissension of the leftists, who by 1966 threw their full support behind Nasser. The leftists' installation with the press was also prompted by Nasser's proclamation of Egypt as a "Socialist, Democratic, and Cooperative" country. Thus, the "Arab Socialism" concept came to the fore, and who would be more able to sell this concept to the masses than the leftists themselves? These writers, therefore, indeed even the non-leftists, went to great lengths explaining to the Egyptians the compatibility of socialism, Islam, and Arab nationalism. Socialism was depicted, not only in the press but also in books and periodicals, as "the revival of the great Islamic past . . . and that the prophet Muhammad was the first socialist."[21]

Due to the repetition of such themes as Arab socialism, Arab unity, revolutionary spirit, imperialism, reactionary elements, and the people's gains; and due to the absence of any criticism of Nasser or his regime, the press acquired the unflattering reputation of being dull and predictable in handling domestic affairs. Even after Egypt's disastrous defeat in the 1967 war with Israel, the press lacked the moral courage to level serious criticism. Journalists were so timid in their writings that Nasser's confidant, Mohammad Hassanain Heykal,[22] began "urging his colleagues to abandon their ingrained habits of self-censorship and speak out."[23] His advice, however, fell on dea ears, since, in a country where all publications were government controlled, a journalist might be risking his only means of livelihood by voicing criticism which might be interpreted as anti-revolutionary. Thus, the only "licensed" critic remained Heykal himself who, because of his closeness to Nasser, was able to write more openly on such matters as the mediocrity of some U.A.R. air force and army generals, the secret police, and Egyptian diplomats. On occasions, Heykal not only refused to abide by the Arab Socialist Union's dictates but also attacked the Union for its tight press control which "suppressed objective reporting and created a credibility gap between the public and the press."[24] Heykal continued to be the outstanding critic even after Nasser's death in 1970, for he also enjoyed a good relationship with Sadat.

It is not intended here to suggest that the press was void of any criticism of domestic affairs. Theoretically, at least, the press was to act as a watchdog for the people, uncovering corruption and threats to the revolutionary goals by government bureaucracy, industrial management, reactionary elements, and foreign agents. Criticism of such matters occasionally cropped up in the press, and was characterized as criticism within the system, not against it. Since Nasser and his regime were exempted from any criticism the Egyptians, lacking a truly responsive press, often resorted to the *nuktah* (the joke) as a safety valve. Indeed, after the 1967 war, the *nuktah* was so much relied on as a political and social commentary that "Nasser publicly admonished the population for showing such levity at a time of crisis."[25]

In treating foreign affairs, the press was much freer in criticising foreign governments considered unfriendly to Egypt. Comments on these matters were practically uninhibited and thus constituted the most lively aspect of the Egyptian press. In this respect, *Al-Gumhouriyah,* a left-wing paper speaking for the Arab Socialist Union, was noted for its ferocious attacks on foreign governments and personalities. *Al-Ahram,* expressing Nasser's views, took a more moderate stand, whereas *Al-Akhbar* generally expressed conservative views. Foreign governments' and newspapers' responses, however, were never reported in the Egyptian press.

Undoubtedly, the quality of the press—the freedom to pursue an independent line from the government—had been adversely affected by nationalization. Quantitatively, however, the nationalization had some positive effects. Scores of newspapers and periodicals were published by the government in such diverse fields as education, economics, industry, finance, agriculture, and politics. In Cairo alone, ten dailies appeared: three in Arabic, three in French, two in Greek, one in English, and one in Armenian. In Alexandria, there were also ten dailies: three in Arabic, three in Greek, three in French, and one in English and French. Circulation went up. Thus, while the average daily sale of papers was about 500,000 before 1960, the figure exceeded 800,000 by 1968, with the average number of copies per 1,000 inhabitants rising from 20 in 1959[26] to 28 in 1968.[27] The increased circulation was largely due to the expansion of education, made possible by the regime's opening of new schools at the rate of one every day; consequently, the total school population rose from 3.5 million in 1961 to more than 6 million in 1968.

The journalists' attitude toward the nationalization was mixed but generally, and at least outwardly, favorable. Some journalists, such as Heykal, appeared genuine in their support of the government's decision and strongly advocated it in their columns.[28] Some others justified the action by explaining that the press was not nationalized but socialized.[29] Fear of government reprisal was of course the obvious reason for such attitudes, but it might also be true that many journalists found it personally rewarding to live under the new system. The nationalization decree specified that half of the profits of publishing houses would be distributed among press employees and the other half would be used to upgrade the press quality. Although the law set an upper limit for profit bonus, many journalists received salaries high enough to support a life of luxury; they have in effect joined the new elitism, generally comprised of army officers and professionals.

A very few journalists publicly expressed discontent with the nationalization act. Notable among these were "The Twins," Mustafa Amin and Ali Amin. Educated in the West, both were known for their sympathy with Western liberalism and free enterprise and were often credited with the rise of the Egyptian "mass" journalism. They started their career in 1944 by publishing the weekly *Akhbar el-Yom* (Today News). In 1952 they published the daily *Al-Akhbar* (The News) which enjoyed the second largest circulation next to *Al-Ahram*. Following the Revolution, the Amins supported the new regime, but in 1960 when the government decided to take over the press, they strongly opposed the move. Consequently, their empire was placed in the hands of Kaml Rif'at, a former minister of labor. Ali was moved to Dar al-Hilal publishing house; and Mustafa, initially forced to retire, was later given a position with Dar al-Hilal. In 1965, however, Mustafa was indicted on charges of spying for the United States and was sentenced to life imprisonment. Although Mustafa was released in 1967, his imprisonment has probably ended his career as one of Egypt's prominent journalists.

DISCUSSION

The press system in Egypt which began as authoritarian under Mohammad Ali has become, after intervals of relative freedom, authoritarian under Nasser's United Arab Republic. In both eras, government control of the press was complete. But why did Nasser have to take such a drastic measure as nationalization when the press was already functioning under tight government control?

Nasser's initial objectives were ostensibly limited to internal reform and development; raising the standard of living, expanding education, and instilling into the masses a keener political and social consciousness.[30] Rather quickly, however, he proved to harbor ambitions both for himself and for his people far beyond Egypt's borders. In *The Philosophy of the Revolution,* Nasser envisioned himself as a leader destined to play an important role in what he termed the Three Circles: the Arab World, Africa, and the Muslim World. He felt that the leadership role, especially in the Arab World, was vacant. Nasser said: ". . . there is a role wandering aimlessly about in search of an actor to play it. And I do not know why this role . . . should at last settle down on our frontiers beckoning us to move to dress up for it as nobody else can do so."[31]

The Egyptians, however, seemed unprepared to assume the role he chose for them. Nasser compared the 1952 Egypt to a caravan led astray and dispersed, with "each group wandering off to a different place."[32] Realizing that Egypt was a house divided against itself, a ground too shaky to shore up his aspirations for regional leadership, Nasser sought first to consolidate his power at home, and utilized a number of devices to create a strong, united public opinion. He adopted the motto "Unity, Discipline, and Work," dissolved political parties, eliminated all opponents, and established the Liberation Rally (later known as the National Union and the Arab Socialist Union) as an all-embracing political organization for the Egyptians.

Unlike the old regime that drew its power from landowners, Nasser sought support from the peasants and workers who comprised 80 per cent of the population. Their sheer numbers would enormously enhance the support he already enjoyed in the army. By providing land to peasants, guaranteeing jobs for the workers, and enabling both groups to play a role in the Arab Socialist Union (by law, peasants and workers comprised half of the A.S.U.'s membership), Nasser sought to cultivate the loyalty of this large, yet previously ignored, segment of the society. In this, he succeeded remarkably.

Now that the masses were drawn into the political process, the expression of opinions acquired a significant new dimension. It was no longer confined to the thin and homogeneous socioeconomic upper class. Rather, the expression of opinions now "may move the masses brought into the political spectrum"[33] and thus could have far-reaching consequences. Determined to mold the masses' opinions to his own liking so that the "Holy March" could proceed without impediment, Nasser wanted the Egyptians to know only what he thought they ought to know. He, in effect, designated himself "the supreme educator of the Egyptian society...."[34] Using the government-controlled radio and TV, the regime began to communicate with the masses more directly and more frequently—creating opinions in them, arousing their passions, and motivating them to strive for the country's goals. The press, while still privately owned, could not be mobilized as fully and effectively as were the other media. To Nasser, press nationalization was the answer.

The press-government relationships from 1960 until Nasser's death in 1970 were perhaps the most stable and consistent in Egypt's modern history. Press ownership remained in the Arab Socialist Union's hands, and journalists continued to abide almost religiously by the Union's directives and guidelines. Other than an occasional shuffling in the editorship and management personnel, the relationship was unmarred by any significant development. Whether Nasser's successors will institute any change that might affect this relationship is an open question.

Press freedom in the United Arab Republic as is often the case in many developing countries, fell victim to a nationalist military revolution. Military leaders have generally proved to be ultra-sensitive to press criticism and seem unable to live with it. It is possible, however, that such leaders might develop a more tolerant attitude toward press freedom after their countries have achieved a reasonable measure of modernity and a sense of national confidence.

NOTES

1.   V. Philip D. Tarrazi, *Tarikh al-Sahafah al-Arabiyah* (History of the Arabic Press), (Beirut, 1913), vol. 1, pp. 48–9.

2.   Ibrahim Abduh, *Tarikh al-Tiba'ah wal Sahafah fi Mistr Khilal al-Hamlah al-Faransiyah* (History of the Press and Printing in Egypt during the French Occupation), (Cairo, 1941), pp. 12–13.

3.   Khali Sabat, *Tarikh, al-Tiba'ah fil Sharq al-Arabi* (The History of Printing in the Arab East), (Cairo, 1958), p. 141.

4.   Ibrahim Abduh, *Tatawwur al-Sahafah al-Misriyah* (Development of the Egyptian Press) (Cairo, –), pp. 261–4.

5.   Abdul Lateef Mohammad, *Al-Tashri' al-Siyasi fi Misr* (Political Legislation in Egypt), (Cairo, 1924), vol. 2, p. 666.

6. Ibrahim Abduh, *ibid.,* pp. 276-8.

7. A. Lateef Hamzah, *Qissat al-Sahafah al-Arabiyah fi Misr* (The Story of the Arabic Press in Egypt), (Baghdad, 1967), p. 183.

8. Nadaf Safran, *Egypt in Search of Political Community,* (Cambridge: Harvard University Press, 1961), p. 194.

9. Don Peretz, "Democracy and the Revolution in Egypt," *The Middle East Journal,* 13, Winter 1959, p. 37.

10. Keith Wheelock, *Nasser's New Egypt,* (New York: Frederick A. Praeger, 1960), p. 59.

11. New York *Times,* May 15, 1954, p. 15.

12. Anouar Abdul Malik, *Egypt: Military Society.* Translated from French by C. L. Markmann (New York: Vintage Books, 1968), p. 116.

13. Raymond H. Anderson, "Nasser Weighing Rigid Censorship," New York *Times,* 17, 1, Feb. 26, 1956.

14. U.A.R., *Al-Jaridah al-Rasmiyah* (The Official Gazette), No. 118, May 24, 1960.

15. Abdul Lateef Hamzah, *Azmet al-Damir al-Sahafi* (The Crisis of Press Conscience), (Cairo, 1960), p. 218.

16. Ministry of the Justice, U.A.R., *Al-Nashrah al-Tashri'iyah* (The Legislative Bulletin), May 1960, pp. 1561-3.

17. Information Department, U.A.R., *Statute of the Arab Socialist Union,* (Cairo, 1962), pp. 3-4.

18. U.A.R., *Al-Nashrah al-Tashri'iyah, op. cit.,* pp. 1561-3.

19. Anouar Abdul Malik, *op. cit.,* p. 147.

20. New York *Times,* May 31, 1960, p. 3.

21. Ali Dessouki, "The Mass Political Culture of Egypt," *The Muslim World,* vol. 61, no. 1, January 1971, pp. 16-17.

22. As a war correspondent, Heykal first met Nasser during the 1948 Palestine war, and an intimacy developed between the two. In 1956 Heykal left his job as editor of the weekly *Akher Sa'ah* to become editor-in-chief of *Al-Ahram* which was on the verge of bankruptcy. Heykal's aggressive leadership and his closeness to Nasser made *Al-Ahram* the largest and the most influential paper in the Arab World. His Friday column, "Frankly Speaking," is widely read by observers of Egyptian politics. In 1970 Nasser made Heykal the Minister of National Guidance; but after Nasser's death, Heykal resigned, retaining his job with *Al-Ahram.*

23. Harry Hopkins, *Egypt, the Crucible: the Unfinished Revolution of the Arab World,* (London: Secker and Warburg, 1969), p. 349.

24. *Al-Amal* (Action), Tunisia, Dec. 21, 1968, p. 12.

25. A. L. A. Marsat, "The Cartoon in Egypt," *Comparative Studies in Society and History,* vol. 13, January 1971, p. 6.

26. Unesco, *Statistical Yearbook 1963,* (Paris, 1964), pp. 383-4.

27. United Nations, *Statistical Yearbook 1970,* (New York, 1971), pp. 794-5.

28. M. H. Heykal, "Al-Sahafah," (The Press), *Al-Ahram,* May 28, and June 1 and 3, 1961.

29. Harry Hopkins, 1969, *op. cit.,* p. 346.

30. Gamal Nasser, "The Egyptian Revolution," *Foreign Affairs*, 33, 1955, p. 208–9.

31. Gamal Abdul Nasser, *The Philosophy of the Revolution* (Cairo: Government Printing Offices, 1958), p. 53.

32. *Ibid.*, p. 44.

33. Morroe Berger, *The Arab World Today*, (New York: Doubleday, 1960), p. 397.

34. P. J. Vatikiotis, *The Egyptian Army in Politics: Pattern for New Nations?* (Bloomington: Indiana University Press, 1961), p. xiii.

The Mass Media
and the
Great Campaigns *

WILBUR SCHRAMM

WILBUR SCHRAMM holds a doctoral degree from the
University of Iowa. He is Professor Emeritus and formerly Janet M. Peck Professor of International Communication, Adjunct Professor of Education, and Director of
the Institute for Communication Research at Stanford
University. He has been a consultant to several government agencies and foundations because of his preeminence
in communication research. He is the author of fourteen
books on communications, including Television in the
Lives of our Children, Mass Media and National Development, Responsibility in Mass Communication, and Classroom Out-of-Doors.

◎ ◎ ◎ In practical terms . . . there are
some development tasks in which the mass media can be of more direct help than in others, and . . . whoever uses mass communication to
help bring about social change had better know the culture he is trying to alter. In countries where people have had the most experience
in using the media for economic and social development there is,
however, less talk of "media" than of "campaigns" or "systems."

---

*Reprinted by permission of Unesco from Mass Media and National Development (Stan-
ford, Calif.: Stanford University Press), pp. 145–74. © 1964 by Unesco.

This is because it is recognized that the great battles of development are continuing ones, and the results come less from the impact of single messages or single media than from a succession of impacts of related messages and reinforcing channels. Campaigns to modernize some part of a society will almost invariably make use of face-to-face communication as well as the media. Whenever possible, they will require different channels or combinations of channels. For example, early in a campaign a medium like radio may be most useful in making the people aware of needs and opportunities; later in the campaign, the emphasis may have to be on face-to-face demonstration or discussion, to help the people come to a decision on a proposed change. Thus, the planners of development campaigns find themselves thinking of communication *systems* rather than media. What *combination* of messages and channels, in what *order,* will be of most help in bringing about the changes that need to occur? This is the planner's question.

Professor René Dumont, of the French Institut National Agronomique, studied the agricultural needs of French Africa and decided that the primary channel for communicating the messages of change to the rural population in that part of the world should be the public schools rather than the media or the field workers. And not the public schools as they now exist, but a radically different kind of school to replace the kind which is now, he says, "a major brake on agricultural development." Professor Dumont continues:

The African school, especially because of caste privileges, is now considered as a source of culture, it is true; but it is regarded even more as a means of access to the "paradise" of government and administration. Many Africans, when they come to France, are astounded to see whites having the social status of peasants and workers and themselves manipulating the pitchfork and the plough. They had been apt to imagine the whites as all being on the pattern of colonial administrators, that is, free of servile tasks, the idea being that education ought to enable the Africans, too, to rid themselves of the disgrace of manual work.[1]

He proposes therefore a new educational institution, designed as transition to a truly African system. This is a rural school for village boys between the ages of 10 and 14, who have been unable to go to a traditional school. Very few, if any, of these students would have a chance to go on to secondary school, the professions, and bureaucracy; rather, they would become the kind of farmer Africa so desperately needs—the modern cultivator who looks to the future, is not ashamed to work, and is prepared to take the advice of technicians and instructors. The school would be comparatively cheap to maintain. The school itself and the teacher's house would be built by the villagers and the students themselves, as an exercise in their education. "Such expensive obligations as the need to learn French, which is a foreign language in Africa," would be dispensed with, he says. The students would work on the land four hours a day and go to school four hours a day. The curriculum would be basic and practical. "A rural school of this kind," he says, "would very soon become the real center of agricultural progress in the village."[2]

After the effect of the new school system begins to be felt, he suggests, then the African countries can use an agricultural field service, agricultural radio, agricultural bulletins, and the other communication channels effectively. But they will not really be effective *until* a change in the schools brings about a fundamental change in attitudes toward manual labor.

It is not necessary for us to decide whether Professor Dumont has the correct solution, or whether he has underestimated what the mass media can do. The point is that he has gone about reaching his solution, not by putting the question, How should we use the mass media (or the field staff, or the schools, or rural discussion groups)? but rather by asking, *How can the needed change be brought about?*

This is where systems thinking necessarily begins. The planner has to know the culture well enough to know how the given change can be brought about: what can be done by information and persuasion, and by what kind of information and persuasion; and what must be done by allocating resources or providing opportunities other than symbolic ones. Then he has to plan some sequence of events. The physical resources and the informational resources have to be brought to bear when they will help each other, and when the audience needs them. So far as the informational part of the program is concerned, at given points in the campaign certain people will need to be reached, and the best channels will have to be found to reach them. Whenever possible, more than one channel will be used for a given purpose, to make sure that the word gets through, and, if possible, to permit one message to reinforce others. Beginning with the question of how a desired change can be brought about, the planner of a development campaign therefore finds himself working with an entire communication system, trying to use all its resources in the best combinations and sequences.

In a typical development campaign, audiences are usually first made aware of a problem or an event by the swifter media. Then come the more detailed treatments, the expressions of opinion, the arguing of different positions, the provision of more information, from whatever channel will appropriately provide those services at the times they are needed. Thus the sequence of need is met—first, for awareness; then for additional details, so that the conditions of decision will become clear; then for arguments pro and con, so that

opinion can begin to form; then for additional information with
which to undergird opinion; and finally, for the expressions of con-
sensus and decision.

We know from studies of innovation in highly developed countries that the first step in this process is usually a contact with the
mass media which provides information about a potentially rewarding new practice (and at the same time suggests the inadequacy of
existing practices).[3] At this point, the prospective innovator is the
more passive participant and the media are the active participants in
the process. But if the message interests the innovator, then he becomes active. Typically he checks the information with persons he
respects, or with other mass media. Usually he wants more details on
what the practice involves. He wants to know what other people
think about it and what they are planning to do. Above all, probably,
he would like to see the practice in use; and therefore, about this
time, a demonstration will be useful. If group decision is required, a
meeting or a discussion forum will be helpful. If the innovator decides to try the new practice, he will then need really detailed information and guidance. For this he may go to an expert, a more experienced farmer, a "how to do it" poster or magazine, or a technical
booklet. And so on. The point is that there is a sequence in which
these different kinds of information are needed, the appropriate
channels for different purposes and different targets at different
times.

So if a developing country is to make best use of its facilities in
the great campaigns of development, early in any given campaign
someone will have to look at the problem broadly—more broadly,
that is, than from the viewpoint of radio, or the extension service, or
schools, or newspapers, or films. Someone must look at the needs for
change, at the likely dynamics of change, and at the resources available, and then design the system of messages, channels, and events
that promises to be most efficient at bringing about the change desired.

FOUR CAMPAIGN AREAS

Agriculture

One example of a broadly conceived development campaign is the
Intensive Agricultural District Program, the so-called "Package Program" in India. This activity, which is designed to reach some millions of cultivators in selected districts in various parts of the country—one in each state, generally—is operated by the Government

of India with some financial aid and technical assistance from the
Ford Foundation. Other institutions are also assisting. The chief representative of the Ford Foundation in India has described the program in a thoughtful paper, from which we shall quote a few passages.

The Package Program includes, for one thing, a "package" of
related practices:

Agricultural improvement work in India in recent years has stressed the adoption
of single practices, such as use of improved seed, or of green manure, or sowing
of paddy rice in rows instead of broadcasting the seed. The Package Program,
however, emphasizes the simultaneous use of a "package" of several related
practices, such as use of better seed, seed cleaning and treatment, better seedbed
preparation, use of fertilizers at the right times and in the proper quantities,
better water use, and suitable plant protection measures. The "package" of practices varies between areas, but always includes a group of interacting practices
that are much more productive than any single practice can be when applied
alone. The practices involved are those that are feasible for cultivators to perform under existing conditions, that can be supported with adequate technical
guidance and supplies, and that the cultivators themselves agree to undertake.[4]

Another aspect of the "package" is logistic support sufficient
to keep innovators from experiencing the frustration of adopting a
plan and then not being able to carry it through. A soils laboratory,
an implement workshop, a supply of fertilizer and seed, and opportunities to obtain credit for purchases are available close at hand.

All this is in addition to, but by no means separate from, the information "package." The intent is to make the information program as local as possible, and responsive in every way to the needs
and culture of the villages. Therefore, each district in the program
has its own information unit. Much reliance is placed on the Village
Level Workers, who devote most of their time to agriculture, and on
the block and district staff members who conduct meetings and have
many individual contacts in the villages. The technique most used is
that of demonstration:

The program relies heavily upon field demonstrations to educate cultivators in
the use of new practices in tillage and planting, application of chemical and
organic fertilizers, use of seed treatments and better selection of seed, water use
and drainage, plant protection, and harvesting, drying, and storage of grains.
From several hundred to several thousand field demonstrations of improved
crop production practices were carried out in each of the seven districts during
the crop year just past. . . . Inauguration of "demonstration villages," special
demonstrations in water use, and development of "demonstration cooperatives"
for service to cultivators are also planned.[5]

The program of demonstrations will be geared into a wider range of
information activities:

A new avenue of mass education is now being opened up by the establishment of Package Program information offices at each of the district headquarters. According to official plan, the work of these information offices will be conducted as part of an integrated center-state-district information service. These units are the first district agricultural information offices to be established in India. It is their function to develop and use the available channels for mass dissemination of technical and program information to cultivators and the general public. They will produce and distribute simple visuals, leaflets, photographs, posters, and slides for use in their districts, and will aid in training of extension workers. To the extent feasible, they will make use of newspaper and magazine publicity, public speeches, radio programs, exhibits at fairs and melas, and motion pictures and film strips. They also will assist in activities with schools, youth groups, women's groups, local cooperatives, business groups, and the Panchayati Raj [village council] institutions so as to extend program information as widely as possible. . . . Together all these activities will result in the continuous communication of improvement information and ideas to cultivators, as well as the creation of necessary mechanisms for "feedback" of information to program officials. This work must close the existing gap between the cultivators and the sources of knowledge and inspiration about new practices and their benefit.[6]

Thus a wide variety of media and interpersonal communication channels are combined to achieve a well-thought-out goal, based on knowledge of the local culture and supported by ample logistics. It is too soon to be able to assess fully the results of this activity, but the early increases in productivity are very encouraging.

Not every developing country, of course, can have an agricultural development program as well supported as the one we have described. In many countries, however, there are very interesting developments on a less elaborate scale, only a few of which we can mention. Many of these involve in an important way the use of radio. It is not difficult to see why radio should be particularly useful in rural development programs. It covers great distances and leaps all kinds of natural barriers. It is swift in reaching a listener. It is the cheapest of the major media in production, and reception can also be inexpensive. Now that transistor receivers are widely available, radio communication can be received even where there is no electricity. It is equally effective with literates and illiterates. And it lends itself to a great variety of content and forms.

For these reasons radio is very widely used, and in a number of different program styles. One of the simpler uses can be represented by the early morning farm broadcast from Radio Amman, in Jordan. This comes on the air daily at 6:15 a.m., and is largely made up of answers to questions. About 300 questions come in from farmers each week. "How do I treat the sickness that makes my cow have a calf before her time?" "What do I do about the insects that make the bark of my orchard trees fall off?" The broadcaster, a former agricultural extension agent, selects the most urgent of the questions and, when necessary, discusses them with specialists at the Ministry of Agriculture or elsewhere. When the best answer is determined, he reports it on the morning program, conversationally, in a friendly and interested manner. The number of questions that flood in to him testifies to the usefulness of the broadcast.[7]

It is worth pointing out that the Jordan program is *two-way* communication. Before the radio broadcast is prepared, the audience sends in its questions. The cultivators are therefore conducting a continuing dialogue with the agricultural experts, telling them at any given time what problems are causing trouble on the farm. When the cultivators don't understand advice, they ask another question. Doubtless it is this two-way circuit that keeps the program so practical and so popular.

Even in highly advanced countries, face-to-face communication takes precedence over the mass media at the point in the campaign where farmers are deciding whether to adopt a new practice. The farmers rely mostly on the media for information about new farming ideas, but when it comes to deciding whether to accept a new practice in their own farming, they consult other farmers or expert advisers.[8] The decision to change, whether the country is little developed or far along in development, is going to be made locally; it is going to involve discussion, advice, and personal influence; and it is much more likely to be a lasting decision if it is made on a group or community basis.

For this reason, the development and perfecting of the rural radio forum, combining expert advice with community discussion and decision, are most promising for the whole field of rural development. The forum need not be restricted to agricultural information; it can be, and has been, used for a variety of community development programs. It can be, and has been, used either with radio or with television. In any of these forms, it is potentially of great value in changing group-anchored attitudes and behavior, because the discussion permits an entire group to change without requiring an individual changer to deviate from the group. That is to say, it works this way in most countries. In cultures where discussion is regarded as a game, or a way to sharpen and demonstrate one's wit, a lecture will accomplish more than a planned discussion. But for most countries, the combination of mass media and group discussion is a most fruitful one, as was discovered in Canada, where the Farm Radio Forum was first started in 1941.

After ten years of the Forum in Canada, Unesco invited the sponsors to evaluate the practice as an instrument of adult education. It was concluded that the programs had been notably successful in developing leadership, in encouraging cooperation among farmers, and in creating a "sense of community."[9]

In France, rural discussion groups were organized around television. These were carefully evaluated and found to do precisely what it was hoped they would accomplish: carry information to their members and result in desirable attitude change. The evaluators discovered another thing of some importance about the clubs: they are more effective when the broadcast topics are selected and the programs planned in cooperation with prospective viewers.[10] This is another vote for "localness" in development information.

Japan also organized a number of forum groups around television. Interest was very high. The groups developed into community social centers. Said the evaluation report: "Though it was cold mid-winter, the villagers, old and young, heads of households, wives and children, came to the community hall every Thursday evening. . . . [They] began to take an interest in the more serious subjects rather than in gossip and idle chatter. Television helped the farmers to open their mouths, to express their thoughts and to learn that it is not, after all, such a difficult thing to talk in the presence of other people. Moreover, after expressing their thoughts, they had a sense of satisfaction."[11] When Unesco's subsidy of the experiment came to an end, the Japanese government decided to continue the clubs under its own support.

The most extensive trial of the rural forums has taken place in India. Beginning with a pilot project of 20 programs broadcast to 150 village listening and discussion groups in five unilingual districts of one state, the activity soon spread to 3,500 village forums throughout the country. The third five-year plan provides for adding forums at the rate of 5,000 a year. In addition to the rural farmers' forums, there are about 1,400 women's listening clubs, and about 2,000 children's clubs in rural areas of the country.[12]

The research report on the rural forums was glowing: ". . . a success beyond expectations. Increase in knowledge in the forum villages . . . was spectacular, whereas in the nonforum villages it was negligible . . . Forums developed rapidly into decision-making bodies, capable of speeding up common pursuits in the village faster than the elected *panchayat*. Frequently they took on functions halfway between those of a panchayat and a town meeting. . . . The forums thus became an important instrument of village democracy, and enabled many more people to partake in the decision-making process in the village. . . . The demand that [forums] be made a permanent feature was practically unanimous."[13]

The effectiveness of these forums, demonstrating the uniquely powerful combination of mass media and related group discussion, has encouraged the government of India, and other governments as well, to go ahead with plans to spot community radio receivers in as many rural villages as possible. In India, the central government subsidizes 50 per cent of the cost of village sets, up to a maximum of $25. Of the remaining 50 per cent, the village is usually asked to pay one-fourth; the other three-fourths, and the costs of installation, are ordinarily paid by the state. About 100,000 such community receivers have now been placed in villages in India, in addition to the somewhat larger number that are privately owned.

It must be emphasized again that rural forums are not used solely for information and decisions on agricultural production. Indeed, enlightened agricultural information programs of whatever kind are much broader than farm techniques. They are concerned with health, living conditions, education, literacy, participation in public affairs, and other topics which are only indirectly related to greater farm production. Ultimately, of course, anything done to meet these indirect goals will also be reflected in productivity. But the most successful agricultural information is addressed to the farmer as a man, rather than merely as a planter and cultivator.

Health

It is not necessary to speak at length of health improvement or other community development campaigns, inasmuch as these present almost exactly the same problems as the agricultural campaigns already discussed.

Linwood Hodgdon, a social anthropologist who has worked for some years with problems of social and economic development in Asia, had this to say about health improvement programs:

The further we progress with programs of public health education, the more our educational efforts will have to be concerned with the individual, and with the sociological and psychological factors which influence his behavior.

In the initial stages of a malaria control program we are not directly concerned with either cultural values or individual attitudes and beliefs. Our efforts are concerned with doing things *to* people or *for* people, rather than *with* people. However, when we are interested in promoting a family planning program, or in changing the dietary habits of a group of people, we impinge directly upon the realm of individual attitudes, values, and beliefs. We must strive to help the people make a fundamental change in their personal behavior. In these instances we will find that progress can be made only as we understand and work through these values and attitudes. We will also discover that public health programs cannot be legislated into existence, but rather the focus must be upon the educational process.[14]

In health campaigns, then, as in agricultural improvement programs, so long as we are concerned with doing something *to* or *for* people, the task is not too difficult, and an information campaign, while useful, is not crucial. But as soon as we come to the point where it is necessary for the villager to make a decision and change his behavior, then effective information is crucial. And at this stage, as health development officers have discovered, if we expect our campaign to succeed and our information to be effective, then (1) we must base the whole campaign on an understanding of the life, beliefs, and attitudes of the villagers, and the social factors that help to determine how they live; (2) we must expect to provide face-to-face communication with field workers or other individuals who understand the village and villagers as well as the dynamics of social change, and use the mass media to support and extend the work of this field staff; and (3) we must use a combination of communication channels, employing each in such a way and at such a time as to contribute most to the total usefulness of the information.

A report of the Central Health Education Bureau of India indicates how that organization goes about applying information to the speeding up of community development in health practices. In the first place, there is an active field staff of public health workers, with traveling doctors and health clinics spaced over the country. To these people the Bureau and the state offices furnish a stream of materials, in the planning and selection of which the field workers presumably have a voice. The Bureau uses all the media of mass communication to reach the public health workers, the health educators, and the general public. It maintains a film library on health subjects, previews new films to advise other users, and helps the Information Ministry in the production of films on health problems. It also stocks filmstrips. It arranges radio talks and publishes the scripts in a monthly journal, *Swasth Hind*. It is beginning to experiment with India's one television station. It publishes pamphlets, carefully pretested with a target audience; issues press releases; takes advertisements; publishes posters. It has participated in a number of health exhibits. Now it plans a new nontechnical health journal in a vernacular language for people with minimum education. In a typical campaign, such as the one aimed at smallpox vaccinations, it produces brochures and pamphlets for popular use; posters on the need for vaccination for six different target groups; handbills, bus panels, and chalk board explaining about vaccination; feature articles and press conferences for newspapers; "talking points" and technical background material for the field staff; a special number of the journal; some radio features, advertisements, and a group of slogans for campaign use.

To the extent that facilities and personnel are available, a public health campaign in almost any developing country will resemble what we have just described. That is, it will be a broad spectrum effort with the mass media in support of an intensive interpersonal campaign. In dealing with rural, often illiterate, people, health information planners have found film and radio especially effective in support of public health workers. We can conclude with an example of each of these.

The government of the Philippines has been operating 22 mobile film vans, built on trucks, and carrying their own power generators, as well as projection screens, loudspeakers, microphones, and exhibits, pamphlets, and other supplies as needed. These vans go from community to community, showing films on health and sanitation, better agricultural practices, government organization and citizen responsibility, and so on. After the film showing, the microphones and loudspeakers of the vans are often used for a discussion of the problems introduced by the film. People throng to see the films. Audiences range from 500 to 3,000. In the course of a year, millions of people are reached.[15]

In South Korea, in an area where electricity and radio receivers were scarce, ingenious use was made of a limited number of inexpensive battery-powered radios. Twenty such receivers were obtained, and a 50-watt transmitter was built for a few hundred dollars. A program was designed to implant some needed information about tuberculosis, typhoid fever, and intestinal parasites, in an area where those were the principal health problems. This information was featured in a three-hour program, which also included a considerable amount of entertainment—a singing contest, local bands, a "man on the street" interview, and the like. The program was broadcast three times a day. After each broadcast, volunteers moved the receiving sets to another community. Thus, in three days, the broadcast on the 20 sets was heard in 180 different locations.

The broadcast was a huge popular success, and it taught the information it was intended to teach. A sample of viewers was pretested and post-tested. After the broadcast had been heard, less than half as many people as before believed any longer that tuberculosis was hereditary, almost everyone had learned how encephalitis is transmitted, and 50 per cent more than previously knew the source of typhoid fever.[16]

This, of course, does not guarantee that an audience in a developing country will necessarily learn from the mass media exactly what it is intended they should learn. One experience of the Peruvian Hacienda project . . . is a case in point. As a part of the health program, a color film was shown on the transmission of typhus by lice. The hacienda dwellers were plagued with lice, and it was desired to point out some of the dangers of the situation. The film was previewed and judged to be effective. But when people were questioned about the film a week after the showing, it became apparent that the message had not been understood. People said they had seen many lice, but never one of the giant kind shown on the screen. Therefore, they judged that the dangerous animals must be a different kind of lice! Furthermore, they had seen many people sick with typhus, but never any like those in the film, who had a strange and unpleasant white and red color. They judged, therefore, that it must be a disease that afflicted other people but not them.[17] What was learned was obviously not what the film was intended to teach. The incident illustrates why it is necessary for a mass communicator to know his audience, and for mass communication in a developing country to be pretested whenever possible.

Literacy Learning

In a thoughtful and enlightened paper considering the contributions various media could make to the teaching of literacy, the French National Commission for Unesco advanced the general hypothesis that literacy in the developing countries "must be regarded as a practical matter and, indeed, as a means to an end"; and from this hypothesis it derived the following points to consider in the fight against illiteracy:

First, the task of eliminating illiteracy must take different forms according to the social groups, the sectors in which development is aimed at, and the object in each case.

Second, in determining when literacy campaigns should be begun, development plans for these groups and sectors should be taken into account; in other words, the elimination of illiteracy is not necessarily the first step to be taken in a movement toward modernization and development.

Third, a literacy campaign must be regarded as part of a wider complex of measures which must be coordinated and consolidated.

Fourth, steps must therefore be taken to carry out the necessary preparatory work (a study of existing needs; measures to arouse a demand, based on existing interests, in places where the need for literacy is not yet felt; the production of more reading matter; the framing of a written form for languages which as yet have none; the production and distribution of supplies such as exercise books, pencils, etc.). To a greater or lesser degree, such problems as these will involve the structure of the economy as a whole, both in the sphere of production and in that of external trade; at a different level, they raise the question of priorities. For what use would it be to teach the people of a country to read if there were no printing-works capable of producing books or newspapers for those who have learnt to read, or if there were no organized distribution of imported newspapers and books, or if—as has happened on several occasions—the language taught in literacy class were not the one used in the current newspapers and books? Another essential aspect of the preparatory work, follow-up, and incidental features of a literacy campaign will be the training of general and technical staff and the administrative services required before, during, and after the campaign.[18]

This serves to emphasize again that any information campaign aimed at broad social change must be grounded in the local culture and the local situation, related to other developments, and adequately supported by planning and logistics. Success in one of these campaigns is by no means assured when one has a high-power transmitter, or the equivalent. As essential as the mass media are in any of these campaigns, they must march in an army and be assigned the tasks they can do best in relation to the other tasks and other channels.

Few campaigns are more closely related to the social setting and the other development plans than a literacy campaign. Literacy, as the French commission said, is a means to an end. It is a means to create more useful, more productive citizens, and to speed up national development. Therefore, its content must relate to the needs of the community and the development plan. Its incentives must grow out of assurance that to learn to read is a good thing from the point of view of the community and the individual, and will pay a reward in jobs and position within the community. The follow-up reading material must be related in a practical way to the life, problems, and opportunities of the community, or else the new literate is likely to decide the effort wasn't worth it, and give it up. In other words, as literacy experts from the Marxist-Leninist countries have often said, "literacy is a social problem," and when one begins to think about literacy information one begins first with the social situation.

When is a society ready for a broad literacy campaign? That is to say, when is it in position to make use of new reading and writing skills and to reward their possessors? Who should learn to read? Is there some group that needs it more than others? Is it sufficient to teach the children to read, and disregard the adults? *What* should new literates learn to read? They will be reading about *something* as they learn; cannot literacy learning be treated as a part of general community development, and used to impart knowledge of health, farming, citizenship, arithmetic, or whatever knowledge is most needed by the society at the time? Questions like these come up *before* one decides about information channels.

When one begins to think about channels, however, one finds three general patterns in use, of which two emphasize face-to-face communication and only one emphasizes mass communication. One of these is the great volunteer campaign. The countries with mass parties and with literacy already fairly well along generally have found it easier to concentrate a large number of people on the job of teaching others to read than to devise other campaigns. In Poland, for example, the electronic media played a supporting role—helping to build incentive, praise accomplishment, and so forth. The printed media made a very great contribution by furnishing primers and by printing materials with easy words and adult ideas to bridge the gap for new literates between literacy-class reading competence and newspaper reading competence. But the chief information channel was the volunteer teacher, who taught the illiterate the letters and the phonics, and monitored his early efforts to read and write.

A second pattern is to leave the whole job to the school. This means that many of the children will learn to read, but few adults will. The printed media will furnish the indispensable primers and readers, and there may be some help from films, radio, or television. But here the chief information channel is the schoolteacher.

The French Commission Report, quoted earlier, contains a paragraph on the school as center of literacy teaching:

The question may arise, therefore, whether the attainment of literacy in the countries requiring rapid development should be regarded as essentially or mainly a task for the schools. Schools are valuable—indeed indispensable—but their rate of achievement is too slow and the numbers they reach are too small to meet the urgent needs of those [developing] countries. While ceaselessly working for the extension of their school systems, they cannot rely on school education alone to lay the foundations of their future development. They need the new techniques and media, and, more particularly, television. Nor is there any conflict between such aids and the work of the schools. A literacy campaign conducted through the medium of television may well be based on school syllabuses, at least in some cases; or it may to some extent use the material facilities available in schools; or it may lay the foundation for school attendance. It is undeniable, however, that a teaching medium such as television is more flexible and more adaptable to individual, rapidly changing situations than is the school system. To give but one example, it would more easily reach the fluctuating population of rural adolescents without vocational qualifications or possessed only of a kind of training that is of little use in their actual circumstances—a group which is growing larger every day in the main cities of Africa and will long continue impervious to those forms of education and training which enjoy more traditional methods.[19]

To greater or less degree, most developing countries have felt the force of this argument and have tried to supplement their school teaching of literacy with out-of-school classes based on television, radio, or film. This is the third pattern of literacy teaching. At the time of the Unesco Expert Meeting on Literacy, in June of 1962, 13 of the 67 countries replying to a questionnaire reported that they were broadcasting literacy courses by radio, and the same number said that they were providing literacy courses by film. The precise number of countries now teaching literacy by television is not known but it includes Italy, Brazil, Mexico, the United Arab Republic, Guatemala, the Ivory Coast, the United States, and Kenya.

In literacy classes taught by media, the general practice has been to try to station a teacher, or at least a volunteer chairman and supervisor, at as many centers as possible where students come to hear or see the literacy program. This is especially important in the case of radio, which is unable to present simultaneous sight and sound. Such a teacher needs little training, because the expert teacher on the broadcast or the film can carry most of the work. The local supervisor has proved to be helpful, however, both in explaining to the student and in feeding back student learning problems to the broadcaster.

Television is an appealing vehicle for literacy teaching, because it can present sight and sound together and because it is new enough to be especially appealing. The most extensive test of television as a vehicle of literacy teaching has been made in Italy. As late as 1960, there were still almost two million illiterates in Italy, mostly in the rural southern part of the country. Furthermore, there was a great deal of resistance among these people to literacy teaching. The Italian broadcasting system and the Ministry of Education combined their efforts and facilities to try to solve the problem. They created a continuing television program called "It's Never Too Late." This program was carefully designed so as not to embarrass or antagonize adult viewers. The teacher's desk and classroom never appeared in the picture; the teacher was chosen for his friendliness and for his resemblance to an ordinary person rather than an intellectual. Care was taken not to offend adult pride by talking down to the audience, by "playing games" with them, or by treating them like pupils. The program was leavened with humor, and with useful information in addition to the skill of reading. It was accompanied by specially prepared reading materials, and followed by additional courses which the student could take if he so wished. The Italians found it useful to station a teacher at each class meeting place to guide the students' drill, supplement the television teaching, and answer questions.

The Italian experiment, then, was an effort to teach a literacy class mostly by television to adults who were predisposed to be resistant. What were the results? Nearly every one of the adults who regularly followed the course at the viewing posts learned to read and write—some, of course, better than others. No precise data could be gathered on the progress of students who had viewed the course in their homes, but there were reports that some of them had greatly missed the help of the local teacher in correcting the students' own drill. The experiment, said the Ministry of Public Instruction, was very economical. The number of regular viewing points reached 4,000, and the number of viewers was approximately 563,000—more than one-fourth of all the illiterates in Italy, assembled at one time to be taught by one expert teacher.[20]

All adult literacy programs, and most particularly those that have leaned on media like television, radio, and film, have depended heavily on special, easy-reading materials for use following the class itself. Without them, the student quickly forgets his newly won skill. Furthermore, if these materials are well planned, they can disseminate a great deal of useful information about agriculture, health, sanitation, citizenship, national history and government, and other subjects of high priority in national development.

Different nations have handled these materials in different ways. Puerto Rico, for example, produces annually four books, several booklets, four issues of a poster, and eight to ten posters, all easily read and geared to the development program. Liberia sells (for three cents) a multilith monthly, *New Day*, written with the 1,200-word vocabulary of the literacy course. In Northern Nigeria, a group of tabloid news sheets, each eight pages in length, are available for new literates. In Lucknow, India, Literacy House assembles village libraries of books with simple vocabularies, publishes books suitable for new literates, and issues a fortnightly easy-reading family magazine. In other countries, special newspapers have been published once a week or once every two weeks to furnish news in easy-to-read form, and thus build the habit of news reading and civic interest. In still other countries, existing newspapers have carried a column or more of material especially written for new literates. These and other methods are satisfactory for delivering the material; the problem is to *prepare* material that new adult literates will consider useful and interesting and that will be easy to read, without being "written down."[21]

The functions of the mass media in literacy learning, then, become important at three stages of the process. They can help build interest and incentive to learn to read. When the students have been brought into the class, the media can play either a supporting role (as in Poland) or the main role (as television does in Italy). When the students have mastered the skill enough to read a little on their own, the mass media must supply easy material to bridge the gap from class to normal adult reading.

Formal Education

Schools and teachers form one of the largest items, except for industrialization itself, on the cost sheet of a developing country. The planner's question is, therefore, how can the mass media multiply scarce resources in this field? Any contribution that modern communication can make to reducing the cost per student taught, raising the efficiency of instruction, or extending it beyond present facilities will be an economic contribution of considerable importance.

Every school system in the world depends on printed materials, and audiovisual aids are used to the extent that schools can afford them.[22] Textbooks and teaching films do not appear automatically in a developing country, of course. There must be a book-publishing industry and skilled textbook writers if the country is to have its own textbooks, and a film-making industry, or at least arrangements for importing suitable instructional films and projectors, if a country is to have films for its schools. Failure in these respects is the reason why suitable textbooks are scarce and teaching films are much less used than they could be in many developing countries. But the efficiency and usefulness of these media in formal education are broadly recognized.

The newer media of radio and television are less well proved in schools in the developing regions, but they offer certain extremely attractive possibilities. To a country where highly trained teachers are scarce they offer the opportunity to share its best teachers widely. Where few teachers are trained to teach certain subjects, these media offer hope that those subjects can be taught even before qualified teachers become available. Where projectors and films are scarce, television can serve as a "big projector" for hundreds of schools at the same time. And where schools are not yet available, or for people who, for one reason or other, cannot go to school, radio and television can offer some educational opportunity without schools.[23]

Henri Dieuzeide, research chief of the Institut National Pedagogique of Paris, has summed up what he calls substantial agreement already reached on the educational advantages and disadvantages of radio and television. On the one hand, he says, certain positive characteristics derive from their power of diffusion and penetration:

a) distribution of a single . . . message over the whole of a receiving network;

b) immediate, instantaneous, automatic dissemination of the message;

c) regularity of delivery, making possible the dissemination of a coherent series of messages permitting a coordinated action of an institutional character.

There are also some psychological advantages:

a) the character of particular immediacy and authenticity of "direct" messages which coexist with the psychological attention span of the spectator;

b) the personalized, intimate character of the message;

c) the feeling of belonging to a community of "receivers" and of participating in an activity of national importance.

On the other hand, there are some negative characteristics, stemming from the difficulty of adapting the broadcast message to the individual needs of the user:

a) fixed timetables which tie the audience to a specific hour;
b) uncertainty (more or less great) [on the part of the teacher] before the broadcast as to what the message will contain;
c) predetermined and immutable presentation of the message (structure, rhythm), all revision being impossible.[24]

Dieuzeide then lists four educational uses of radio and television which have been successfully undertaken in many places throughout the world. These are:

the *enrichment* broadcast, which is integrated into classroom teaching and makes a *qualitative* improvement in the teaching;

the broadcast designed to *palliate the deficiencies* of an existing educational system—for example, substituting for unqualified teaching staff or upgrading present teachers—and thus making a largely *quantitative* improvement in the system;

the *extension* broadcast, which extends or prolongs educational opportunities for individuals in their homes or groups of individuals formed for educational purposes, the individuals in this case having already had some schooling;

the *development* broadcast, designed to carry education to communities where there has never been a school. In this case radio and television conduct a mass educational activity which really *precedes the school.*[25]

The electronic media have been used successfully for years, in most or all of these forms, by the relatively highly developed countries.[26] During the last few years, a sufficient number of experiments and case studies have come in from Asia, Africa, and Latin America so as to leave little doubt that the developing countries, also, can with great effect use these media for education.

Concerning the usefulness of the electronic and film media for enrichment and palliative purposes in the developing countries, there can hardly be any remaining skepticism. Talks and music by radio, demonstrations and films by television have been used effectively in so many countries that it is useless to name the places. Research studies back up what has been reported from the trials. For example, Japan tested a course in English by radio in the seventh grade and found that the classes taught in part by radio were significantly superior to the conventionally taught classes.[27] They found also that third and fifth grades, whose classes in Japanese language were enriched by radio, did as well as or better than conventionally taught students in all test periods.[28] In Thailand, large groups of second-

and third-grade pupils, and sixth- and seventh-grade pupils, were tested with and without enrichment broadcasts in music and in English language, respectively. The music students who had the broadcasts scored significantly better than the classes without broadcasts. The students of English who were assisted by the broadcasts did as well in aural tests as, and better in tests of reading and writing than, those who did not have the broadcasts.[29] In Delhi, India, two eighth-grade geography classes were compared on a 24-day unit of study. One of the classes was shown a number of films during the experimental time; the other class was not. Tested at the end of the unit and again some weeks later, the class that had seen the films did significantly better.[30]

In Turkey, rather than trying to develop a new course in physics, Istanbul educators adapted for use by Turkish school children the 162 half-hour lessons of the Harvey White physics course which had been broadcast successfully on television in both the United States and England. In Turkey, the programs were shown on film, and were intended to find out how programs of this kind might help to fill in the scarcity of well-qualified teachers. The experiment was therefore designed to compare what *lycée* students would learn (1) if taught by experienced teachers with the aid of the films, (2) if taught by inexperienced teachers with the aid of the films, (3) if taught by correspondence but given a chance to view the films, (4) if taught by the best teachers without the films, (5) if taught by average teachers without the films, (6) if taught by the films alone. It was found that students taught by the best teachers, using such teaching aids as they wished but not using the films, did indeed score somewhat higher than students who had the films but no classroom teacher. However, there was no significant difference between the test scores of students taught by *experienced* and by *inexperienced* teachers *if the films were a part of the course!* There was no significant difference between scores made by students taught by *correspondence* and film, and those taught by experienced *teachers* with the films. Students taught either by inexperienced teachers or by correspondence, using the films, did significantly better than students in another city taught by average teachers *not* using the films. These results are a remarkable testimony to the effectiveness of televised or filmed teaching.[31]

In 1942 an experimental radio school went on the air in Chile, supported at first by advertising on commercial stations. Its function was primarily enrichment of curriculum, but it soon branched out into extension broadcasts on such topics as "Knowing Our Children" and "Education for the Home," along with programs for teachers and other professionals. With each year, the school gained more acceptance and support. The Ministry furnished official backing and a considerable increase in staff. Teachers on their own raised money for receivers and amplifier systems. The Asociación de Radiodifusoras de Chile (Chilean Broadcasting Association) placed at its disposal a chain of 14 stations, covering the whole country, for 26 programs a week. The general verdict on this experiment is that it played a highly useful and significant part in the establishment of the new curricula and new methods in Chile.[32]

In New Delhi, over 30,000 students are receiving enrichment lessons in language and science by the use of about 500 television sets placed in the schools. Reports are encouraging. Both teachers and administrators are quoted as saying that the television lessons, and in particular the lessons in Hindi, provide as much learning for the teachers as for the students.[33]

Western Nigeria has been broadcasting school television for nearly three years. It has faced many of the problems that are likely to recur in any school television program recently established in a developing country, and a study of the Nigerian experiences would be most useful to developing countries. The evaluation of results, however, has been generally favorable, and the teachers and station personnel have been able to produce more programs than expected.[34]

One of the general results of instructional television and radio is to upgrade teachers and improve classroom teaching. Henry Cassirer discussed this in a lecture to the 1961 Purdue Seminar:

Somebody mentioned to me that in Oregon a science teacher wrote to the television teacher and said: "This year I'm not going to take you in my class any more, because I've watched you for two years and I think I can do the same thing you do and I don't think I need you any more." To my mind this is exactly as it should be, particularly if the television teacher didn't introduce physical elements that could not be reproduced in some form in the classroom. If the classroom teacher has the assurance that she can do it, then that is very good. And if she learned it from television, so much the better. Another occasion when I was in Pakistan, this question came up: "Should television be used for primary education?" Obviously, it poses enormous problems to have a television set in every primary school. There's no electricity in the villages, there are thousands of primary schools, the cost will be very great, the economics and many other aspects make it rather difficult. But if you can use television to train the teachers, you have the double effect of, first of all, using your television medium, but then also of avoiding some of the handicaps of the television medium, namely the lack of contacts between the teacher and those who are taught. So I think we should give considerable attention to the use of television as a means of teacher training, pre-service, and particularly in-service.[35]

This kind of teacher training is a by-product whenever radio or television is used for enrichment or palliative broadcasts. But teacher training may also be done directly by media. For example, in Sarawak, experts from the teacher training college broadcast twice a week a program called "Talking to Teachers," which discusses methods of teaching the primary curriculum. Supplementary talks for teachers are given on a variety of subjects—the design of school buildings, the Book Box plan, medical care, national development, and other topics designed to widen the horizons and deepen the knowledge of the teachers in the schools.[36]

In addition to broadcasting radio courses three times a day to 140,000 pupils in 2,200 classrooms, the School Radio and Television Service of the Ministry of Education in Morocco broadcasts four model lessons in the evenings, two lessons in Arabic, two in French, for teachers. The Director of the Service reports:

Some broadcasts, for example, explain how to teach languages orally. They have contributed notably to the success of reforms in the teaching of French. You see, many teachers have had to change their methods completely. They were accustomed to teaching a literary language. Now, they have to teach a utilitarian one, where the part played by oral exercises has become much more important.

Moreover, many young Moroccan instructors responsible for teaching spoken French often experienced difficulties, as their pronunciation and intonation were not up to the level of their knowledge of the written language. These model lessons in French have enabled them to improve their pronunciation, while at the same time showing them how to conduct language courses properly and efficiently. Primary school inspectors have noted that pupils of teachers who follow our broadcasts regularly speak much better and more fluently than others, and that their teachers are also much more at ease in the classroom.[37]

Television receivers are not yet widely distributed in Morocco, but television has been used both to encourage students to go on to secondary school and to promote teacher training.

Use of radio and television for extension takes numerous forms. In Italy it became the Telescuola (the *television school*, not television *for* school), which provides education in a variety of subjects for children and adults otherwise unable to study. The success of the alumni of the Telescuola in the public school examinations is testimony to the effectiveness of their television teaching. In 1961, 69.6 per cent of the television candidates were accepted for admission to the second year, compared with 81.6 per cent of the classroom pupils. For the third year, however, 73.2 per cent of the television pupils passed the promotion examination, compared with 69.9 per cent of the classroom students.

Iran used educational television successfully to transmit a six-week summer make-up course in physics to students who had failed the course during the school term. Seventy-two per cent of the students who took the summer course made passing grades when they took the course examination over again in the autumn.[38]

Evidence at hand concerning what Dieuzeide calls "development broadcasts," which go to regions where schools have not yet been established, is scarce. Chiefly it is about literacy-teaching programs. We have already mentioned some of these. It should be added that radio has been used for literacy programs in a number of Latin American and African countries, and that in many of these cases it has carried a great deal of development material as a part of, or alongside, the classes in literacy. Colombia is a good example of this, and Behrman's "The Faith That Moves the Mountains" is a good account of the Colombian experience.[39]

"Television is certainly better than radio for school instruction," said the Director of the Moroccan Service. "But television also poses a problem of equipment since each school must be supplied with a receiving set."[40]

There is no doubt that television fills the dreams of many of the developing countries today when they look to the media for help in meeting their educational problem. This is true despite the much wider availability of radio, its relative cheapness, and the greater number of technicians and producers to use radio. Television receivers cost roughly ten times as much as radio receivers. Television maintenance is higher. Television transmitters, studios, and production cost more. To make good television programs takes more personnel and more skilled training.

Nevertheless, television, as Cassirer says, "has proved so powerful in impact, so effective for the communication of information and education, so commercially attractive, so significant for national prestige, that its march around the globe exceeds all predictions."[41] Most Latin American, most Middle Eastern, about ten African, and eight Asian countries have television at this writing, and the numbers are increasing month by month. Therefore, a substantial number of developing countries have television at hand, usually with a number of daytime hours (and perhaps others) available for educational use. Their television is not country-wide, in most countries, but it covers a large population.

What television costs, of course, depends on what it can do. The Chicago Junior College found that there was a break-even point somewhere between 300 and 400 students. Fewer than that could be taught more cheaply in the classroom; more than that, by television. The Jefferson County, Indiana, schools also found a break-even point beyond which television actually saved money. It is hard to put a financial figure on *improved* education or upgraded teachers, but when one figures the great cost to many developing countries of training and paying expert teachers, then, indeed, there seems to be good reason to think that television's ability to multiply such good teaching as there is may lead to substantial savings. Furthermore, technical developments are making it possible all the time for television to cover more area. Low-cost boosters are now available. An airplane, flying over northern Indiana, is successfully broadcasting to five states and some millions of school children. And there is a good chance that within ten years television satellites may be available to distribute educational programs very widely.

It is more than probable that the opportunity for developing countries to use television for educational purposes is going to be much greater in the next ten years than anyone could have predicted only a few years ago.

"Is there in fact today any other human undertaking, besides radio and television," Dieuzeide asked in the article we have quoted, "which appears capable of helping a society in transition to cross so quickly and effectively the difficult threshold of the second half of the century: of providing a modern education on a world-wide scale?"[42]

Some people think there may possibly be one—in programmed instruction.

This new method of automated learning has come very swiftly into use in the United States, Western Europe, the Soviet Union, and Japan, and is now beginning to be tried in the developing regions. Two workshops on programmed instruction were held in the summer of 1963, under the auspices of Unesco in Nigeria, and of Unesco and the United Nations Relief and Works Administration in Jordan. In these sessions, more than 60 teachers and national development officers were introduced to the methods of writing and using programs, and during the workshop periods they made and tried the first programmed instructional materials ever produced in and for developing nations. A sense of excitement pervaded those two meetings, especially as the new programs were being tried out. It is too early yet to say how much either the new programs or the method will contribute to education in the new countries, but the workshop participants, and also the people who looked over their shoulders, are very hopeful. They point out that programmed instruction has certain qualities that recommend it especially to developing regions and their educational systems:

1. In regions where teachers are scarce, it emphasizes pupil self-teaching.

2. In regions where governments and educators are anxious to revise curricula to make education fit the national need, programmed instruction requires a close study of teaching objectives and methods, as a part of the construction of programmed materials.

3. In regions where men are in a hurry, it provides a means whereby people can learn and progress at their own fastest rates.

Regardless of whether programmed instruction lives up to its first notices, and whether television proves financially feasible for education in the developing regions in the near future, still it looks as though the new educational media are going to contribute a considerable amount of excitement to the development of education in the next decade. For, as observers have pointed out, introducing the new media into a relatively new and rapidly growing system is not accompanied by the same restrictions as introducing them into a well-developed system where patterns of education have hardened. If the new countries take the challenge presented them, they will look imaginatively at the "new" media, and at their educational problems in relation to the media.

Let us dream with them a moment.

Suppose that a new country were to feel free to design precisely the curriculum it needs (not necessarily the one it inherited), secure in the belief that the new media could help it teach whatever curriculum it chooses.

Suppose that the country were to share its very best teachers as widely as possible, so that every student, by television, would have access to a considerable proportion of really masterly teaching.

Suppose, in addition to this, that the country would divide teaching duties according to abilities, with a few master teachers on television, others conducting classroom drill and discussion, still others (with very little training, perhaps) monitoring, correcting papers, keeping records.

Suppose that the country were to unfreeze the repetitious pattern of building schools with every room the same size. That is, suppose that the country were to observe that there are many learning activities a student needs to do by himself, and others for which he can efficiently use a very large room (for example, for televised classes), and still others for which he needs a discussion-sized room— and build accordingly.

Suppose that a country, with programmed instruction available, would make it possible for as many as possible of its young people to go forward in certain subjects at their own pace, so that the bright ones might go much further in the same time, and the slow ones would learn better what they have to learn.

Suppose that a country, short of secondary schools, long in dropouts, were to provide programmed correspondence courses, so that many of the young people who are in a region with no secondary school or who are forced to drop out of school for other than academic reasons, might still go further with their education.

Dreams? Perhaps. But not beyond possibility. The early years of a country are years to dream ahead. The early, pliable years of an educational system are good times to dream of how to use the new educational multipliers in support of the national goals. This is the time for educators in the developing countries, despite their pressing problems of budget and teacher training, to be imaginative about the new educational media. For as Robert Lefranc says:

Some countries, very little developed economically, have made colossal strides, passing without any intermediate stage from the age of the wheelbarrow and the bullock cart to the age of the aeroplane. We need have no fear that these countries, at least, will make the same slow pilgrimage to the temple of culture which has taken European countries some hundreds of years. On the contrary, they should undertake forced marches, and fight ignorance and illiteracy with modern methods and techniques, not with those available to Socrates, Montaigne, Rousseau, and Jules Ferry.[43]

NOTES

1. René Dumont, "Accelerating African Agricultural Development," *Journal of Agriculture*, 3 (1959):231-53.

2. *Ibid.*

3. For example, Everett M. Rogers, *The Diffusion of Innovations* (Glencoe, Ill.: Free Press, 1963).

4. Douglas Ensminger, "Ways of Overcoming Obstacles to Farm Economics in the Less Developed Countries," (paper presented to American Farm Economics Association, Storrs, Connecticut, 1962), p. 25.

5. *Ibid.,* pp. 27, 32.

6. *Ibid.,* pp. 27, 28, 32.

7. Wilbur Schramm and G. F. Winfield, "New Uses of Mass Communication for the Promotion of Economic and Social Development" (paper presented at the United Nations Conference on the Application of Science and Technology for the Benefit of the Less Developed Areas, Geneva, 1963) (Washington, D.C.: *U.S. Papers for the Conference,* Vol. 10, 1963). With the consent of Dr. Winfield, I have borrowed quite closely in places from this paper.

8. For example, a very large survey of the use of different communication channels in agricultural adoption in the United States is reported in E. A. Wilkening, "Roles of Communicating Agents in Technological Change in Agriculture," *Social Forces,* 34 (1956): 361-67. See also Everett M. Rogers, *The Diffusion of Innovations.*

9. See J. Nicol, A. A. Shea, G. J. P. Simmins, and R. A. Sim, *Canada's Farm Radio Forum* (Paris: Unesco, 1954).

10. R. Lewis and J. Rovan, *Television and Teleclubs in Rural Communities* (Paris: Unesco, 1955); also J. Dumazedier, *Television and Rural Adult Education* (Paris: Unesco, 1956).

11. Unesco, *Rural Television in Japan* (Paris, 1960).

12. J. C. Mathur and Paul Neurath, *An Indian Experiment in Farm Radio Forums* (Paris:

Unesco, 1959). Also P. V. Krishnamoorthy, "Broadcasts for Rural Audiences in India," *Rural Broadcaster*, September 1962, pp. 11–12.

13. Mathur and Neurath.

14. Linwood L. Hodgdon, "Psychological and Sociological Factors in Rural Change" (paper presented to the 16th General Assembly of the World Medical Association, November 13, 1962, Bombay, India), p. 7.

15. Report to US/AID.

16. G. F. Winfield and P. Hartman. "Communications—the Way to Health Improvement," *The Multiplier*, 4, No. 3 (1961): 2113.

17. Reported in George M. Foster, *Traditional Cultures and the Impact of Technological Change* (New York: Harper and Row, 1962).

18. Paper prepared by the French National Commission for Unesco.

19. *Ibid.*, p. 4.

20. See Evelina Tarroni, "A Programme on the Struggle Against Illiteracy," *Television and Adult Education*, 6 (1962): 3–8; also Maria Grazia Puglisi, "The Contribution of Italian Television to the Campaign to Eradicate Illiteracy Through TV Broadcasts. 'It's Never Too Late' " (paper presented to the Unesco Meeting of Experts on New Methods and Techniques in Education, March 12–20, 1962).

21. See two useful publications by Unesco, *Publications for New Literates: Seven Case Histories*, Reports and Papers on Mass Communication, No. 24 (Paris, 1957), and *Publications for New Literates: Editorial Methods*, Reports and Papers on Mass Communication, No. 22 (Paris, 1957).

22. For a review of research on the effectiveness of audiovisual materials, see W. H. Allen, "Audio-Visual Communication Research," in *Encyclopedia of Educational Research* (New York: Macmillan, 1960).

23. See Schramm and Winfield, p. 13.

24. Henri Dieuzeide, "Notes for a Rational Theory on the Use of Radio and Television for Educational Purposes," *EBU Review*, 75B (1962): 45–58.

25. *Ibid.*, p. 46.

26. See the report submitted by the Soviet delegates to the expert conference on new media for education, March 1962, in Unesco, *New Methods and Techniques in Education* (Paris, 1963), pp. 35–40.

27. NHK Radio-Television Cultural Research Institute (Japan Broadcasting Corporation), *The Listening Effects of "Radio English Classroom," April 1954–March 1955* (Tokyo, 1956). Abstracted in Benjamin Duke, ed., *Survey of Educational Media Research in the Far East* (Washington, D.C.: U.S. Office of Education, 1963), pp. 103–4.

28. NHK, *The Effects of "Radio Japanese Classroom," April 1954–December 1955* (Tokyo, 1956). Abstracted in Duke, *Survey of Educational Media Research in the Far East*, pp. 102–3.

29. M. L. Tooi Xoomsai and P. Ratamangkala, *A Survey of Results of Using School Broadcast as a Teaching Method* (Bangkok: Department of Educational Research, College of Education, 1960).

30. National Institute of Audio-Visual Education, *Effectiveness of Films in Teaching* (New Delhi, India, 1961). Abstracted in Duke, *Survey of Educational Media Research in the Far East*, p. 136.

31. See *Istanbul Physics Film Report: Technical Report and General Report* (Ankara, 1961). This account follows closely the United Nations paper by Schramm and Winfield.

32. Maria Teresa Femenías Loyola, "A Ten-Year Experiment in Chile," *Shiksha,* 11, No. 3 (1959): 37–43.

33. Personal report from Mr. Douglas Ensminger.

34. George L. Arms, "Diary from Nigeria," *NAEB Journal,* September-October 1961, pp. 11–21; *End of Tour Report to US/AID* (Nigeria, 1962).

35. Henry R. Cassirer, Address in *Report of the International Seminar on Instructional Television* (West Lafayette, Ind.: Purdue University, 1962), p. 112.

36. See *Program Bulletin of the Asia Foundation,* 26 (1963): 3.

37. Reported in *Unesco Features,* No. 424, September 20, 1963, pp. 12–14.

38. R. S. Hadsell and G. K. Butts, "Educational Television in Iran," *The Multiplier,* 4 (1961): 28, 31.

39. Daniel Behrman, "The Faith That Moves the Mountains," in *When the Mountains Move* (Paris: Unesco, 1954), pp. 31–44.

40. *Unesco Features.*

41. Henry R. Cassirer, "Radio and Television in the Service of Information and Education in Developing Countries," typescript prepared for *World Radio Handbook,* 1963.

42. Dieuzeide, p. 56.

43. Robert Lefranc, "The Audio-Visual Media: Their Place in the School," *World Screen,* 3 (1961): 39.

PART TWO

GLOBAL VILLAGE

INTRODUCTION

The term global village was popularized by H. Marshall McLuhan. It is used here to refer to the world's communication net—the telephone, telegraph, radio, and satellite facilities that permit almost instantaneous communication from one point on the globe to another. This, together with jet aircraft, breaks down the relationship between time and distance, effectively "shrinking" the globe. In 1870 the New York Herald sent correspondent Stanley into "darkest Africa." It took him fourteen months to locate Dr. Livingston on the shores of Lake Tanganyika and a further time lag to get his story out. Today, we could get the story in hours from a wire service or relay it to the world live by satellite. One hundred years after Stanley's mission the world's television audience was able to view man's first moon walk as it happened.

The first three articles in this part deal with these international communication linkages. The cable system described by Cherry reflects the world's distribution of power and wealth: the strongest links are between Europe and North America. Although we can speak of a global system, the poorest countries still have far less than optimum services at their disposal.

The basis for the most up-to-date communications web in the free world is Comsat, the controlling interest in American satellite operations. Like many other endeavors in the defense/space arena, the United States government's satellite activity is deeply entangled in the corporate world because of its reliance on private contractors. Satellite technology was developed as a result of political pressures, corporate lobbying, and government expenditure. It was then turned over to a monopoly, Comsat—a consortium of established communications carriers with American Telephone and Telegraph the dominant partner—to run as a profit-making enterprise. The government meanwhile continues to subsidize and guarantee the profitability of the corporation, both by military use and by recommending it to overseas media! Why the benefits of such nationally financed enterprises should not accrue to the public generally is one of the recurrent mysteries of the American political economy.[1]

Satellites are one of the sophisticated communication technologies now urged on poor countries as a shortcut solution to their media deficiencies. For example, a United States Agency for International Development report has recommended satellite use for Indian television.[2] The international organization set up to facilitate the use of American satellites is Intelsat, a consortium that includes Comsat and non-American government and private communication enterprises. (The communist bloc countries have their own satellite system.) The article by Hultén outlines the Intelsat operation and its use. Like the ground cable system, it is generally too expensive for widespread use in the underdeveloped world, and primarily serves the developed countries.

The main news-gathering organizations that use international communication technology are described by Hester. The big five, AP and UPI (American), Reuters (British), AFP (French), and TASS (Soviet) collect and edit world news and distribute it to newspapers, radio stations, and television stations around the globe. The flow of world news is primarily in their hands. News of Brazil, for example, is edited in New York and wired back to Argentina, giving Latin Americans news of each other through an American filter. Similarly, Africans hear of each other via British, French, or American intermediaries; and Eastern European news has a Russian slant. And, as Hester makes clear, it is the news agencies that determine what is newsworthy and what is not.

The remaining articles in this volume deal with the operations of governmental, quasi-governmental, and private organizations that conduct media campaigns for foreign audiences. Third World populations are a primary target for such propaganda from the contending world powers, while the cold war communications battles of the developed countries continue.

After reviewing international broadcasting organizations, their growing audiences, and their future, a high official in Radio Liberty and formerly in Voice of America finds the outlook is one of continued challenge and expansion.[3] A more critical way of stating the trends is to say that violations of national sovereignty and external mind-management attempts are being escalated. The trend in television and film, described by Rubin in the first article in this section, is to retreat from "hard" propaganda to a softer, cultural form. This may be seen by recipients, especially in poor countries, as a form of cultural imperialism. Rao takes up this issue as it relates to the printed media, in the next article, and lays bare considerable support for concern.[4]

The remaining selection deals with private overseas influences. The commercialization of broadcasting is Schiller's topic. He shows that many countries now operate their media systems along American commercial lines instead of choosing one of the noncommercial alternatives. Nor is this accidental, for United States media and consumer goods corporations are active around the globe. Programming, financing, and advertising in many countries are of American origin. Cultural and educational uses are pushed aside for the sales pitch. The poor, Schiller concludes, are being given a glimpse of modern commercialism, when they clearly cannot afford modern luxuries without severely distorting their economies. Such media use may have some very disturbing long-range consequences affecting the whole international community. A growing awareness in underdeveloped countries of such media misuse, however, may rectify the situation in the future.[5] But it will be a struggle against formidable odds.

Before turning to the international networks and the overview of propaganda efforts, let us examine here the structure and activities of the chief American government agency engaged in communications overseas—the United States Information Agency.

THE UNITED STATES INFORMATION AGENCY

The USIA was established in 1953 as an executive office to coordinate previous official communications operations and to initiate new ones. In 1968, senior staff were given career foreign service status thereby giving agency employees parity with officials in the State Department.[6] The director of the USIA is appointed by the President, with the approval of the Senate, and is responsible to him. The current director, James Keogh, was appointed by President Nixon in December 1972.[7] He is a former newspaper man and executive editor of _Time_, campaigner for Nixon in 1968 and subsequently special assistant to the President. He is the author of two pro-Nixon books. The reasons for his appointment, then, are not hard to find.

The agency's mission centers primarily around the task of explaining government policies, particularly foreign policies, and American life to people overseas. A presidential memorandum in 1963 stated that the agency should "help achieve United States foreign policy objectives by (a) influencing public attitudes in other nations," and (b) serving as an adviser and information source to policy-making organizations.[8] To this end the agency maintains liaison with the Department of State and is consulted before any government programs affecting foreign media are begun. It is responsible "for the conduct of overt public information, public relations and cultural activities" for all government agencies except the Department of Defense, which manages these tasks for itself.[9]

Overseas nationals often claim that USIA is a propaganda organ of the United States government. That is precisely what it is set up to be, and as such it has been quite successful. A former director, for example, has boasted: "I can report proudly that the exhibits, broadcasts, telecasts, films, books, pamphlets and periodicals produced by the U.S. Information Agency are now regarded as models by the professionals engaged in the arts and crafts of persuasion."[10] He goes on, however, to deny that the United States is participating in a worldwide "propaganda contest"; it is engaged only in "persuasion."[11] The difference is a significant one for the agency. During the tenure of relatively enlightened directors, it has tried to give an objective view of the United States and its policies and thereby retain a semblance of credibility. Within the confines of its official task it has generally succeeded and on occasion has incurred the wrath of other government agencies for its integrity.

The agency has a staff of a little over 9,000 persons; 1,823 are Americans serving abroad, with the support of 4,834 foreign nationals. They provide information through most of the media channels with a 1973 budget of $206.8 million.[12] The agency's operations and objectives are extremely diffuse and by no means simply fulfilled, given these staffing and budgeting limitations. There are 168 overseas posts in 100 countries offering personal contacts, maintaining libraries, and distributing subsidized books to schools, colleges, and individuals. They also support "binational centers," where private United States citizens living abroad assist in educational (primarily language training) and cultural programs. The posts send information to local newspapers and magazines in a weekday radioteletyped release of United States news and commentary, running from 10,000 to 15,000 words.

The USIA is also charged with promoting all official large scale exhibitions abroad, publishing magazines, and operating the Voice of America (VOA) broadcasting facilities. The VOA has forty-one transmitters in the United States and seventy-four overseas, broadcasting 858 hours per week in thirty-six languages to an estimated audience of more than fifty million people.[13] Magazine publications include America Illustrated (monthly) for the Soviet Union and Poland, Topic for Africa, Horizons for Southeast Asia, and Al Majal for the Near East. Two magazines are produced for world distribution—Dialogue (quarterly) and Problems of Communism (bimonthly). A new quarterly, Economic Impact was scheduled for general distribution in 1973. Its aim is to present the positive aspects of the United States economy. Altogether, the USIA publishes forty-seven magazines in twenty-seven languages.

The agency also runs a film and television service. Until 1959, limited television activities were undertaken by the Voice of America. In that year a separate television project was inaugurated. In December 1965, the television and film services were merged, to enhance efficiency and reduce costs: thirty-three positions were eliminated and over $1 million "saved" during the following two years.[14] The service produces, buys, or otherwise obtains approximately 500 programs per year for distribution to about 2,000 television stations in 100 countries having a total potential audience of 500 million.[15] Unlike the VOA's radio activities, however, no television transmitting stations are owned by the agency.

The programs distributed may generally be classified as either series or special documentaries. In the former category the most prominent are the weekly news series, "Washington Correspondent" and "Correspondent Commentaries," produced in thirteen languages for forty-five countries.[16] These series are tailored for each country by the use of native commentators. Another series, "Enfoque las Americas," was produced for Latin America to publicize the Alliance for Progress. Recent specials include the Spanish language "Decision: 1968," a documentary on the United States presidential election, which was carried by television stations in nineteen Latin American countries; "Richard M. Nixon: The New President," a thirty-minute television film, and "Nixon: A Self-Portrait," produced by CBS and acquired by the agency for world distribution. Teletapes of United States space programs have also been distributed by the USIA. President Nixon's visits to China and the Soviet Union spawned twenty-minute documentaries entitled "A Journey for Peace" and "A Summit of Substance." The agency clearly is a publicity organ for the executive, not the legislative, branch of government.[17]

The agency is currently responsible for issuing export certificates for educational audiovisual materials and it similarly supervises imports of such material into the United States.[18] This gives it some regulatory authority over United States private communication organizations overseas. But most commercial material is still authorized by the Commerce Department, which is probably more concerned with increasing sales than ensuring the quality and suitability of American media exports. The agency is therefore <u>not</u> an overseas equivalent of the Federal Communications Commission. Rather, its former director saw it as supplementing the image of the United States produced by the activities and public relations of private expatriate corporations.[19] Indeed, the agency is subordinated to private enterprises by congressional legislation that restricts its operations to activities that do not compete with United States mass media exports and corporations overseas. (Nor can the agency compete at home; its programs cannot be shown legally in the United States.) This is not too great a constraint, however, because few of the commercial exports deal with public affairs matters.[20]

Nonetheless there are areas of conflict between the agency and private enterprise. The capacity of United States commercial television to represent United States <u>national</u> interests abroad has been questioned by Walt Dizard, a career officer with the USIA and a former writer-editor for Time, Inc.[21] His objections to the media corporations center primarily on the content and educational influences of their programming. In part, his criticism reflects a conflict over United States image-building. The USIA, he says,

shows aspects of U.S. life which are intended to generate respect, admiration, and emulation of our democratic political system in other nations. For U.S. television networks and film companies to inundate these same nations with programs which do the opposite appears inimical to our total national objectives.[22]

Which source is giving the most honest image is perhaps a matter of perspective, but it is clear that the corporations themselves are not unduly conscious of a public relations role on behalf of the nation. But legally the image field is all theirs, should they ever choose to exercise their option. Clearly neither the USIA (image-building) nor commercial interests (profitable operation) make the needs of foreign countries a major objective. And their own organizational imperatives give them no reason to do so.

OTHER GOVERNMENT COMMUNICATION AGENCIES

The United States Information Agency has not been the only government agency involved in mass communications. There are several others for radio broadcasting. Centered in Munich, Radio Free Europe was one of the first projects undertaken by the Central Intelligence Agency, when it was set in motion by Congress in 1949. In 1955 RFE was broadcasting to communist Europe from twenty-nine transmitters, primarily medium-wave in Germany, but including a powerful short-wave station in Portugal. It was set up as a private nonprofit (tax-exempt) organization, which served as a rather transparent front for its CIA funding and the policy guidance of the State Department.[23] By 1966, RFE employed about 2,000 people. The Munich organization alone had a $3 million budget.[24]

Organizations similar to RFE were set up for broadcasting to other parts of the world: Radio Free Asia in 1952, using short-wave transmitters in Taiwan and the Philippines, and Radio Liberty in 1953, broadcasting to the Soviet Union from German stations.[25] In the Western Hemisphere, Radio Swan (later renamed Radio Americas) began its operation for the liberation of Cuba from its 50,000-watt station on Swan Island in 1960. Like the other stations, it has a civilian "front" office in New York, in this case headed—none too tactfully for

Latin sensibilities—by a former president of the United Fruit Company.[26] Under allegedly "absolute CIA control,"[27] the station played an intimate part in the unsuccessful Bay of Pigs invasion of Cuba. The funding of Radio Free Europe and Radio Liberty by the CIA has been publicly acknowledged and is now under congressional review.[28]

Other national governments are also active in international communications. Britain, Germany, and France engage in operations similar to those of the USIA through the Central Office of Information and British Information Services, Deutsche Welle, and OCORA respectively. The communist countries, of course, also exert influence wherever they can.

Such then are the external influences on communication in the Third World stemming from foreign governments. These together with private interests help shape the way their media operate, and often deflect the media from their basic aims.

NOTES

1. For a useful account of the formation of Comsat, see H. L. Nieburg, In the Name of Science (New York: Quadrangle, 1970), pp. 305–24.

2. Wilbur Schramm and Lyle Nelson, Communication Satellites for Education and Development: The Case of India, prepared for the U.S. Agency for International Development, Washington, D.C., Aug. 1968.

3. See Francis S. Ronalds, Jr., "The Future of International Broadcasting," Annals, Nov. 1971, pp. 71–80.

4. Herbert I. Schiller has similarly argued, in "The Electronic Invaders," Progressive, Aug. 1973, pp. 23–25, that the widespread rejection of the "free flow of information" by Third World leaders stems from their recognition of ongoing cultural imperialism.

5. While there are nationalist reactions to American media influence in several Latin American countries, the process was probably most advanced in Chile prior to the military coup. See, for example, Herbert I. Schiller and Dallas Smythe, "Chile: An End to Cultural Colonialism," Society, Mar. 1972, pp. 35–39, 61. Cuba, of course, has long since removed commercial and American influences on its domestic media.

6. USIA, 31st Report to Congress, July-Dec. 1968, p. 23.

7. He replaced media careerist Frank J. Shakespeare, Jr., another Nixon insider, who served for four years as director. At the time of his appointment as director of USIA, Mr. Shakespeare was president of the service division of CBS-TV. He was also a key member of President Nixon's 1968 campaign team. See Joe McGinniss, The Selling of the President, 1968 (New York: Trident Press, 1969), especially chap. 3.

8. USIA, President's Memorandum, July 25, 1963, quoted in The Agency in Brief (1969), p. 3.

9. Ibid., p. 4. Nonetheless, most other government agencies have overseas activities of their own. See Kenneth R. Sparks, "Selling Uncle Sam in the Seventies," Annals, Nov. 1971, pp. 113–23.

10. Leonard H. Marks (Director, USIA), 30th Report to Congress, Jan.-June 1968, p. 4.

11. Of course successful propaganda results in persuasion. The cold war and what President Johnson referred to as "a battle for the hearts and minds" of the world's uncommitted were patently propaganda struggles. Mr. Marks is here limiting the term to persuasion that employs untruths rather than part-truths. See Dale Minor, The Information War (New York: Hawthorn Books, 1970), pp. 12, 40. For serious studies of propaganda see Terrence H. Qualter, Propaganda and Psychological Warfare (New York: Random House, 1962), and Jacques Ellul, Propaganda, trans. by Konrad Kellen and Jean Lerner (New York: Knopf,

185

1966). Some critics believe the United States would be better served without the current persuasion efforts. See, for example, Arthur Goodfriend, "The Dilemma of Cultural Propaganda: 'Let It Be,' " Annals, Nov. 1971, pp. 104–112.

12. Information in this and the next paragraph is from USIA Fact Sheet, July 1973.

13. USIA, Office of Public Information, The Voice of America in Brief, July 1973. The broadcast time has dropped seventy-four hours per week since 1969 although thirteen transmitters have been added. The United States trails the Soviet Union, China, and the United Arab Republic in official overseas broadcasting. The armed forces network (radio and television), which came under direct military command in 1967, also broadcasts on a global scale. Although this network is ostensibly for American armed services personnel, its "eavesdropping audience of foreigners [is] estimated at twenty times that of Voice of America English-language broadcasts." Charles C. Moskos, Jr., The American Enlisted Man (New York: Russell Sage Foundation, 1970), p. 101.

14. USIA, 30th Report to Congress, Jan.-June 1968, p. 24.

15. USIA Fact Sheet, July 1973.

16. USIA, 38th Report to Congress, Jan.-June 1972, p. 6.

17. The 38th Report to Congress is an open celebration of this fact.

18. Executive Order no. 11311 (Oct. 14, 1966), pursuant to Public Law 89–634; The Agency in Brief, p. 7.

19. Leonard H. Marks, 30th Report to Congress, Jan.-June 1968, p. 37.

20. W. Dizard, Television: A World View (Syracuse, N.Y.: Syracuse University Press, 1966), p. 126.

21. Ibid., especially p. 284.

22. Ibid., p. 195. Another ex-USIA man, Don R. Brown, has taken issue with this point, but deals primarily with United States effects on viewer satisfaction in developed countries, in "The American Image as Presented Abroad by U.S. Television," Journalism Quarterly, summer 1968, pp. 307–16.

23. See Erik Barnouw, The Image Empire (New York: Oxford University Press, 1970), pp. 89–91.

24. Ibid., pp. 103–4; for an account of RFE's role in the Hungarian uprising, see pp. 105–8.

25. Ibid., pp. 91–92; for samples of Radio Liberty's programming, see pp. 170–73.

26. Ibid., pp. 137–46.

27. Ibid., p. 187.

28. See U.S. Senate, Hearings before the Senate Foreign Relations Committee, first session on S. 18 and S. 1936 (May 24, 1971) and second session on S. 3645 (June 6 and 7, 1972).

INTERNATIONAL WEBS
OF COMMUNICATION

The International
Cable System*

COLIN CHERRY

COLIN CHERRY is Henry Mark Pease Professor of Tel
communication at Imperial College, London. He has
published over 100 papers in journals of engineering,
psychology, linguistics, and other fields. His books include On Human Communication, and World Commun
cation: Threat or Promise?

The international planning for the global cable system of telephony ... [relates to] three major sphe of interest (see Figure 1); first, the North Atlantic for common Am ican, Canadian, British, European and Middle Eastern Connexion; second, the British Commonwealth system linking continental area of common trading and political interests;[1] third, the system servir the United States' interests in the Pacific sphere.

The first of these cables was laid across the North Atlantic in 1956, by joint U.K. and U.S.A. enterprise and its message capacity was taken up very quickly, because the need for high-quality, relial speech communication had long been urgent. The North Atlantic route is by far the busiest in the world, for both message and aircra traffic. (Telephone traffic alone is growing at the rate of 15 per ce per annum.)[2] A second and similar cable was laid in 1959, this tim to Paris and Frankfurt, and a third in 1961 from Britain to Canada

---

*Reprinted from *World Communication: Threat or Promise?* New York: Wiley-Interscie
pp. 87–88, 90, 93–94. Copyright © 1971 by John Wiley and Sons, Ltd. Used by permiss

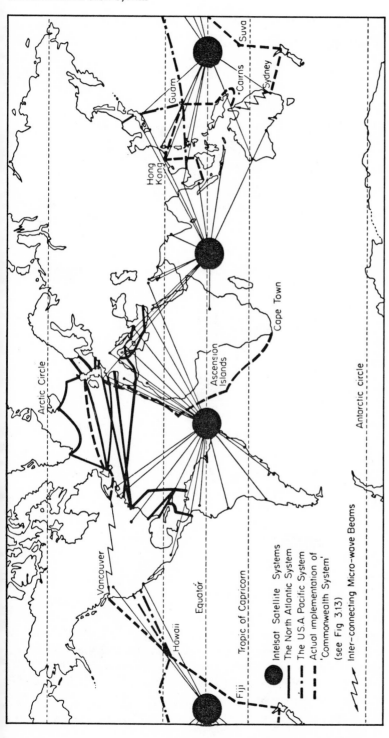

FIGURE 1. The World's Principal Intercontinental Trunk Routes (Cable and Satellite) for Telecommunication (Telephony, Telex, etc.) as of April, 1970.

followed by others. Each cable laying has been paced by a subsequent
rise of traffic demand. The situation in 1970 is shown on the map,
Figure 1.

The growth of North Atlantic traffic channels since 1950 may
be seen from Figure 2, which shows also an official prediction of the

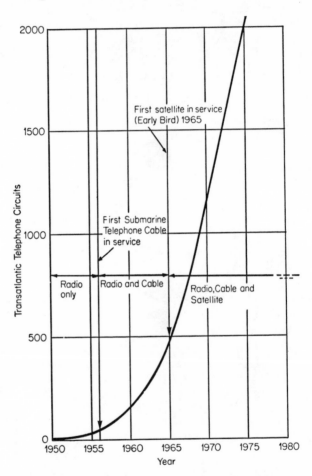

FIGURE 2. Official Prediction of Telephone Circuits
on the North Atlantic (the "Rome Plan").

channels then thought likely to be needed up to 1975.[4] Such predictions, made in situations of such rapid change as today's must always be regarded as liable to revision; there is reason to believe that,
these predictions are underestimates,[5] probably large underestimates

The second sphere of overseas cable development serves in the
first place the needs of the British Commonwealth,[6] where good

quality overseas speech communication has always been lacking. Responsibility for promoting telecommunication services within the British Commonwealth has, since 1949, been vested in the Commonwealth Telecommunication Board.

In July 1958 the Commonwealth Communications Conference was held in London, at which it was recommended that a "round-the-world" submarine telephone cable should be provided . . . forming a complete girdle round the earth. Political happenings have forced changes upon this original tentative plan and the cable system which has actually been laid, at the date of writing, is that shown in the composite map Figure 1.

If we look at this simple map and consider the millions of human beings living on each continent and then at these scarce and slender lines of communication, carrying but a few persons' conversations at any one moment . . . a curious picture may appear. It is a picture of isolated nation islands, some intensely busy with their own internal affairs and some much less so, carrying on mutual trading in conditions of the greatest difficulty, each knowing little of the others in any depth, perhaps frightened of each other, with nearly all their social attitudes and relations decided for them by various official institutions. Even if we regard all the other forms of world communications, telegraphs, radio, ships and air travel, tourism, satellite television and all else, the picture seems little different. The *rates* of growth of all these media may have been truly explosive since the last War, but their magnitudes are small; the facilities they offer are still comparatively slender, though some will undoubtedly continue to grow even faster. But it is the very suddenness with which these facilities for world communication have appeared and been used, especially by institutions and organizations, which suggests a desperate act to overcome the effects of past restrictions.

From such considerations of the world picture of intercontinental communication, we can draw one conclusion of major importance: *all the signs indicate that the nations of the world have been socially deprived in the past through lack of means of communication*; their means, such as have existed, have been utterly inadequate to assist them to resolve their mutual involvements in stable ways, *however much they may have wished to do so.*

I should hasten to add that this is far from saying that now, when our means of communication are beginning to expand at last, we are using them for their best purposes or in the wisest ways. This would be expecting too much of technology!

This is a question of great importance: are international relations, at all the various levels, trade, diplomacy, personal attitudes and education, and others, seriously handicapped by inadequate means of communication, even *today*? Suppose that a fairy-tale wish could be fulfilled by some miracle of economy and these means be increased tenfold overnight; would it be for the better or worse? . . . The explosion *could*, in theory, proceed too fast and be disastrous. There may be some optimum rate of expansion, but there is no doubt that we have been, and still are, far below this ideal.

Writing in 1961, Telford and Isted commented, after surveying the U.K. and the U.S.A. and other intercontinental traffic: "To the authors the most striking lesson is that present facilities for long-distance telephone communication are, in the majority of cases, utterly inadequate for the needs of the world today and tomorrow."[7] Six years have passed since then and great progress has been made, but the conclusion remains true, namely, that both the existing facilities for world communication and their rates of growth, however rapid, can scarcely be said to reflect the more explosive growth of our detailed international involvements and suggest still a preoccupation with local, national affairs.

Which comes first, the *demand* for communication (the social need) or the *means* to make it possible (the technical facility)? No technology develops in a social vacuum but to some extent, greater or less, is created out of the urgent social needs of the day; sometimes it is created far too early in history and is still-born. Inventors must to some extent be motivated by their past experiences, or must believe that there is some *chance* that their inventions will be welcomed, that is to say, believe that some need exists (whether it be realized by the public or not) which they can satisfy. Nevertheless demand and facilities are like chicken and egg;[8] one creates the other . . .

Evidence . . . suggests a *regenerative* growth, meaning that each further improvement in technical facilities not only satisfies an existing demand but creates new conditions which give rise to yet further increase in demand. Such "regenerative" growths are typical of *service* industries of all kinds and are in distinction to the growths of *consumer* industries, in which demand may simply increase with increased wealth merely to be satisfied; consumer growths are represented typically by straighter graphs. Service industries, like capital investment, can be creators of new wealth.

The routes of world communication of various kinds have not evolved haphazardly but are closely related to international trade and political relations. For example, Timmerman *et al.*[9] have published the noteworthy fact that Britain's gross revenue from her communication services (telephony, Telex and telegraphs combined) with, at least, France, Netherlands, Belgium, Germany, Norway, Sweden and the U.S.A. bears a fairly constant ratio to her trade values with each of these countries.

Just as the early telegraphs were built alongside railway lines, so our North Atlantic telephone traffic correlates with the heavy aircraft traffic on that busiest overseas route. Much of today's traffic, of various kinds, follows the general directions of traditional trade routes, of which three form the main arteries .... First, and busiest today, across the North Atlantic; second, from Britain and Europe through the Suez Canal to the Far East (i.e. prior to its closure); third, from Britain and Europe to South America. As well as these, other and newer communication routes are developing especially for aircraft, satellites and submarine cables: e.g. traffic is growing across the Pacific and we must expect a very rapid growth between North and South America too.[10] (See Figure 3.)

Examination of the world's main intercontinental telegraph routes, as they existed already last century, would also show them to have a certain correlation with the shipping and even the aircraft routes of today ..., based on the tripod skeleton (1) transatlantic (2) Europe to Far East (3) Europe to South America. ...

This rough correlation between the principal ship, airways and telegraph traffic routes held until very recent years, the routes being determined mainly by trade and political relations, coupled of course with geography, rather than by technology. Thus aircraft, in theory unconfined by sea coasts, nevertheless have their most dense traffic following the *general* routes of shipping, and message traffic naturally follows.

Thus these same three "legs" of world traffic form the basic skeleton of global telephony and Telex traffic too. Figure 1 shows how the very busy North Atlantic traffic is carried by both cables and the mid-Atlantic satellite system; this same satellite system carries the Europe/South America traffic also. The satellite system over the Indian Ocean carries the Europe/Far East traffic. However, the Pacific satellite system represents a more recent strengthening of global communication—a fourth leg.

The expected traffic growths along these principal world routes of communication are shown in Figure 3 which is based upon the official International Telecommunication Union predictions.[11] The absence of any direct Europe-Far East traffic route is very obvious in this diagram (what has been called the "second leg" here); however, these I.T.U. predictions were made in 1963, before the possibilities of satellites were at all clear.

I have been using the word *traffic* a good deal, without making much distinction between its use to mean *transport* (aircraft, ships, etc.) and to mean *message traffic* (telegraphs, telephones, etc.) It is a convenient word to use to mean "communication activity," without specificity.

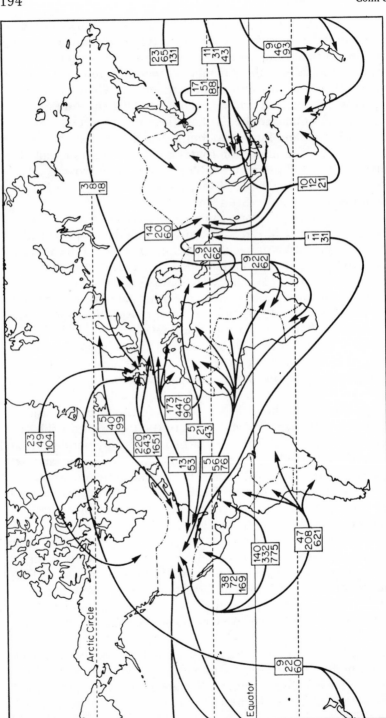

FIGURE 3. "The Rome Plan," 1963. The Principal Intercontinental Flows of Telephone Traffic, or Equivalent Telex and Equivalent Telephone Channels in Years 1962, 1968, 1975.

As the quantity of message traffic grows, in ways such as those illustrated by graphs here, so it becomes less possible, in general, to distinguish between the various forms, because any one technical system, whether cable, satellite, microwave beam, or other, may be used for carrying several forms of traffic: e.g. telephone messages, Telex traffic, television, data, etc. Systems of communication like satellites and intercontinental cables are of a global scale of size and so costly that the economics of their use demand this *traffic diversity*. That is to say, they must be designed to carry various different kinds of message traffic so as to increase the chance that they are used 24 hours in the day, by planned allocation.[12]

It is this diversity of present day traffic needs of the industrialized countries, leading to the design of these gigantic global systems, having flexibility of usage, that has made at all possible the likelihood that poorer countries may share these services. Their traffic demands are at present small and more specialized, but under such planning as that of Intelsat, sharing does become a theoretical possibility.

In the meanwhile, the overseas communication needs of these poorer areas have most economically been met by using short-wave radio, as all countries did before 1956, but this situation cannot be expected to persist.[13] Satellites do indeed offer hope to such areas,[14] a fact which was recognized early in the history of experimental satellites. Small, transportable, satellite ground receiving stations were already made and being tested in 1962 using the experimental satellites Telstar and Relay.[15] Small satellite ground stations may be designed to suit the limited traffic needs of the developing countries, operating with internationally owned satellites[16] though, unfortunately, . . . such stations may be far less economical to use than large ones.[17] Similar remarks might be applied to the possible use of satellites for communication with aircraft and ships, a technical possibility, but expensive.

Since the Commonwealth telephone cable (Figure 1) now connects mainly those areas of the world which already had some forms of communication before, because of their past political and trade relations, satellites will have special value to the non-Commonwealth developing areas of Africa, the Middle East and South America; to these we might add the Commonwealth countries, Pakistan and India, whose overseas radio-telephone and telegraph communications are often unreliable, because of atmospheric radio conditions in the tropical belt.

. . . Modern overseas communication systems are very expensive, whether for message traffic, or aircraft transport. The large capital should not be laid down too early by installing systems before there is enough traffic demand to make some use of them, nor should traffic growth be inhibited by lack of new systems. Prediction of future traffic is a very important matter therefore but, unfortunately, it is singularly difficult to do with any accuracy, partly because owing to the unprecedented rates of growth there have been inadequate experiences to call upon. As already mentioned there is a further reason that the growths of demand for each specific form of traffic (i.e. telephones, telegraphs, aircraft, post, etc.) *within* each country seem not to be correlated with identical social factors within the various countries.[18] The habits and environment of each are varied. Predictions of international traffic growth must be made, for simple economic reasons, but they cannot be made with accuracy for more than a few, say five, years ahead whereas the operating lifetime of a new system may be expected to be 20 years or more. The International Telecommunication Union's appropriate body, the Comité Consultatif International de Telephonie et Telegraphie, recommends 3–7 years for "short-term forecasts" and 15–20 for "long-term," in their *Manual on National Telephone Networks*. For certain aspects of planning fifty year forecasts are recommended! (Geneva, 1964).

There is a third difficulty in the way of accurate prediction. In our present industrial stage, with its proliferation of new ideas, new methods, new materials and inventiveness, especially in electronics, there is no feeling of certainty that a newly designed system will not be out-of-date and uneconomic to use before it has paid for itself. . . . Neither is it known beforehand just what stimulus may be given to traffic demands by the introduction of a new system.

Such difficulties as these of course face any industrialist of today, in most fields of technology; the important point about communication being that each system newly introduced is both enormously expensive and essentially international in its function.

NOTES

1. Institute of Electrical Engineers (U.K.), Several papers concerning the Anglo-Canadian Telephone Cable (CANTAT), *Proc. I.E.E.*, 110, July 1963, pp. 1115–1164.

2. H.M.S.O., *Satellite Communications* (White Paper), Her Majesty's Stationery Office, August 1964.

3. I.E.E., *op. cit.*

4. Chapuis, R., "Work of the Plan Committee in the Intercontinental Sphere" (Rome, Dec. 1963), *Telecommunication Journal,* 31, No. 4, April 1964, p. 98.

5. *Ibid.*

6. Halsey, R. J., "British Commonwealth Ocean Cables," *I.E.E. Trans. on Comm. Tech.*, Vol: Com-12, No. 3 (Sept. 1964), p. 6.

7.   Telford, M. and G. A. Isted, "Predicted Future Expansion of Intercontinental Telephone Traffic," *Point-to-Point Telecommunications,* Vol. 6, Oct. 1961, p. 4, Marconi Wireless Teleg. Co., England.

8.   Schramm, W., *Mass Media and National Development,* Stanford: Stanford University Press & Unesco, 1964.

9.   Timmerman, W., *et al.* "Expanding Global Submarine Cable Network," *Electrical Communication,* 41, No. 1, 1966, p. 77.

10.   International Telecommunication Union, *General Plan for the Development of the International Network for 1963-68* (the full and official Report of the Rome Committee: the first global plan), Geneva, 1964.

11.   Chapuis, *op. cit.,* and *Ibid.*

12.   Chapuis, *op. cit.*

13.   Timmerman, *op. cit.,* p. 77.

14.   Chapuis, *op. cit.*

15.   International Telephone and Telegraph Corp. Journal, *Electrical Communication,* 36, 1964; 45, 1970.

16.   Chapuis, *op. cit.*

17.   I.T.T., *op. cit.*

18.   Bogaerts, R. F., "Probable Evolution of Telephony," *Electrical Communication,* 38, No. 2, 1963, p. 184.

The Uses
of Intelsat *

OLOF HULTÉN

OLOF HULTÉN holds an advanced degree from the
Stockholm School of Economics where he specialized in
mass communication research. He is now working with
the Swedish Broadcasting Corporation's Audience and
Program Research Department. He is coauthor of the
Swedish-language book Man and Mass Media.

evelopments in satellite technology
have awakened a good deal of optimism in the public debate surround
ing international mass communications, and broadcasting in particular
Utilization of satellites is commonly foreseen to increase telecommunications capacity and to permit reduced costs, thereby promoting
intercultural exchange and production of broadcasts for international
audiences. Indeed, communications satellites are generally cited as on
of the most hopeful prospects towards the promotion of a "free flow
of information." As regards the communications needs of the technologically less developed regions, satellites have virtually been cast in
the role of deus ex machina.

Nevertheless, the scale of costs of satellite utilization in the exist
ing systems of international scope is such that use of the system by
broadcasting organizations is restricted to transmission of items of

*Reprinted from "The Intelsat System: Some Notes on Television Utilization of Satellite
Technology," Gazette, 19, no. 1 (1973), pp. 29-37. Used by permission of the publisher
and the author.

the highest "news" priority, transmitted by and for only the most well-to-do broadcasting organizations.

The operations and tariff policies of the Intelsat consortium— the only such system operating on a commercial basis—comprised the focus of this study, which was commissioned by the International Broadcast Institute and completed in the spring of 1971. Special attention was devoted to present utilization of the system by broadcast organizations and prospects for future use. Although some of the facts and observations might have changed during the past 12 months, the general tendencies no doubt hold. The development in the satellite utilization field is seemingly very fast, but the underlying political, economical and institutional patterns have not changed and are not likely to change quickly.

The Intelsat consortium presently comprises some 80 member states. Since its inception in 1964 it has developed and operated four "generations" of satellites. A consortium, Intelsat is jointly owned and operated by its members, each member or member-group wielding a vote proportionate to its share of Intelsat traffic.[1] During the so-called interim period since the birth of the organization the actual business operations of the consortium have been in the hands of Comsat, the US public corporation for civilian satellite development. This arrangement is to be formally terminated according to recent agreement.

The volume of Intelsat telecommunications capacity has multiplied many times over during a very short period.[2] Demand for telecommunications service—generated by a complex interaction of political, economic, trade, social and cultural relations among nations— has tremendously increased in recent years. The normal rate of growth of interregional telecommunications traffic is high, between 10 and 20% annually, some routes showing even higher growth rates.

Intelsat is presently served by satellites of the third and fourth generations. Their configuration, through the lifetime of Intelsat IV, will remain as follows: two over the Atlantic Ocean, two over the Pacific Ocean and one over the Indian Ocean. Although the basic function of the satellites (through Intelsat IV) remains the same, namely point-to-point communication between standard ground stations, technical developments have allowed ever greater capacity and flexibility. And, while initial investment per satellite has quadrupled between the first and fourth generations, the growth in capacity has been still more rapid, resulting in a considerably lower satellite investment cost per circuit year.

Two aspects of the Intelsat system are vital to an understanding of the prospects of satellite mediated international mass communication. First, Intelsat was created and is operated in the interest of telephone and other telecommunications traffic rather than for broadcasting. Indeed, broadcasting accounts for but 2 to 3% of Intelsat traffic. This fact has direct consequences for Intelsat tariff policy, which in turn affects utilization patterns.

Secondly, Intelsat's formal jurisdiction as well as the consortium's tariffs apply only to the "space segment" of satellite mediated transmissions (see figure 1). An examination of the cost structure of such transmissions reveals that Intelsat's share of costs is on the order of a mere 10 to 15%. The remainder is accounted for by the ground stations' land lines and switching costs—services under the authority of the respective telecommunications organs of the member states.[3] Consequently, often-voiced calls for a reduction in Intelsat rates cannot be expected to significantly alter the exclusive costliness of international broadcasting by satellite.

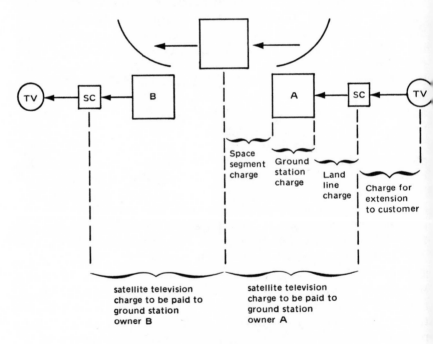

FIGURE 1

As demand for international telecommunications service is a direct function of economic development and international engagement, the general patterns of Intelsat traffic are reflected in the broadcast utilization of the system. While Intelsat traffic has grown impressively during its short history, this utilization is unmistakably concentrated to those areas of the world where the telecommunications infrastructure is already at an advanced stage of development. Roughly three-quarters of present leasable telephone capacity goes to or from the United States. This proportion will be sustained in the foreseeable future, i.e. through 1975. Only some 10% of total utilized capacity did not go to or from the United States or Western Europe in 1970.

As for television utilization, present technology permits point-to-point transmission or multiple-point service.[4] From a modest beginning in 1965, television traffic has increased some 25 times over. (One should keep in mind that television nevertheless presently accounts for but 2 to 3% of total traffic.) As in the case of other telecommunications traffic the Atlantic region heavily dominates television traffic, in terms of both time and number of programs.

TABLE 1. Television usage in hours, 1969, for each INTELSAT region

Region	Number of programs	% of total	Transmission time	% of total
Atlantic	460	52.1	449	58.9
Indian	9	1.0	12	1.6
Pacific	347	39.3	229	30.1
Atlantic/Indian	4	0.5	14	1.8
Atlantic/Pacific	1	0.1	2	0.3
Pacific/Indian	62	7.0	56	7.3
Total	883	100.0	762	100.0

The main flows of traffic in the Intelsat system are, in descending order of magnitude (per transmission time): USA to Puerto Rico, USA to Hawaii, Europe to USA and vice versa, and USA to Latin America.[5] Domestic US traffic (US Mainland to and from Puerto Rico and Hawaii) accounted for about 37% of total transmission time, but only about 10% of transmissions in 1970. (The relatively long transmission times derive from the almost exclusive use of these routes for transmitting sports events from the US Mainland.) The Europe–USA route in 1970 accounted for about 20% of total transmission time, and 34% of transmissions, which reflects the predominance of news items on this route.

In the Pacific Ocean region the westward traffic flows primarily from the United States to Japan and Australia, while at present about two-thirds of the flow eastwards emanates from Hong Kong to the United States. (The content is primarily news from the wars in Indochina.) Ground stations in the Indian Ocean region originate or receive a negligible number of programs.

Without going into details of the actual costs of broadcasting via satellite, we may say that they are high, and, indeed, almost prohibitively high for the regions most in need of satellite service. In at least two aspects the present structure of the Intelsat system is poorly adapted to the needs of broadcasters.

First, a technological detail, which can be traced to the imbalance in the ownership structure of the consortium: namely, that Intelsat satellites require expensively large and powerful ground stations. As noted above, control of the system is distributed according to the member's respective share of the traffic. In practice, this has meant that heretofore the United States had had more than 50% of the interest in Intelsat and thus has stood for more than 50% of the costs of the consortium. While the United States is bound to pay more than 50% of all costs arising in the space segment, costs arising in the ground segments are borne by the respective common carriers, and ultimately by Intelsat's customers. Thus, it has been in US interest to economize in the space segment (i.e. the satellite), while relying on more powerful ground stations to pick up Intelsat signals. One nation's cost-benefit balance would thus appear to have determined the structure of satellite services to the detriment of both a. small nations, who must invest inordinately large sums in ground stations to receive a relatively slight flow of traffic and b. broadcasters, who as customers of Intelsat assume the higher costs of larger stations.

The other complaint broadcasters raise against the Intelsat system concerns the system employed in deriving charges. Broadcasters base their demand for lower charges on the fact that broadcast transmissions make up a so insignificant fraction of total traffic. Claiming that ground station capacity—and the concomitant investments—would be the same even without television service, broadcasters demand not to be charged in the same way as the other telecommunication services. Ground station owners, on the other hand, aim to recover at least the marginal costs incurred by television service. The controversy arises over how sizable these marginal costs actually are. The situation is further complicated by technical differences in ground stations, which result in quite varying marginal costs.

There are also other criticisms raised against the system of charges employed, particularly from members in the Third World. But, pressure must be raised on the influential common carriers if any change is to be effected.

Use of satellites for television broadcasts actually represents a decision on the part of the broadcaster to "buy time." Indeed, one newsman described his organization's use of satellite technology as "putting on an airmail stamp." Content broadcast via satellite is thus primarily that which is extremely time-sensitive or for which the send of "actuality" of "simultaneous presence" is important. Thus, two types of transmissions have become common: the short news "flash," transmitted between the major news centers of the world, and longer special events type programs. Satellite transmissions of news is increasing, but at a slower pace than during the first years, as the high charges strain the budgets of most news departments. The high charges likewise limit the transmission of special events to such programs as are of particular interest to certain broadcasting organizations (e.g. national sports team abroad) or, in commercial systems, such programs as can easily be sponsored. Multiple receptions and syndications are increasing.

The activities of the European Broadcasting Union and Eurovision provide an example of broadcasters' optimized response to the technical and cost structures of Intelsat service. First of all, it should be noted that European broadcasters are confronted by two particularly adverse circumstances, which perhaps have elicited EBU's efficiency: 1. The common carriers in the European region, strongly organized in the Conference of European Postal and Telecommunications Administrations (CEPT), have taken an ungenerous attitude toward satellite broadcast service. They charge, for example, 80% more for ground station service than does their US counterpart. 2. Because of the proliferation of national entities (and therewith national telecommunication administrations), the European area is served by an unnecessarily large number of ground stations. The extra costs arising from this proliferation are naturally borne by European customers.

The exchange and cooperation under the Eurovision program has been expanded to include satellite broadcasts. By this means the members of EBU have managed to rationalize their use of European ground stations and have created an effective means of sharing costs. In addition to coordinated broadcasts of special events of broad general interest, Eurovision also coordinates exchange of short news items originated outside Europe. The volume of this traffic has grown.

In the regular Eurovision exchange of news items the larger European countries dominate as originating sources, while the smaller broadcasting organizations act as receivers. In the case of reception of satellite-fed news items, however, another pattern appears to emerge: all countries utilize the coordinated service via Eurovision to about the same extent, with possibly a slight bias in favor of the larger organizations. All in all, the majority of EBU members take the opportunity to provide their viewers with news material transmitted via satellite. EBU also arranges satellite feeds in the regular exchange with Intervision when members of the East European Broadcasting Union so wish.

Generally speaking, cooperating, either on the part of receivers (e.g. Eurovision) or among producers and/or sponsors (syndication), can achieve economic benefits. Given the present tariff level only such "cooperative" transmissions would appear to have any sizable growth potential.

An important feature of broadcast utilization of satellites, namely, the world-wide traffic pattern of various types of program content, should not be overlooked. Generally speaking, satellite broadcast content is subject to the same social, cultural and economic factors as is other broadcast content. In the case of satellite mediated broadcasts, however, the extra expense acts as an additional filter in the selection or editorial process.

To summarize the flows on the principal routes of traffic: Taken as a whole (that is, including domestic US traffic), the largest share of transmission hours from US sources has no doubt been devoted to the space voyages and sports. Many transmissions have also been devoted to US political events. Among transmissions to the United States, the Middle East crisis in 1967, the Pope's journeys, and the political events in France in 1968 took a large part of total time. Most transmissions to the United States carry news. Sports events dominate the route from the United States to Latin America, and sports and entertainment programs dominate the route between Europe and Latin America as well.

The choice of types of program content for satellite transmission as well as traditional "news values" are, of course, products of the social and cultural context in which broadcasting organizations operate. Satellites do not and probably cannot effect changes in these non-quantitative factors.

The world-wide flow of news may be described as falling into three major categories:

1. between the news centers of the world, that is the political and economic capitals as well as hubs in the international communication network;

2. between these news centers and the "minor" news areas of the world, i.e. those which only sporadically generate any flow of news. Among the minor news areas are the less developed countries, but almost all small countries in the developed areas of the world fall into this category as well;

3. between the minor news areas.

As for the first category, satellites have helped to expand the flow and have speeded it up.

The flow of news between major and minor news areas remains unsatisfactorily one-sided. News agencies, press wire services and television news services are often owned and controlled from the major news centers. Satellites have only provided these organs with another means of distributing their wares. The transmission of news from the periphery is scant, and what little news is generated is generally related to disasters, revolutions or such news as affects people or institutions in the major news areas. If anything, satellites have only confirmed the traditional patterns of flow.

The distribution of news between countries in the news periphery is even more rudimentary than the patterns described above.

Underlying these traditional news flows are traditional news values. In the words of one broadcaster, "Satellites can and will do a lot for us. They will certainly do it faster and take it further. They won't necessarily do anything better."[6] While satellites make possible television news from countries previously inaccessible, the new technology would not appear to alter underlying news interests and news evaluation patterns.

Seen from the perspective of developing countries, satellite technology poses a complex of advantages and disadvantages, of promise and potential dangers. Satellite technology has been hailed as a new means of breaking the traditional telecommunication isolation of countries in the Third World. Theoretically, at least, satellites do offer effective telecommunication facilities in these regions characterized by low traffic density and often vast or difficult terrain, since these obstacles pose less of a hindrance to satellite communication. Operating at the same economy, independent of Earth-surface distances, absorbing traffic from large regions, and with low marginal costs of expansion, satellites are indeed a promising technology for the developing regions of the world. But, the present international satellite communications system, developed to fit the scale of operations of the rich and advanced countries, requires expenditures—particularly for ground stations—far greater than can be justified by many developing countries. Some countries, however, value the social and political opportunities offered by satellite links so high as to justify the otherwise uneconomic investment.

Broken isolation, increased involvement in international flows of communication—oft-voiced "advantages" offered by satellite technology—may also be seen as potential threats to national culture. Developing economies not only lack resources for investments in telecommunications, but the budgets of broadcasting organizations in these countries are also often very meager. Unable to finance original production of programming, they are vulnerable to the forces of so-called cultural imperialism. At best, economically disadvantaged broadcasters can merely decide whether or not they wish to receive someone else's information. Particularly the growing trend toward commercial syndication of programs—especially commercial products of well-to-do Western societies—present tempting low-cost alternatives to local production of programs. Furthermore, many powerful institutions in the economically advanced countries, among them broadcasting organizations, advertising and national information agencies, are using and planning increased use of satellites, including direct broadcast satellites. Centripetal forces mount.

Thus, improved technology in the service of an imbalanced, and in many ways "imperialistic" international mass communications structure is feared by many in the Third World. Until this imbalance is redressed, and until the economics of broadcasting via satellite can be placed within reach of the developing countries, Intelsat will not contribute to a truly "free flow of information," but rather merely to an increased and lubricated flow along present channels.

One should be careful not to overlook the positive potential which communication satellite technology offers. But socio-politico-cultural factors—ethnocentric tendencies in combination with an imbalance of wealth among the nations of the world—conspire to limit the content and direction of information flows, preserving traditional privileges and prejudices. Social and institutional factors at both ends of the satellite "bridge" are crucial for the development of television utilization of satellites, and these factors change slowly, if at all. Our modern belief in technological solutions must not blind us to these facts.

NOTES

1. As recently amended. Previously, voting strength was based on members share of *total* international telecommunications traffic, an arrangement which favored large nations served by both satellite and cable at the expense of small powers who perhaps are totally dependent on satellite links.

2. Capacity is measured in terms of the telephone, or "voice-grade" circuit. The telephone circuit can, of course, be utilized for other telecommunications services (telex, facsimile, etc.). A television transmission with full sound accompaniment uses some 240 circuits.

   Illustrative of the enormous expansion of international facilities is the fact that while satellite circuit capacity has burgeoned during the period 1965–70, cable circuit capacity (measured in circuit-miles) has trebled.

3. It may be noted here that television tariff policies of the common carriers (i.e. ground segment operators) vary considerably around the world. Particularly striking is the contrast between the philosophy of CEPT in Western Europe and that of the U.S. ground station operator, Comsat.

4. Multiple-point service, i.e. one station simultaneously transmitting to multiple receiving stations, is becoming more and more common.

5. The 1970 traffic *from* Latin America was of comparable magnitude due to broadcast of the World Soccer Championships.

6. W. S. Hamilton of Australia in *EBU Review*.

International News Agencies*

AL HESTER

AL HESTER is Assistant Professor at the Henry W. Grady
School of Journalism at the University of Georgia, Athens.
His background includes thirteen years as a reporter and
editor for the Dallas Times Herald and other newspaper
and free-lance writing. He holds a doctorate in mass communication from the University of Wisconsin. His areas
of interest include international communication, with an
emphasis on Latin America; the teaching of newswriting;
and mass communications research. He has conducted
several studies of the international news operations of
global news agencies.

N̸o news-gathering operations influence
more persons throughout the world than do the complex, multi-mil-
lion-dollar activities of the global news agencies. Hundreds of millions
of persons each day receive a large part of their news through the
efforts of a handful of world news agencies.

A college student in the United States, a rancher in Australia, a
minor government official in Ghana, and a secretary in a Paris business
office—all are dependent to a high degree upon the international
news agencies for their foreign news. When users of the mass media

*This previously unpublished article was prepared specifically for this volume at the editor's
request. The author acknowledges the generous help of Theodore E. Kruglak of the School
of Journalism, the University of Southern California, Los Angeles, California. Used by permission of the author.

think of news, they frequently picture television commentators, newspaper reporters, or radio broadcasters. Rarely do they think of the news agencies and their thousands of employees who gather and transmit international news from hundreds of bureaus over the face of the globe.

WHAT A NEWS AGENCY DOES

What is a news agency and why is it important in a study of international communication? The news agencies—also called news services or wire services—are adjuncts to the mass media. They are connected to the media and play an extremely important role, but they are not primarily in the business of presenting the news to the ultimate consumer. An agency's job is to gather information anywhere in the world in as timely and accurate a manner as possible and to relay it to the mass media using the agency. The individual mass medium then selects what it wants from the news agency stories and photographs and passes these along to the reader, viewer, or listener. The agency material may be cut, rearranged, or combined to suit the purposes of the individual newspaper, radio, or television station. Sometimes reporters working for the news agencies write stories on the events covered, which are then transmitted to the agencies' mass media clients. At other times, the agencies merely relay or retransmit stories obtained by reporters in the mass media or by other news agencies with which they have exchange agreements. For instance, the Reuters News Agency has an exchange agreement with Canadian Press, a national news agency, and can use stories from CP.

It is easy to see the importance of the global news agencies. Few newspapers, radio stations, or television networks have the money to pay for more than a very limited number of their own correspondents to bring international news to media users. Most of the mass media depend heavily on the news agencies. A newspaper or radio or TV station may be able to cover most of the important local stories in its community, but it cannot afford the high cost of gathering national and international news. One news agency alone—the Associated Press—spent $78.2 million in 1973 to get and transmit the world news.

It has been estimated that three of every four international news stories used by the mass media are world news agency stories.[1] The other stories come from the foreign correspondents of individual mass media, from syndicates, or from miscellaneous sources.

A world or international news agency can be defined as one that spans the globe with its services and has the capability to cover events in all major areas. The world news agency also has clients, members, or subscribers throughout the globe. There are national and regional news agencies, too, but these have less importance in international communication.

When this definition of a world news agency is used, five news agencies qualify: Agence France-Presse (AFP), the Associated Press (AP), Reuters, Telegrafnoie Agenstvo Sovetskavo Soiuza (the Soviet Telegraph Agency or TASS), and United Press International (UPI). Each of these agencies has hundreds or thousands of employees and makes reports available to millions of mass media users. Hsinhua (the New China News Agency) is considered by some authorities to be global in nature. Dr. Theodore Kruglak notes that it is rapidly expanding and has many foreign bureaus now. The author does not consider NCNA to have the scope or capability of AP, UPI, Reuters, TASS, or AFP, however.

A number of countries have national news agencies operating as arms of the government or as monopolies for disseminating foreign news. These agencies select news from the global news agencies and pass it on to the media within the country and ultimately to the nation's media users. In many countries, the media are not free to obtain reports directly from the international news agencies, but must receive them through the national agency.

The global news agencies can be considered furnishers of "raw material" of news to be used by individual mass media or smaller news agencies. It is up to the mass media or agency editors to select what they need from the vast outpouring of news agency material. Then, of course, it is up to the individual to select from the media what interests him or her. Thus the opinions of individuals concerning international news events are largely formed on the basis of information made available through the media and news agencies.

In many nations, the ultimate support for or rejection of national foreign policy comes from the citizens. Accurate and balanced information would be a first requisite for them to form intelligent opinion on issues. Obviously few of us can have firsthand knowledge of world events; we must depend on others to be our eyes and ears. The international news agencies assume this role to a degree not shared by other news-gatherers.

How do the stories and photographs travel from the news services to the mass media? Each world news agency has a complex system or network for gathering and transmitting news within its organization and to outside users. The material is generally sent electronically over land telephone and telegraph lines, by submarine cables, via radio, or by communications satellite. Not only are words recreated from electronic impulses, but so are photos. The mass media have access to the information flow by teletype or photo transmission devices that include facsimile and even more advanced methods of printing. In other words, the material that the news agencies have collected is distributed over their own networks of communication and then "piped" into the newsrooms of thousands of newspapers and radio and TV stations throughout the world.

Millions of words of news and hundreds of photos pass each day over the distribution systems of each global news agency. A small daily newspaper may receive 20,000 to 30,000 words a day of news from a single agency. A metropolitan daily may subscribe to several agencies and get hundreds of thousands of words of news and many photos daily. No one news medium receives all the potential news available from any one agency. Some of it would have little interest for the medium's users. For example, Latin American soccer

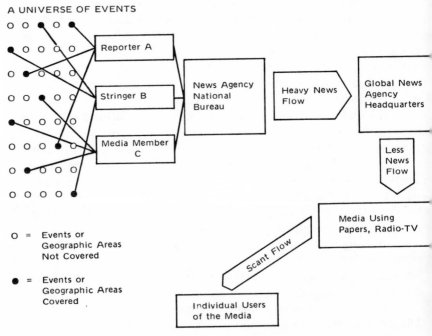

FIGURE 1. International News Flow Via a News Service Of the many potential news events, only some are covered by reporters, "stringers," or members relaying stories to the bureau of the global news agency. Editors there forward important news items to the world headquarters of the agency. Editors at world headquarters select what they think newsworthy and pass it on to the media. Editors in each medium further select what they believe most newsworthy. Finally, the individual reader, listener or viewer decides what international news he will be attentive to. What began as hundreds of events and items has gradually dwindled to only a handful.

football scores are very important to daily newspaper readers in South America, but would be of little interest to readers in Calcutta, India.

Figure 1 gives some idea of how news flows from a given nation through the world news agency, to the mass media and ultimately to the media user. The diagram is much simplified, but it shows how events in many areas may not be covered, or how stories about them will be cut from the news flow before it reaches the user.

Nevertheless, because the media are tied in to the vast news agency networks, each user *can* be informed of important news occurring anywhere in the world. One of the most important reasons for the existence of news agencies is their ability to transmit a news bulletin within a few moments after an extremely important event has occurred almost anywhere in the world.

The desire for quick distribution of major news has become almost a fetish with some news agencies. Few businesses are as competitive as news agencies. United Press International will congratulate itself fervently if it scores a "beat" of a few minutes over arch-rival Associated Press, and vice versa. The headquarters of a news agency will send up a "rocket" to a bureau that misses a story or is slow in getting one. Throughout the world, employees of a news agency dread the thought of a reprimand for not "being on top" of a major news story. Although there are hazards in too much emphasis on speed, it is important for the global news agencies to move fast. If the President of the United States becomes ill or a violent earthquake kills thousands in Japan, we expect to know about it quickly. This desire to obtain news quickly from far away was a major reason for the development of world news agencies.

DEVELOPMENT OF THE INTERNATIONAL AGENCIES

The news agencies first came into being in the nineteenth century, although precursors certainly existed much earlier. The sixteenth-century Fugger Newsletters, which contained news of commercial interest, were examples of the international gathering and transmission of information. These private letters went not to newspapers but to individuals interested in trade, shipping, or developments in government, who were willing to pay for such news.

In colonial North America, an early cooperative news-gathering enterprise operated in the field of shipping news, according to one authority.[2] In 1811, Samuel Gilbert at his Exchange Coffee House in Boston began compiling "news books" containing shipping information for his customers.[3] Soon a young assistant, Samuel Topliff,

Jr., took over the job. He didn't wait for the news to be brought in by ships' officers but paddled out in a small boat to meet arriving ships and then returned to post information in the news books. One book contained general news, both foreign and domestic, and the other carried commercial shipping news. Soon newspaper owners began to use the news from these compilations in the reading rooms of American coffee houses.[4] An annual fee was collected from the persons using the books.

A few years later, in 1825, Charles Havas, a young Frenchman of Hungarian extraction, organized a news bureau in Europe, with correspondents in various European capitals to gather news for private subscribers including businessmen, financiers, and diplomats. A year later, Havas suggested to some newspaper publishers that his service could benefit them, but not until some years later, when the papers saw that the Havas agency's use of semaphore signals and carrier pigeons could get them faster news, did they begin to use its services.[6]

Havas's idea led others to follow. In 1848, Bernard Wolff, a former Havas employee, set up a joint news operation among German and Northern European papers, starting what would later be the Wolff News Agency.[7] Still another former Havas worker, Julius Reuter, opened a news office in the London Royal Exchange in 1851 after he had tried to set up a news service in continental Europe. He offered financial news to businessmen and speculators, but the London papers were slow to see their need for a news service. Not until 1858 did they subscribe to Reuter's service.[8]

Reuter early entered into a close relationship with the British government by furnishing his news telegrams free to high officials and to Queen Victoria. He was later able to make favorable arrangements with the government for use of the submarine cables laid to link the British Empire.[9] Much of Reuter's news concerned events within the British government and Empire, and this helped foster the idea that world news agencies sometimes serve as agents of imperialist expansion. The long and friendly relations between Reuter and the British government further benefited the agency when the cable press rate was reduced to about a penny a word between points in the British Commonwealth.[10]

Havas, Wolff, and Reuters all sold their news as a commodity to make a profit. In the United States, however, at about the same time, further attempts were being made at cooperative news-gatherin Competitive newspapers were finding out that getting the news— especially foreign news—was too expensive and took more resources than they had individually. During the 1840s United States papers sometimes shared the costs of obtaining news faster. In 1848, the leading New York papers agreed to obtain foreign news in common via the newly perfected telegraph from Boston. This "Associated Press," as the group called itself, was the forerunner of the modern wire service of that name.[11] Within the next few years it became known as the New York Associated Press.

While this American news cooperative was establishing itself in New York, the European news agencies were developing into complex, powerful organizations. In 1859, the Reuter, Wolff, and Havas agencies worked out an agreement with the New York Associated Press for a news exchange. Again in 1870 an agreement was signed by the four agencies, this time in reality setting up "news preserves" for each agency—exclusive areas for gathering and distributing the news.[12] The areas were: Havas—France, Switzerland, Italy, Spain, Portugal, Egypt (with Reuters), Central and South America; Reuters—British Empire, Egypt (with Havas), Turkey, the Far East; Wolff—Germany, Austria, the Netherlands, Scandinavia, Russia, the Balkans; and New York AP—the United States.[13]

Newspapers had little choice but to take the news service for their area of the world, whether they liked its methods of operation and quality of news or not.

In the latter half of the nineteenth century the New York Associated Press began to share its news service with other United States papers to lessen telegraph costs. These papers, organized into groups or regional associations, included the Western Associated Press, the Southern Associated Press and the New England Associated Press. The new members did not feel that the New York AP had their interests at heart, and in 1885 the Western AP withdrew from the cooperative.[14] It was reorganized as the Associated Press of Illinois in 1892, and the old New York AP went out of existence. The new Associated Press signed an exclusive contract with Reuters, Havas, and Wolff, although its members were not really satisfied with the arrangement and wanted their own representation abroad.[15] After losing an antimonopoly suit in Illinois, the AP of Illinois was reorganized in New York in 1900, keeping its cooperative nature. This was the basis for the present AP.[16]

The newly organized agency soon had some competitors in the United States. It was set up so that only one newspaper in a given circulation area could have the right to its services. As newspapers increased at the turn of the century, many found themselves denied membership in the AP because there were already AP papers in their areas. The exclusive contract was disliked by many, among them Edward Wyllis Scripps, then building up a group of newspapers. He organized the Scripps-McRae telegraphic service to serve his papers in 1897.[17] The Scripps-McRae Association later bought out a rival

group and in 1907 formed a new agency—the United Press Associations—which was to become the AP's greatest rival in news-gathering
throughout the world.[18] The new UP was to be a profit-making venture, not a cooperative, and, since it was not a party to any "spheres
of influence" agreements with other major news agencies, it soon had
bureaus in various world capitals. The AP, too, was flexing its muscles
and had established some overseas bureaus, although it was hampered
by interagency agreements.

The assertiveness of the UP was to give extra stimulus to the AP
to break the bonds of the world news cartel. In 1909, another world
news agency, the International News Service (INS), was formed to
serve the Hearst newspaper chain in the United States.[19] It, too, had
overseas bureaus and was not a party to the news cartel agreements.
It operated until it was absorbed in 1958 by United Press to form
the present-day United Press International (UPI).

In 1918, the Soviet government saw the need for a state news
agency and established ROSTA which later became TASS. From its
beginning, TASS differed from the other global agencies. It is an
integral part of the Soviet government, helping to serve national and
international policies. In 1972 the director of TASS was given ministerial rank, and TASS was organized as a state committee, the
equivalent of a ministry.[20] A TASS spokesman has said that TASS
considers itself an official but unsubsidized agency.[21]

Not only does TASS act as a global news agency, but its correspondents have also been accused of espionage activities on occasion
in different parts of the world.[22] It makes its services available at
very little or no cost in some countries. Few nations outside the communist group depend completely upon TASS as a world news agency
since its news is sometimes politically colored. It is, however, used as
an important supplementary service by many mass media outside the
communist nations.

It was not until the early part of the twentieth century that UP
and Hearst's INS gave much worldwide competition to the news
cartel of which Reuters, Havas, Wolff, and AP were major members.
But as news media desired more and better coverage during World
War I, the concept of exclusive news preserves began to crumble, and
in the 1930s the near-monopolies of news finally ended.

Today, Havas, Wolff, and INS have faded away. Havas, the
French agency, was transformed into and revitalized as Agence France
Presse in 1944. Wolff, the German agency, ceased its existence in
1933, and INS merged with UP in 1958. Reuters is no longer a profit
making organization, having changed its status in 1941 to a cooperative trust owned by the British press and Australian and New Zealand
media. The AFP was forced to seek financial aid after World War II,

and it was subsidized directly by the French government. In 1957 it became an autonomous organization with eight directors from French newspapers on its board. Its ties with the French government remain close, however.

The global news agencies as they currently operate may be characterized as follows: profit-making—United Press International; cooperative—Agence France-Presse, Associated Press, and Reuters; integral part of a national government—TASS.

A number of supplemental news agencies also have considerable importance, although they cannot be classified as truly global agencies. These include the mainland Chinese government's New China News Agency (Hsinhua); Novosti, a Soviet feature service; Deutsche Presse Agentur (DPA), the West German agency; and Prensa Latina, the Cuban agency.

In the 1970s the global agencies have increased in size and in number of clients. The Associated Press, for example, claims that more than one billion persons outside the United States see or hear its news every day.[23] The agencies have also added services specifically for the needs of radio and television with special broadcast wires and audio networks.

Table 1 gives a rough idea of the magnitude of operations of the global news agencies. Estimates of the number of bureaus, subscribers, and employees are the best available and should be considered only an approximation. The AFP estimate of users, for example, seems much exaggerated. The agencies are very competitive and do not always define bureaus or subscribers in the same way.

TABLE 1. Size of the Global News Agencies

News Agency	Foreign Bureaus	Media Users	Employees
Agence France-Presse	165	17,000	1,800
Associated Press	53	8,500	3,300
Reuters	55	4,450	1,660
TASS	100	3,000	2,500
United Press International	238	6,546	10,000*

Source: Reports to the author by news agency spokesmen in 1973.

*Includes both full- and part-time employees. Other agencies supposedly gave full-time workers only.

THE FLOW OF INTERNATIONAL NEWS

The global news agencies have linked all parts of the world in complicated news-gathering and transmitting networks. Several major characteristics of these networks stand out. The headquarters are all located in developed, industrial nations: AP and UPI have their world headquarters in New York City; Reuters's main office is in London; AFP's home office is in Paris; and TASS is headquartered in Moscow. Each agency's network is primarily based on an east-west transmission axis, around the globe. The main lines of world communication are laid out in this same direction, linking the more industrially developed areas such as North America and Europe. Trade and political ties have for long periods linked these areas, and the flow of communication has been heavy among the nations along the east-west line.

Other lines of communication feed into the main east-west flow, transmitting news to and from areas to the north or south of the main channels. Africa, Latin America, much of Asia, and much of the Pacific are on "feeder lines" bringing more information into the east-west flow, or taking it out. News agency communications do not flow as heavily between Latin America and the United States, for example, as between the United States and Europe.

Another general characteristic of the global agency communication pattern is that much of the information originating in Africa, Asia, or Latin America is funneled into collecting points along the east-west axis (such as New York or London) before it is relayed elsewhere in the world.

Some of the lines of communication follow communication patterns set up in the nineteenth century between colonizing European powers and their holdings in Africa and Asia. Latin America was linked in that century to the United States and Europe by telegraph and cable. The active interest of the United States in commercial relations with Latin America has strengthened lines of communication between the two continents. In parts of the world off the main east-west communication axis, however, it is often difficult to communicate even with nearby countries. For instance, telegraph rates are often higher between neighboring countries in Africa than they are between former French colonies there and Paris and back to East Africa. The old colonial communication routes still tend to be more efficient and cheaper.

Another characteristic of the communication pattern of the agencies is that they have bureaus scattered all over the world. An event covered by reporters in one bureau is placed in the news agency's world network of communication if the story is important. For instance, when Salvador Allende was elected the first Marxist president of Chile, the story was sent as a bulletin from the Santiago, Chile, bureau of the Associated Press via its channel to the New York AP headquarters. From there the news was relayed on different AP channels throughout the United States and to other countries. Within a matter of minutes the news had been carried to the ends of the earth.

Since the early 1960s, the communication process has been made more efficient by the use of communications satellites. Signals are sent by land line and radio from various bureaus to satellite ground stations that send them to satellites, which relay the signals to ground stations near the news agencies' headquarters. Before satellites were used, agencies relied on short-wave radio, land lines, and cables. Satellites offer increased international transmission channel capacities. They are less subject to unfavorable conditions in the ionosphere that affect radio waves, and do not suffer from thunderstorms, which cause static on radio frequencies. Radio-teletypes, telegraphs, and cables are still widely used, but the communications satellite, with its freedom from radio transmission problems, is assuming more and more importance.

The international news agencies have also begun in the 1970s to use computers to speed the flow of information. They are used to store and retrieve information, to produce stories for transmission in printouts with even right hand margins (justified lines) and proper hyphenation done much more quickly than a human being can produce them. The volume of stories is becoming so great that some news agencies are transmitting short summaries of international news, from which a bureau selects the stories it desires to receive and pass on to media users in its area. The requested stories are called up from storage in the agency's computer. Computers connected to high-speed printers can make stories available much more rapidly than the old teletype transmission method, which outputs about sixty-six words per minute.

The news agencies, like the mass media, have been hit by a revolution in communications technology that emphasizes speed and ease of news production and transmission. Some of the global agencies are already using new devices such as the cathode ray tube in video display terminals that take the place of the reporter's typewriter and the editor's pencil. The reporter writes his story on a video display terminal and sees it appear on a screen much like a TV set, while it goes into a computer that prepares it for transmission and printing. Editors make corrections and update stories on the same video display terminals, rather than laboriously by hand. The system eliminates several steps in the process of getting a story written, transmitted, edited, and set in type, if that is needed. It makes a much greater volume of international news potentially available to the mass media.

Another general characteristic of the world agencies is their strong tendency toward centralized control of the flow of international news. Key editors decide what will be sent along the communication chain. Only a handful of individuals determines whether a specific news story will be written, transmitted from a bureau to the news agency headquarters, and then relayed throughout the world.

When a news story is received by a newspaper, radio station, or television station from the news agency, an editor decides whether to use the story. It is edited to fit the needs of the medium; for example it may be trimmed to fit the space designated for it, combined with other stories on the same subject, or rewritten to emphasize facets the individual medium editor believes are especially important.

NEWS AGENCY PROBLEMS

In the 1940s Kurt Lewin, a social scientist, used the concept of a "gatekeeper" to describe how an individual can have great influence on the flow of information from the source to the ultimate receiver.[24] The gatekeeper can open or close the "gate," allowing information to pass through or stopping it. He may pass a communication along unchanged, or shorten it, alter its emphasis, or abort it—breaking the chain of communication.

Studies of mass media and international communications can profitably focus on these gatekeepers, because all of what we read, see, or hear in the media is determined by them. Nowhere is the gatekeeping process more noticeable than in international communication, where the communication chain is longer than in local communication, and there are more opportunities for the story to be distorted, cut, or stopped altogether because more gates must be passed. In a way, we can compare the transmission of news to the old-fashioned game of "Gossip," in which each person in the circle is a gatekeeper in the flow of information. The content of the original message is easily distorted or changed, and this gives the game its twist. The news media and global news agencies of course take pains to be accurate, but gatekeepers still play key parts in moving information and have ample opportunities to change the message, either on purpose or accidentally.

Thousands of persons are busy every day throughout the world gathering and sending the news in the world news agencies. Millions of words are written in the original stories, but obviously all of this news cannot be sent through the teletype circuits, via satellites, or in other modes of transmission through the world. There simply is not enough channel capacity to pass all of it on at every "gate," even if it would be desirable to do so. Some of the news is of interest only to a particular region, and it would be ridiculous to pass it on to other areas. Editors in the bureaus of the agencies act as gatekeepers, sifting and winnowing the news, deciding what to pass on to the next gatekeeper.

What standards do these editor-gatekeepers use? When asked, most of them will say something like, "I transmit what is newsworthy, what I think people will want, or what my main office wants in news." Thus the choice of news transmitted across the globe via the wire services is basically determined by subjective judgments.

One of the biggest problems—not only for the news agencies but for the mass media—is: What constitutes news? Does the definition of news meet the need of mass media consumers to be informed? Will the average citizen be able to form intelligent opinions about major events if he receives information that is tailored to meet the concept of newsworthiness?

Some professionals in the mass media and in mass communication research believe that well-rounded and balanced presentations of events are the information most needed by mass media users. Other professionals argue that what is most untypical and nonrepresentative makes the most interesting and important news.

Another question that has been asked is: What effects, if any, do the biases, education, age, professional experience, etc., of the gatekeeper have on the way he works his gate? Very little study has been done concerning gatekeepers in international news, and it is quite difficult to show that a gatekeeper's bias may have a dramatic influence on whether he lets a specific piece of news through his gate. Several studies suggest that biases directly influence selection of the news.[25] This writer believes a more practical way to study the effects of the gatekeeping process may be to study on a large scale the flow of news in volume and content before it enters a specific gate and after it leaves. Such a news flow study will indirectly throw some light on the values gatekeepers have as they transmit the news. A few studies of this nature have been done on the global news agencies. In one, news was traced from its origin in foreign news bureaus, through transmission to the headquarters, and then onto the teletype circuits going to members.[26] This study, made in 1971, involved most of the Latin American bureaus of the Associated Press, its New York headquarters, and editors there who relayed the news to media receiving the AP main trunk wire services. During the three weeks of the study, more than a third of a million words in 1,636 items were transmitted to New York from the Latin American bureaus. There, the Latin American news had to compete with news from the rest of the world, for selection for further dissemination. One of the major characteristics of international news flow via wire service quickly became apparent: the very drastic decrease in news flow. Only 7.8 percent of the Latin American news items were re-transmitted by New York onto the main AP trunk wire, which serv-ices thousands of papers and broadcast stations in the United States. In the competition for news space on the AP wire, United States news of course predominated, and nearly two of every three stories sent were domestic. Of the remaining third, Latin American news clearly had a low priority during the study. Western European items made up 38.5 percent of the foreign news, Asian news 25.8 percent, news from the Middle East and Latin America 9.9 percent each, African items with 7 percent, Eastern European stories 6.4 percent, and news from a scattering of other points accounted for the rest.

This order of priorities reflected the AP gatekeepers' concep-tions of what world areas were of most interest to AP members (and, by extension, to millions of media users).

A brief, three-day survey of the United Press International wire serving the Georgia media also revealed a predeliction for Western European news emphasis.[27] Foreign news made up about 16 percent of the total news on the wire during the survey, and of the foreign items, nearly 61 percent were from Western Europe. Asia followed with 17.6 percent, North America outside the United States account-ed for 8 percent, Eastern Europe 5.4 percent, Latin America and the Middle East 4.1 percent each, and Africa received no mention at all.[28]

A study by the International Press Institute in 1953 also found that most wire service coverage centered heavily on just a few coun-tries, and that most of the foreign news used by United States papers was from a handful of major nations such as the United Kingdom, Germany, France, and the Soviet Union.[29]

The heavy emphasis placed on news from and about the highly developed industrial nations has caused concern among some mass communication scholars. Cataclysmic events have a way of occurring in the underdeveloped nations, but little advance warning of these is given. The mass media user awakes to find that genocide has taken place in Pakistan, or hundreds of thousands are dying of starvation in sub-Saharan Africa. He is bewildered to see the United States dragged into nasty wars at the far ends of the earth—and cannot understand why American interests are even involved.

The global news agencies frequently give only superficial and spot coverage of the "news storms" that blow up in underdeveloped areas. And little space is given to one of the most important stories of our time—the shape and direction of development of the new nations. Observation by this writer concerning news service opera-tions in Latin America and Africa indicates that many agency correspondents tend to cover the more dramatic and overt stories—such as earthquakes, civil wars, and criminal violence. A news editor for one Latin American agency bureau, criticizing his own performance, said:

Terrorism is over-emphasized. Yet each day I check first for what terrorism has occurred in the country, and push it [on the wire] if it seems at all noteworthy. I know it will receive attention in New York. It is also a damned sight easier to write than, say, a story about education or agricultural problems.[30]

A comparative study found that one global news agency transmitted seven stories from developed nations to every three from the developing nations.[31] Wilbur Schramm, who has studied the news flow from developing portions of the world, believes that such unbalanced coverage "in some cases at least . . . tends to ignore important events and to distort the reality it presents."[32]

In justice to the world news agencies, it must be said that frequently their mass media clients fail to use the stories that *are* made available about Africa, Latin America, and Asia. Editors seem to believe that the average citizen has very little interest in what happens in the developing portions of the globe. An investigation into the perceptions of editors of fifteen Wisconsin daily papers of small to medium size found they gave low priority to news from such areas because they felt most readers were uninterested, except when United States interests were directly involved.[33]

Some writers for world news agencies are frustrated by this apparent lack of interest among mass media editors and consumers. One writer noted that news from Latin America had to fit the preconceptions of United States media users before it had much chance of being carried. The stereotype of that part of the world is of a place of violent natural and man-made acts, where instability makes events rather incomprehensible to United States residents. A former AP bureau chief said:

Latin American news must fit certain preconceived notions of readers and editors before it has much chance of use. Earthquake stories are almost always used, as are other natural disasters, accidents, revolutions and coups. Then there's the "dancing bear" type of human interest story which tickles the readers' fancies. They like to say, "Oh, look how interesting and quaint those little brown-skinned people are!"[34]

The 1971 study of Latin American news previously cited found that nearly half the news stories retransmitted to United States users of the AP main trunk wire were in one category—crime and criminal violence. While news from the bureaus covered seventeen categories, only twelve were retransmitted (see table 2). The survey of

TABLE 2. Subjects of AP Latin American News

Subject Categories	From Latin American Bureaus %	On U.S. AP Trunk Wire %
Accidents	3.01	2.34
Agriculture	0.86	1.56
Art, culture, and entertainment	1.16	0.00
Crime and criminal violence	13.81	47.66
Disasters	3.61	11.72
Domestic government and politics	15.65	14.06
Economics and business	7.58	2.34*
Education	1.04	0.00
Foreign relations	19.19	6.25
Human interest features	2.81	5.47
Labor	2.20	0.00
Military and defense	1.16	0.00
Miscellaneous	1.04	0.78
Prominent people	1.47	3.91
Religion	0.79	1.56
Science and medicine	1.34	2.34
Sports	23.23	0.00*
Totals (percent) †	99.95	99.99
Number of items	1,636	128

*A few sports items were retransmitted on AP sports wires in the United States. A few business items were used on the AP–Dow Economic Wire.

†Totals do not equal 100 percent because of rounding.

UPI foreign news indicated that the Georgia UPI wire used only ten of the seventeen categories. Crime and criminal violence stories made up more than 20 percent of the foreign news (the largest single category), and news of military and defense subjects was the second-highest category used, making up nearly 18 percent of the foreign stories.[35]

Thus not only is the news transmission from certain areas thin, but it is also bunched into few categories. Categories receiving little emphasis seem to be art, culture, and entertainment; education; labor; religion; and science and medicine. These are all "soft" news categories and are not generally involved in big, spot news stories. Yet they are important subjects for giving a well-rounded picture of the life of mankind.

Another problem the global news agencies have is lack of manpower to staff news events in all parts of the world. The largest staffs are in the developed nations. When manpower for gathering the news is allocated, coverage is likely to be heaviest where the most sub- scribers to the services are. Where there are few clients, as in Africa, Asia, and Latin America, the agencies often rely on roving corres- pondents to cover big stories. Newsmen from other areas are sent to report on breaking stories. William A. Hachten has noted that "jet correspondents" fly quickly in and out of Africa, and "Africans resent . . . that London and Paris continue as Africa's major news centers."[36] He finds:

The . . . agencies are sorely undermanned and inadequate to cover African news with speed, accuracy and comprehensiveness. Professionally trained correspond- ents are too few, and there is much reliance on stringers, most of whom are either professionally incompetent or too involved with local governments to report news objectively.[37]

Some Third World spokesmen criticize what they see as "wire service nationalism" and link the Western news agencies with the colonialist past. Whether the world news agencies present news that is detrimental to Third World interests or that does not suit their needs is still unanswered. It is apparent, however, that much of the world news is written by Europeans or North Americans to appeal to the parts of the world where the most agency clients are. The key gatekeepers in the agencies are generally (although not always) citi- zens of the more developed nations.

The bureau official or agency correspondent reporting the news presents another problem. A foreigner serving as bureau chief may not have a basic understanding of the country and may make mis- takes in news judgment. A bureau chief native to the area may have better understanding of local news but may be more subject to pres- sures from his own government not to print critical items. Some news agencies depend heavily on local "stringers" who work part- time for the agency. They frequently have conflicts of interest, and agency coverage may suffer.

Several news agency officials have noted that heavy demands are made on a bureau chief to be a salesman of his agency's services and a hand-holder of clients who need to be kept happy. Much time is spent by bureau chiefs in nonnews functions, sometimes to the detriment of the agency's news reports.

But, if all these criticisms were answered, it would still be naive to think that the agencies would place heavy stress on stories from areas or on subjects that they believe have low interest to most agency users. Perhaps the most that can be hoped for is a dedication to generating somewhat more complete and rounded coverage than is now given, even though there is no great demand for it from users. If such stories are done well, emphasizing the significant tasks and opportunities in nation-building, the arts, education, and culture, perhaps the general public will begin to take more interest.

Not only are news agencies beset by problems in deciding newsworthiness and in finding manpower to staff stories, but they must also overcome the attitudes of national leaders who see no need for a free press or for cooperation with the agencies. Such leaders see journalists as enemies unless their stories favor the government. This places obstacles in the way of adequate news flow from some nations to the rest of the world and from the world into those nations.

The very competitive nature of news agency work creates some disadvantages, too. The constant battle among agencies to be first with the news sometimes results in hurried reporting and mediocre performance. News agency workers are obsessed with the passage of time and feel they are constantly working under deadlines. Yet it is often immaterial which agency scoops another by five minutes on a story. The emphasis on "go-go" journalism and hurried coverage of spot news events frequently keeps a reporter from doing a more thoughtful and meaningful piece. The news agencies are conscious of this problem and try to do interpretative articles as well, but most of wire service reporting is still a race against the clock with the devil taking the hindmost.

Another problem this writer sees concerns the subject matter usually emphasized. News of war and threatened war, crime, violence and natural disaster must of course be reported. But should so much emphasis be placed on such news? The news services have to a large extent fashioned their news values according to those prevalent in the mass media, since the agencies must serve the media. Yet this writer suspects that the general public frequently tires of such news. A steady recitation of the evils of the world deadens the senses and lessens the impact of such events. News announcers on radio and television recite the most horrid calamities in completely unmoved voices. Editors religiously reserve a place on the front page for the latest war story, whether it has significance or not. We find ourselves narcotized into apathy by the flood of such news.

Perhaps it is time to question somewhat the old news values and to seek out new priorities for informing the public of foreign news. War is easily perceived as a threat to society, and so are crime and violence. But other subjects need on occasion just as great an emphasis: the problems of overpopulation, pollution, and the quality of life for millions of the world's inhabitants. Compassionate reporting is needed about humans as individuals rather than as abstractions and statistics.

A statement by A. M. Rosenthal, managing editor of the *New York Times,* while not given as a commentary about the work of the world news agencies, applies to these services too: "More and more we have to give something considerable in addition to spot news. We have learned that news is not simply what people say and do, but what they think, what motivates them, their styles of living, the movements, trends and forces acting upon society and on a man's life."[38]

The international news agencies in actuality reflect many of the flaws and virtues of the mass media to which they are adjuncts. We would be severely hampered in getting knowledge of the world without them. We have come to expect quick dissemination of major news wherever it occurs. Most news agency workers are dedicated professionals attempting to do the best job possible, often under poor conditions. Yet they must be severe self-critics and reach always for more responsible performance.

NOTES

1.   John C. Merrill, Carter R. Bryan, and Marvin Alisky, *The Foreign Press* (Baton Rouge: Louisiana State University Press, 1970), p. 34.

2.   Victor Rosewater, *History of Cooperative News-Gathering in the United States* (New York: D. Appleton and Company, 1930), p. 5.

3.   Ibid., pp. 5-6.

4.   Ibid., pp. 7, 12-13.

5.   United Nations Educational, Scientific, and Cultural Organization, *News Agencies: Their Structure and Operation* (Paris: Unesco, 1953), p. 11.

6.   Ibid.

7.   Ibid.

8.   Ibid., pp. 11-12.

9.   Graham Storey, *Reuters: The Story of a Century of News-Gathering* (New York: Crown Publishers, 1951), p. 35. Also, Llewellyn White and Robert D. Leigh, "The Growth of International Communications," in *Mass Communications,* ed. by Wilbur Schramm (Urbana: University of Illinois Press, 1960), p. 77.

10.   White and Leigh, *Growth of International Communications,* p. 73

11.   Edwin Emery, *The Press and America,* 2d ed. (Englewood Cliffs, N.J.: Prentice-Hall, 1962), pp. 254-55.

12.   Unesco, *News Agencies,* p. 18.

13.   Ibid.

14.   Ibid., p. 43.

15.   Ibid.

16. Ibid.

17. Joe Alex Morris, *Deadline Every Minute* (Garden City, N.Y.: Doubleday and Co., 1957), pp. 17-19.

18. Ibid., p. 19.

19. Unesco, *News Agencies*, pp. 49-50.

20. "TASS Ministerial Rank," *New York Times*, Jan. 11, 1972, p. 6.

21. Letter from Harry Freeman, assistant manager of the New York Bureau of TASS, July 31, 1973.

22. The best treatment of TASS is Theodore E. Kruglak's *The Two Faces of TASS* (Minneapolis: University of Minnesota Press, 1962). Kruglak gives much detail on the two missions of the news agency—gathering and transmitting news and obtaining intelligence and at times apparently carrying on espionage. He believes the espionage function is becoming more and more subordinate.

23. Don Huth, "World Services by Satellite, Landline or Bicycle," *The AP World* 28, no. 1, summer 1971, p. 12.

24. The gatekeeper concept is explained in Lewin's "Channels of Group Life: Social Planning and Action Research," *Human Relations* 1 (1947): 143.

25. Probably the earliest of these and one of the best was David Manning White's "The Gate Keeper: A Case Study in the Selection of News," *Journalism Quarterly* 27 (autumn 1950): 383-90. See also Walter Gieber's "Across the News Desk: A Study of 16 Telegraph Editors," *Journalism Quarterly* 33 (fall 1956): 423-32.

26. Al Hester, "The News from Latin America via a World News Agency" (paper presented to the International Communication Division, Association for Education in Journalism, Fort Collins, Colorado, Aug. 20, 1973).

27. Al Hester, "Points of Origin and Subjects of UPI Georgia Wire Foreign News," (mimeo) Henry W. Grady School of Journalism, University of Georgia, July 1973.

28. A similar two-week study of the Wisconsin AP wire in 1970 showed it contained 19 percent foreign news, and that Western Europe also predominated. See Al Hester, "An Analysis of News Flow from Developing and Developed Nations," *Gazette* 17, no. 1/2 (1971): 29-43.

29. *The Flow of the News* (Zurich: International Press Institute, 1953), p. 8.

30. Hester, "The News from Latin America," p. 17.

31. Hester, "An Analysis of News Flow," p. 43.

32. Wilbur Schramm, *Mass Media and National Development* (Stanford, Calif., and Paris, France: Stanford University Press and Unesco, 1964), p. 65.

33. Hester, "An Analysis of News Flow," p. 42.

34. Hester, "The News from Latin America," p. 17.

35. Hester, "Points of Origin and Subjects," table 2.

36. William A. Hachten, *Muffled Drums* (Ames: Iowa State University Press, 1971), p. 68.

37. Ibid., pp. 66-67.

38. "If Everybody Screams, Nobody Hears," a pamphlet adapted from Rosenthal's memorandum to his staff when he became managing editor in September 1969, and later published by the *New York Times*.

INTERNATIONAL
COMMUNICATION
AND GLOBAL
PROPAGANDA

International Film and Television Propaganda*

BERNARD RUBIN

BERNARD RUBIN holds a doctoral degree from New York University and is currently Professor of Governmental Affairs, School of Public Communication and the Graduate School of Arts and Sciences, Boston University. He has been a consultant to the Agency for International Development and the Internal Revenue Service. His publications include Public Relations and the Empire State, and Political Television.

Scientists at work on plans for the next generation of communication satellites, devices which will probably be in wide service within a decade, have announced completion of engineering designs for direct satellite-to-receiver broadcasting. Much more efficient operation in respect to national, continental, and global communications is forecast. The prospects are that television will be equally available to the hinterlands and the urban centers. In short, what has recently been accomplished with radio technology through transistors and other sophisticated miniaturizations, and through battery-powered receivers, is on the verge of being surpassed with television.[1]

---

*Reprinted from "International Film and Television Propaganda: Campaigns of Assistance," by Bernard Rubin in volume no. 398 of The Annals of The American Academy of Political and Social Science. Copyright 1971, by The American Academy of Political and Social Science

Every village in Pakistan or the Sudan will be drawn into direct contact with all other centers of mankind. Countless villagers and city dwellers will be dragged mind-first into the twentieth century, without adequate preparation.

The existing bases of international law provide no remedies for what could quickly evolve into a communications environment that would permit quick and easy intra-national communication as well as international communication that would respect no frontiers.

In times of peace, competitive international propaganda, by virtue of increased volume and new target audiences of all levels of maturity, will prompt new forms of instant misunderstanding. In war, films and "live" productions geared to this new technique of military psychology are nightmare twins to the conceptualization of a better world, in part created by satellite television.

For the industrialized nations, the new technology increases the already high pace of development and promises new levels of proficiency in informational, educational, and entertainment links. To planners and politicians in the less developed areas, the new technology is seen as the way through formerly impassable communication barriers. In short, all concerned with nation-building and modernization are irresistibly drawn to satellite communications.

Indicative of that interest is the *International Telecommunications Satellite Consortium* (Intelsat), an international venture which began on August 20, 1964, when eleven countries agreed to establish a global system of commercial communications satellites. By 1969, there were sixty-three Intelsat members which originated over 90 percent of international telecommunications traffic. The Soviet Union has shown interest but has not joined.[2]

PROPAGANDA AND NATIONAL DEVELOPMENT

In the past decade, international propaganda has increased in direct proportion to advances in communications technology. However, technical innovations have so far produced exceedingly moderate social advances of benefit to mankind. Regarding international propaganda programs of major and minor powers, increased access to foreign audiences has so far accelerated the pace of rather traditional approaches to communications, with few conceptual developments paced to electronic prowess. We witness, at this stage, the domination of the "hardware."

Every discussion of motion pictures as a propaganda device must include consideration of television because this medium, incorporating cinematography as it does, is the most efficient delivery system for bringing films to the masses of the world's populations.

Motion pictures, shown around the world in theaters or on television, are often condemned for introducing noxious social ideas and, by repetition of these themes, forming bases for hatred between men and nations. For example, many films from the commercial sector of the United States are condemned as vehicles for the export of the idea that "to be white" is an infinitely more desirable human state than any other. Such films as *Beyond Mombasa* and *The Naked Prey* are seen as typical examples of gross distortions of African life. Even such an "innocent" product as *To Sir, With Love* has been criticized as bringing a subtler version of the "color line" to worldwide audiences.[3]

Inasmuch as propaganda in its basic connotations has to do with the propagation of ideas, both good and bad, one ought not exclusively to comment on the negative aspects. A great deal of positive work in the education, health, and social welfare fields is being accomplished. For example, the United States government has been active since 1960 in American Samoa, Colombia, Jamaica, and El Salvador, among other places, sponsoring educational television projects, and has been working with India toward the day when satellite television will serve that entire subcontinent. The results have been varied, due to local conditions; but planners are learning how to prepare each constituent group for step-by-step change when television is introduced to the schools. One of the prime lessons learned so far is that if television is to perform well and to achieve locally desirable results, it must be in conjunction with "a whole system of accompanying supports, most of which have to be worked out in terms of self-interest of millions of individual citizens."[4]

Disruptive Effects

We must, however, recognize the possibility of certain disruptive effects of television.

1. One of the propaganda themes of the highly developed nations is that their aid programs are designed to help further local modernization ambitions. That theme sounds sour if those who assist educational television expansion, for example, assume that any less developed country is capable of restructuring its educational, economic, or political systems to accommodate the new technology in the style and to the ends pursued by their assisters at home. For one thing, educational opportunities of mass television are still being explored in the industrialized states.

2. The "paraphernalia of modernity" can menace the cultural integrity of entire societies. When an underdeveloped people is given

television equipment and rudimentary capabilities for technical operation of the facilities, the audiences must become pawns to whatever
outside source or sources provide the bulk of the programming. For
one ramification, Herbert I. Schiller warns that

the cultural homogenization that has been underway for years in the United
States now threatens to overtake the globe. . . . Everywhere local culture is
facing submission from the mass-produced outpourings of commercial broadcasting.[5]

3. Antidemocratic or predemocratic established governments
usually try to resist or control sources of popular information. Rarely
is change perceived as in the self-interest of those in power. Status
quo autocracies in the less developed countries do not set a high
priority on nation-building. The elites in such autocracies do not
encourage uses of television and films which create "vertical linkages
between the rulers and the ruled."[6] Thus, the industrialized democracies need to examine what they do when they help to install television in certain less developed countries.

4. Television can have unsettling effects on pre-existing mass
communication structures. When any public is diverted from its customary reliance on other media, power struggles among communication leaders are probable. Local political control mechanisms will
be out of kilter until the establishment itself makes the transition.

5. With the introduction of television and the widespread distribution of films, largely imported, new views of life and manners
in the outer world set up previously unheard-of expectations; these
can lead to enormous frustration when it turns out that the images
are as close to reality as the local population is likely to get for a long,
long while. All sorts of virulent results are to be expected as a sort of
anti-propaganda, bred by the propaganda concerning things in sight
but not in hand.

6. Mass media affect behavior, but we do not know with any
exactness the relationship between portrayals of violence and the
creation of actual civic disorders. Therefore, much experimentation
in behavior is an unwelcome guest, together with television (or film)
depictions, however innocent the packager of that information may be.[7]

PROGRAMS OF DEVELOPED COUNTRIES

The great industrial powers maintain the most energetic programs of
film and television propaganda. To a notable degree, the focus is on
bids for appreciation of their national goals in the less developed

regions. With an increasingly competitive communications situation prevailing in highly developed areas, there is less opportunity for cross-national propagation of governmentally inspired ideologies. The peoples of the developed states are better serviced by domestic systems.

Where the government controls the domestic media, as is the case in the Soviet Union, it is difficult for outside propaganda to penetrate the screens of officialdom. Short-wave radio offers foreign propagandists about the only hope, as they try to reach the Russian masses on a regular schedule. Every effort is made by the Kremlin to counter broadcasts of foreign origin such as Radio Liberty, Radio Free Europe, and the Voice of America. Except for films occasionally admitted under a cultural exchange agreement, the peoples of the Soviet Union are kept free of "capitalistic" motion pictures.

Where there is a free domestic media situation, as in the United States, internal productions tend to be more attractive than importations. Foreign-made documentaries are available from time to time, primarily as fillers for the ever-hungry television maw. Hard propaganda has almost no market.

In Japan and India, huge motion picture industries catering to mass audiences rarely prepare propaganda films for foreign distribution. But they do sponsor films to promote tourism and to make cultural treasures known abroad. Some industrial promotion work is also included. Yet, as against the volume of other films, government propaganda productions are a drop in the bucket.[8]

U.S. FILM AND TV PROPAGANDA

The United States government's television operations began on a small scale in the U.S. Information Agency in 1955. By 1963, Agency Director Edward R. Murrow concluded that

world television has followed the path of the population explosion. . . . Appetite for TV products is voracious. TV reaches a person in the intimacy of his home, in the height of his leisure, when he is most receptive to persuasion and a new idea. We must use this tool lest our competition use it in our absence, and to our eventual loss.

By 1969, the agency was supplying more than two thousand television stations in ninety countries with film clips and videotape programs. In the administration of President Johnson, emphasis was placed on the tailoring of individual programs and series to specific overseas target audiences. Variety, talk, and videotaped documentaries were featured.

Between 1965 and 1968, approximately 174 documentary television "specials" were prepared. Educational television also was stressed. In Vietnam, USIA gave technical assistance to Government of South Vietnam Television (THVN) and by 1965 THVN was broadcasting from Saigon, Cantho, and Hue.

On the matter of communications satellites, USIA pioneered. The first relays of the Tokyo Olympic Games of 1964 were sent to the United States in October, via "Syncom III." The "Early Bird" satellite and the "Intelsat" family of satellites relayed programs to Europe and the Far East.

However, high costs and uncertain USIA goals have kept the satellite relay program modest. If USIA is to embark upon a program similar to its international radio efforts, massive funding and some basic decisions about USIA's future will be needed.

The Motion Picture and Television Service (IMV) of USIA develops its yearly schedule in accordance with "Worldwide Priority Themes," as do the other media units of the agency. Its budget is in excess of ten million dollars a year for personnel, production, and distribution expenditures.[9]

Broad-ranging objectives and themes present problems. Almost all major social, political, and economic topics can be grist for the foreign policy mill. As a result, the agency's film and television activities lack a central purpose and an essential motivation. One positive result is the acceptability of the productions around the world, because the films are quite often ends in themselves, being interesting and informative treatments of subjects for general enlightenment and not being "hard sell" presentations. Thus, IMV is basically a cultural operation. Nevertheless, there are somewhat standardized political obligations which make sense and enhance immediate governmental propaganda needs.

In early 1969, a main task was to inform the world about the President-elect and the new Administration. One film was created: *Richard Nixon: The New President.* Two commercial films were acquired, for worldwide distribution: *Nixon—A Self-Portrait* and *The Nixon Cabinet.* Covering the inauguration, IMV produced and transmitted the first multinational television program to Latin America, sending it from studios in Mexico, Panama, and Chile via satellite. A twenty-minute color film of Inauguration Day was prepared and sent to all USIA overseas posts.

To help explain U.S. foreign policies, all overseas posts regularly receive film prints of presidential press conferences and major speeches, and USIS officials attempt to place them on local television stations and in local theaters. In the Far East and to a lesser extent in Latin America, satellite television is used to transmit the speech or conference to a convenient overseas country, where it is quickly processed and shipped to posts in the area.

Two "specials," *The Silent Majority* and *The Cambodian Decision,* in addition to a documentary on President Nixon's first officia. visit to Europe, *The First Step,* and a film of Nixon's visit to Rumania, are recent IMV products. Compressed in these films are some of the outstanding issues of the day as the American Administration sees them.

An outstanding success story for IMV in 1969 and 1970 was achieved because of the extensive work on the U.S. space program. With the landing of Americans on the moon, U.S. propagandists were able to captivate people in 140 countries. The deed and all of the details of the background constituted one of the biggest stories of the century. The natural interest of all people in the proceedings superseded all sheerly partisan politics. Emphasizing the great steps necessary for the trip, and the landing on the moon as the fulfillment of one of the dreams of all mankind, IMV had little difficulty in draining prestige for the United States from official presentations verging on the modest, under the circumstances.

In August of 1970, USIA began a new live satellite series in cooperation with Brazilian TV.

Special films are made whenever a head of state visits Washington, describing his reception there and all other aspects of his stay in the country. These films are primarily useful in impressing the dignitary's countrymen and in demonstrating the warmth of his visit and the high regard the United States has for his nation. Films on modernization and nation-building subjects are also prepared, but the major responsibility for those areas is held by the Agency for International Development, which has an extensive system for distributing a great variety of practical films.

Effectiveness

Effectiveness of films with foreign audiences is always a problem. Despite the best planning, observers at the agency recognize that many productions fall short due to changing conditions overseas (political, economic, and social), failure to anticipate special local needs or to take account of nuances or prejudices, and the difficulty of producing films for use in more than one country. Artistic treatment often differs radically from the plan originally behind any film's production. The planners of the films tend to be bureaucrats, and the creators, artists. There is always the natural conflict of interest between those who decide the foreign policy needs and those who plan scenarios or camera shots. Often those most aware of an overseas environment don't know how to make films, and those who make the films see environments differently while the film is in preparation. Officials in charge of budgets take certain short cuts which lead to long shots. To add to the over-all problem, no film producers, governmental or private, have devised formulas which apply to works of art. In one sense or another, every film is a work of art.

Estimates of the effectiveness of films or television programs come to USIA from several sources. Perhaps the most significant come from the field reports to Washington, relaying how audiences reacted when the materials were shown in private theaters or on post premises. Experienced Foreign Service Information Officers send reaction information to Washington. The research arm of the agency also commissions polling organizations to sample public opinion on foreign impressions of IMV's products.

Under pseudo-scientific conditions, each USIA post, in an annual "country program" plan that has gone by various names, is required to follow cost-accounting procedures to account on the basis of "exposures" for each film and television program. In general terms, a film is considered effective if enough persons see it to justify its cost. In the cost language known as the Resource Allocation System,

An exposure is one time that one person sees one program film. The total number of exposures is therefore the annual attendance at all film showings. . . . Films shown on TV are to be counted under TV placement.

Each film is also evaluated in terms of effectiveness as an implement of post policy and programming objectives; usefulness to the country-wide film program and to specific target audiences; usefulness for commercial and/or TV placement; and the like. Post reviewers are free to express their opinions candidly, and they do. Negative and positive reactions are carefully studied at IMV and by USIA's top executives.

WESTERN EUROPEAN PROGRAMS

Western European countries have developed sizable film and television programs for international persuasion purposes, emphasizing trade, cultural, and political objectives. France and Britain exchange information with the independent countries formerly in their colonial empires. Both nations look to the maintenance and enhancement of important trading areas within the cultural regions they helped to shape in the past. The Federal Republic of Germany is anxious to win understanding for its political point of view and customers for its commercial and industrial offerings. All three nations are representative of the highly developed democracies whose main propaganda is geared to peaceful exchanges of information and technology.

Great Britain's overseas film and television program is largely directed by the Central Office of Information (COI), which works in close cooperation with other government departments and with relevant private organizations. On the film side, the *Overseas Film Library Catalogue 1970–71,* published by the COI for the benefit of potential clients, offers hundreds of productions dealing with British culture and history, Commonwealth developments, governmental planning and services, science and technology, sports and recreation, the arts, agriculture, industry, and labor.

An essential aspect of the enterprise is the determination of all concerned to "put Britain across" in its export program. A senior British official writes: "The promotion films we acquire—mainly for non-theatrical showings—are most important . . . and the trade theme features prominently in our television programs."[10]

The over-all effort is impressive. In 1968/69 the COI distributed a weekly cinema newsreel to seventy-nine countries, two monthly and one bimonthly cinemagazine programs going to fifty-one countries, and eleven weekly television programs going to ninety-two countries. In that same period, COI completed twenty-six films requested by government departments concerned with home affairs and four on behalf of the Foreign and Commonwealth Office. Two hundred and ten other films were acquired from commercial sources—mostly industrial—and of those, ninety-seven were distributed overseas.

Approximately 150 Commonwealth, colonial, and foreign lands receive COI films each year. To support the imposing oversea work, the COI for fiscal 1970/71 has a television budget of £1 million and a film budget of £500,000.[11]

The Films and Television Division of the COI cooperates closely with the British Broadcasting Corporation (BBC) and the Independent Television Authority (ITV). Reuters, the BBC, and the Australian, Canadian, and New Zealand broadcasting authorities form the partnership known as Visnews Ltd., the news film agency which provides a daily international news service on film to television subscribers in sixty-eight countries.[12] The BBC and the ITV each distribute about sixteen thousand television programs a year to more than eighty countries.

By and large, the COI is reticent about the successes and failures of the film and television productions sent abroad. It states:

No attempt is made to evaluate the total film and television programmes. Comprehensive usage reports are called for each year from overseas posts on a sample range of films. In the television field, user stations are asked to report times and frequency of use.

The Federal Republic of Germany

The Federal Press and Information Office in the Federal Republic of Germany cooperates closely with several quasi-official and private organizations. Inter-Nationes, the German association for the promotion of international relations, is a non-profit institution primarily responsible for cultural programs. Official government missions abroad maintain inventories of films listed in the Inter-Nationes catalogue. Those missions thus act as clearing houses for a wide range of German organizations. They include: *Institut für Film und Bild in Wissenschaft und Unterricht, Institut für den Wissenschaftlichen Film,* and *Deutsches Industrie-Institut.* The only limitations imposed by the missions before they will pass requests along to Inter-Nationes is that the clients order no more than four films from any one organization at a time, and that the order be placed a month ahead of the screening date.

Following other leading Western powers, the West German government maintains film archives in key cities abroad and film depots to serve regional interests. "Kultur" institutes in seven less developed countries also serve as presentation centers for television and film works.

Trans-Tel, the only non-government TV organization partly sponsored by the federal government, is headquartered in Cologne. Its statutes forbid Trans-Tel to distribute in Europe, the United States of America, Canada, Australia, and Japan. Television companies, acting directly through their commercial agents, deal with those markets.

Trans-Tel does not produce anything itself but, from the two German networks, merely selects, edits, and dubs TV programs that promise to be of cultural, instructional, or public relations value in the developing countries. The fees are relatively low.

Because there is no governmental television agency in the Federal Republic, this joint undertaking of the two major and rival West German television services, *ARD* and *ZDF* (Arbeitsgemeinschaft der Rundfunkanstalten der Bundesrepublik Deutschland; Zweites Deutsches Fernsehen), is of prime importance in the success of foreign relations.

For the international market, Trans-Tel

employs international teams of experienced film editors and commentators whose job it is to adapt and tailor the films, synchronizing them in English, French, Arabic, Portuguese and Spanish.

By and large, adaptations of TV programs are handled by the staff of *Deutsche Welle*.[13]

France

The French government's film and television overseas enterprise in the Ministry of Foreign Affairs works closely with other government organizations such as the *Office de Radiodiffusion Télévision Française* (ORTF) and the *Office Français de Techniques Modernes d'Education*, and private companies.

In scope, the program ranges as widely as the American, British, and German, emphasizing distribution of film magazines, cultural films, television program series, theatrical films (several subtitled in English, Arabic, and Spanish), newsreels (Great Britain is the other main supplier of newsreels), educational films, and courses of instruction in the French language.

During 1970, the Ministry of Foreign Affairs with the help of private firms sent out the magazines *France: Panorama, Chroniques de France,* and *Aux Frontières de l'Avenir* (on scientific subjects), while ORTF produced *Pour Vous, Madame* and a magazine devoted to literature. Most of these productions were also prepared for audiences speaking English, Spanish, Portuguese, and Arabic. *France: Panorama* was prepared in a Russian language version in addition to the other languages.

ORTF productions form the mainstay of the general program. Variety, documentary, dramatic, and musical programs are sent to French-speaking countries in the same versions as seen at home, while other countries received dubbed or subtitled versions. A strong effort is made in the area of education. The *Service de la Radio-Télévision Scolaire* emphasizes the sciences.

The volume of programming is impressive: approximately 8,500 hours of film and television magazines a year; 5,783 of ORTF domestic productions in 1969; and, in terms of copies sent out, approximately 1,600 copies of educational programs sent to 69 countries in 1969.[14]

Estimating or speculating about the effectiveness of French television and film work is difficult. In the past few years governmental sensitivity seems to have increased in proportion to the increasingly important role France tries to play as a mediator between and manipulator of powerful opponents. In short, French reticence on the subject of program evaluation is at this time a fact of life.

THE DEVELOPING NATIONS

Films and television programs have been instruments for useful propaganda exchanges between the "have" and the "have-not" peoples. Cultural news has been the main ingredient in those exchanges, and this will continue. Unfortunately, cultural news is primarily one-sided, the "have" nations not learning much, if anything, about the people they communicate with.

However, some small insight as to foreign effectiveness with films is obtained from a limited recent survey (those interviewed were mainly young people considered to be potential technological change-agents), conducted in South America and Middle America. The results which follow (see Table) are in response to the question, "From what country or countries are the films which you see most?"[15]

TABLE 1. Foreign Film Reception in Middle and South America

Source	Middle Americans (n = 119)	South Americans (n = 190)
United States	96	82
France	41	57
Italy	35	51
West Germany	26	12
Mexico	25	4
Great Britain	17	15
Eastern Europe	3	6
Spain	5	3
Argentina	4	3
Sweden	0	5
Japan	0.8	3
India	0	0.5

Note: The respondents in many cases named more than one country, which accounts for total of answers being larger than number of persons interviewed.

At the very least, provisions must be made for film and television propaganda to be mutual, if the general interest is to be served.

In a significant way, film and television propaganda constitutes schooling in development. Will it be effective? Perceptive students are skeptical. Here are a few reasons:

1. For a developing world torn by political difficulties, there

is precious little use of films and television to warn emergent nations about the perils of repeating dreadful twentieth-century experiences of the advanced countries. The newsreels available from abroad have too little relevance to the local needs for news; much so-called news is documentary gloss and lacking in truly educational information. It is a fact that "underlying causes of recurring crises are rarely explored . . . no account is given of what might be done to avoid or alleviate these crises."[16] For both the developing and developed nations, there is a lack of adequate reporting about really serious problems like starvation and brutality. Coverage of the Biafran revolt or its aftermath in Nigeria, or about South African apartheid, are cases in point.[17] Eric Sevareid, one of the few savants produced by the American television industry, says, "As journalists, we are not keeping pace with the realities; we report them but we do not truly understand them, so we do not really explain."[18]

2. Not enough study has been devoted to why development films fail to "contribute vitally to organic progress." We need more films of the type produced in the last decade by the National Film Board of Canada, such as *The Head Men* (which compares village chiefs in Brazil, Nigeria, and Canada), *You Don't Back Down* (a report of a two-year study by a young Canadian doctor in a village of Eastern Nigeria), and *The Stage to Three* (which contrasts leading theatrical personages of Greece, Thailand, and Canada.)[19]

Tulsi Bhatia Saral of the Institute of Communications Research, the University of Illinois, commenting on the host of weaker efforts, declares,

> development agencies—governmental, nongovernmental, national, international—have been helping finance their large-scale production and distribution in the remotest part of the world—wishfully thinking that once the people come out of their shells and expose themselves to these wonderful vehicles of opinion, attitude, and behavior-change, they will feel inspired to change their outlook, if not their living habits, and the task of development will be that much easier. To our great disappointment, however, the miracle does not happen.[20]

3. The developing nations are so caught up in rhetoric about communications technology that key Western leaders translate all worldly needs in terms of their own ambitions, and those ambitions by-pass objectives so necessary to progress in less developed countries. Propaganda becomes a mirror image of the developed West. Robert W. Sarnoff, chairman and president of the Radio Corporation of America, worries about the "social grasp" of communications and about communications satellites in particular. He warns that

If this new device is to realize its full potential, the nations of the world must come together to agree on matters of frequency, rates, copyrights, avoidance of interference, and freedom of access to the system's facilities.[21]

Such contemplation reveals all too dramatically the basic propaganda chasm of our times! The man in love with the idea of the machine is distinct from the man who desperately needs the ideas that are themselves the machines of progress.

NOTES

1. R. W. Hesselbacher, "An Evaluation of Television Broadcast Satellite Systems," *American Institute of Aeronautics and Astronautics* (AIAA Paper 68-1061, October 1968) 11 pp; William K. Stevens, "TV By Satellites Stirs New Debate," *The New York Times,* October 27, 1968; *Modern Communications and Foreign Policy,* Report No. 5, together with Part 10 of the Hearings, Committee on Foreign Affairs, Subcommittee on International Organizations and Movements, House of Representatives (Washington, D.C., April 30, 1967). Note the speech of Mr. P. A. Bissonette, Canadian delegate to the UN Outer Space Committee, September 3, 1970, "International Cooperation in Outer Space," in *External Affairs,* monthly bulletin of the Department of External Affairs, Canada 22, 10 (October, 1970), pp. 364–367.

2. Acting as manager for the space segment is the representative of the United States, The *Communications Satellite* Corporation (Comsat). It is the largest shareholder. Planned for 1971 and beyond is the Intelsat IV series of synchronous orbit satellites, each of which will contain at least five thousand voice grade circuits, or up to twelve television channels. It is hoped that the developing countries will be important beneficiaries. Before the era of satellites, Asia could not communicate directly with Africa and Latin America. At present the concentration of international communications is almost entirely in the latitude of United States-Europe-Japan. The less developed nations which joined Intelsat were assigned very little management control because each member is given voting strength according to a quota system geared to estimates made of its share of international telephone traffic. Their hopes are based on international needs and not organizational control.

3. Lindsay Patterson, "In Movies, Whitey Is Still King," *The New York Times,* December 13, 1970.

4. John D. Montgomery, "The Challenge of Change," *International Development Review* 9, 1 (March, 1967), p. 3.

5. Herbert I. Schiller, "National Development Requires Some Social Distance," *The Antioch Review* 29, 1 (Spring, 1967), pp. 63–67. Also, see his "The U.S. Hard Sell," *The Nation* (December 5, 1966), pp. 609–612.

6. Richard R. Eagen, "Relation of Communication Growth to National Political Systems in the Less Developed Countries," *Journalism Quarterly* 41, 1 (Winter, 1964), pp. 87–94.

7. Eugene R. Black, "Can the Underdeveloped Countries Catch Up?" *Journal of International Affairs* 16, 2 (1962), pp. 192–202; also, Ithiel de Sola Pool, "Communications and Development," in Myron Weiner, ed., *Modernization: The Dynamics of Growth* (New York: Basic Books, 1966); also, Jerome S. Bruner, "Educational Assistance for Developing Nations," in W. Y. Elliot, ed., *Education and Training for the Developing Nations* (New York: Frederick A. Praeger, 1966).

8. See Frederick C. Barghoorn, *Soviet Propaganda* (Princeton: Princeton University Press, 1964), especially chs. 7 and 8; Thomas H. Guback, *The International Film Industry* (Bloom-

ington: Indiana University Press, 1969); B. S. Murty, *Propaganda and World Public Order* (New Haven: Yale University Press, 1968); Arthur S. Hoffman, ed., *International Communication and the New Diplomacy* (Bloomington: Indiana University Press, 1968); Heinz-Dietrich Fischer and John C. Merrill, eds., *International Communication* (New York: Hastings House, 1970); *The Future of United States Public Diplomacy*, Report No. 6, together with Part 11 of the Hearings, Subcommittee on International Organizations and Movements, Committee on Foreign Affairs, House of Representatives (Washington, D.C.: U.S. Government Printing Office, 1969).

9.   For the 1955-1969 period, see draft of Murray G. Lawson (USIA historian) et al., *The United States Information Agency During the Johnson Administration, 1963-1968* (Washington: USIA, 1968), pp. 123-138. For policy objectives and worldwide themes, see United States Information Agency, *The Agency in Brief, 1969* (Washington, D.C.: USIA, 1969), p. 3; and "Fact Sheet" (USIA, 1969). See also annual reports such as *United States Information Agency, 29th Review of Operations, July-December 1967* (Washington, D.C.: U.S. Government Printing Office, 1968); and *United States Information Agency 28th Report to Congress, January-June 1967* (USIA, 1967).

10.   Letter to Bernard Rubin from D. Willcocks, Deputy Director, Policy and Reference Division, British Information Services, New York, N.Y., dated November 24, 1970.

11.   Letter from P. W. Coldham, Head of Overseas Distribution, Films and Television Division, Central Office of Information, London, England, dated December 4, 1970.

12.   Letter, Willcocks, op. cit.

13.   The following sources were utilized in the discussion of West German activities: Letters to the author from Dr. Johannsen, *Press- Und Informationsamt Der Bundesregierung*, Bonn, Federal Republic, dated October 16, 1970, and December 8, 1970; letter from Wilhelm Hondrich, *Zweites Deutsches Fernsehen*, Mainz, Federal Republic, dated January 16, 1971; letter from Dr. Krause-Brewer, *Trans-Tel*, Cologne, Federal Republic; letter from Christian v. Chmielewski, Direktor des Kulturellen Programms, *Deutsche Welle*, Cologne, Federal Republic, dated November 16, 1970.

14.   Letter to author from Alain Chaillous, Director, Press and Information Service, Embassy of France, New York City, dated January 26, 1971. Also, from same source, specially prepared document, 2 pp., "La Production des Films et des Programmes de Télévision Réalisés par le Gouvernment Français a l'Intention des Pays Étrangers." Also, see "Unesco: Global Overview of Film Situation," in Fischer and Merrill, eds., op. cit., p. 402.

15.   See Paul J. Deutschmann, Huber Ellingsworth, and John T. McNelly, *Communication and Social Change in Latin America* (New York: Frederick A. Praeger, 1968), p. 79.

16.   Max F. Millikan and Stephen White, "TV and Emerging Nations," *Television Quarterly* 7, 2 (Spring, 1968), p. 31.

17.   Robin Day, "Troubled Reflections of a TV Journalist," *Encounter* 34, 5 (May, 1970).

18.   Eric Sevareid, "Address to the Massachusetts House of Representatives" (January 24, 1967), House No. 4408, Commonwealth of Massachusetts. Also see, "How Influential Is TV News?" *Columbia Journalism Review* 9, 2 (Summer, 1970), pp. 19-28; Sir William Haley, "Where TV News Fails," *Columbia Journalism Review* 9, 1 (Spring, 1970), pp. 7-11

19.   Jean Marie Ackermann, "Small Actions and Big Words," *International Development Review* 8, 4 (December, 1966), pp. 33-39.

20.   Tulsi Bhatia Saral, "Evaluating Films For Development," in ibid., pp. 39-41.

21.   Robert W. Sarnoff, "Proposal For a Global Common Market of Communications," *Communications News* 7, 4 (April, 1970), p. 8.

Propaganda Through the Printed Media in the Developing Countries*

Y. V. LAKSHMANA RAO

Y. V. LAKSHMANA RAO holds a doctorate from the University of Minnesota. He is Secretary-General of the Asian Mass Communication Research and Information Centre, with headquarters in Singapore. He has served as Senior Specialist at the East-West Center, Honolulu, 1969 to 1970; Program Specialist, Unesco, Paris, 1964 to 1969; Deputy Director, Press Institute of India, 1963 to 1964; Research Fellow, Institute for Communication Research, Stanford University, 1961 to 1963; and news-paperman and broadcaster in New Delhi, India, 1947 to 1957. Among his publications are Communication and Development and The Practice of Mass Communication: Some Lessons from Research.

With the best of intentions, the United Nations Conference on Freedom of Information in 1948 called freedom of information "one of the basic freedoms," and added that free and adequate information was "the touchstone of all the freedoms to which the United Nations is dedicated." Working on

* Reprinted from "Propaganda Through the Printed Media in the Developing Countries," by Y. V. Lakshmana Rao in volume no. 398 of The Annals of The American Academy of Political and Social Science. Copyright 1971, by The American Academy of Political and Social Science.

this premise and with this authority, one of its specialized agencies (Unesco) established agreements to facilitate the free flow of information around the world. Serious thinkers everywhere went along with the idea because in itself it was worth aspiring for.

Reflecting almost to a word Unesco's own preamble, which states that "since wars begin in the minds of men, it is in the minds of men that the defenses of peace must be constructed," Lester Markel wrote in *The New York Times* in 1960 that we

cannot have understanding—and thus peace—among the peoples of the world unless they have better, truer information about one another.[1]

Always true to his profession, Markel also insisted that the main avenue for such information is the newspaper.

It is common knowledge, however, that not all newspapers—or other printed media—are like the one Markel works for! But many of the others also circulate internationally; and they carry a great deal of entertainment and triviality which by itself may not be entirely bad, but it does provide an "image" of the country or the society which it represents. It will, therefore, be apparent that in the relatively one-way flow of information which we shall discuss, it is not merely the receiver that may stand to be affected—one way or another—but also the sender.

Within the context of the free flow of information, and especially at a time when communication is not only fast but also seemingly gluttonous, certain questions must occur frequently to political leaders, communication scholars, and practitioners, as well as to the thinking public. How much of the news, information, and other content is propagandistic? In what direction and in what quantities is it flowing? How is it being received? What are some of the expected, and unexpected, repercussions of such international informational intercourse? Is some of this material really subversive?

Obviously, all these questions cannot be answered without systematic research. There has, so far, been very little such research, especially in the developing countries. The discussion here will be largely confined to the printed media, to the extent that these can be separated from the electronic and other media, including human channels of communication.

ONE-WAY FLOW

The general assumption behind this discussion is that the flow of information in the developing countries is largely one-way and that the leadership is becoming increasingly conscious of this process and is beginning to take a closer look, not always based on research findings or even a detached outlook, but with emotion, with concern, and frequently with fear. At least to some extent, the leaders may be justified.

Their concern and fear have more to do with the printed media, because the electronic media are invariably in their own hands while the press and the publication of magazines and books are in private hands, and it is more difficult to control them. It is not merely political considerations that are making the leaders wary of "imported" news, information, and entertainment; it is also economic, social, and cultural considerations.

In his preface to a book on the United States Information Agency, Robert E. Elder says

Americans distrust propaganda—especially government propaganda—yet they have allowed their government to fashion a powerful propaganda machine. This machine, which costs taxpayers about $170 million a year, is designed to convince people in the rest of the world that the United States policies and actions are helpful to them, or at least not harmful to their basic interest.[2]

Normally it is in this sense that the word *propaganda* has been used. And when used in this sense it is distrusted not only by Americans but by everybody elsewhere.

It is common, in most discussions on "international propaganda," to confine oneself to material put out deliberately for the purpose of convincing somebody about something. But it seems to be more realistic, within the context of the obvious communication "explosion" which has taken place and within the context of the tremendous increase in international intercourse, to deal with this subject in a much broader fashion and include perhaps all communication.

Most discussions on international propaganda, through the printed media or otherwise, also concern themselves almost exclusively with governmental propaganda or propaganda material with a distinct political bias. Only recently has it occurred to governments as well as to the general public that propaganda, insidious by its very nature (in their view), can seriously affect social, cultural, and economic thinking and actions as well, and that a political motive may or may not be the guiding force behind many of the actions in the social, cultural, and economic spheres. Whether or not such a feeling and such an argument have any basis in fact, the interrelationship between political, social, and economic phenomena cannot by itself be denied.

INFLUENCING CONDUCT

Bartlett has said,

Practically everybody agrees that propaganda must be defined by reference to
its aims. Those aims can, in fact, be stated simply. Propaganda is an attempt to
influence opinion and conduct—especially social opinion and conduct—in such a
manner that the persons who adopt the opinions and behaviour indicated do so
without themselves making any definite search for reasons.[3]

As leaders of unsophisticated and relatively less educated masses, the
heads of the developing countries are worried about the effects of
propaganda—whether or not the material made available is propaganda
in its strictest connotation and whether or not it has, in fact, any definite aims at all.

    I define propaganda much more broadly, in the sense of Bruce
L. Smith, who says that

present-day theory considers propaganda a special case of the theory of communication in general, which in turn has increasingly been treated as a sub-
division of the general theory of social systems.

The range of possible behavior studied includes that of the individual
and that of large interest and regional groups, which may encompass
the world as a whole.

    Smith goes on to say:

Hence, modern theory views the current state of the world's social system as
highly polycentric: the cultural patterns, and hence the economic patterns and
political patterns, of its component sub-systems are at once highly interdepend-
ent and highly diverse and often appear more or less incompatible. Yet the set
of sub-systems as a whole shows powerful though slow moving tendencies to
evolve, convulsively, toward global community.[4]

It is this aspect of the flow of information, and of largely unin-
tentioned growth of uniformity, perhaps, which Marshall McLuhan
refers to as "macroscopic gesticulation." The fear of the leaders in
the developing countries is a real fear. Whether or not this is based on
a "true" appreciation of the global communication situation is not th
point. That such fear exists, and therefore might return these countries to informational isolation, is a subject worth studying.

    For such a purpose, it is necessary to include all kinds of propa-
ganda, black and white. One simple reason for this—a very practical
one—is that during a no-war/no-peace time such as the one in which
we are living, the techniques of propaganda and of persuasion have
become so sophisticated that it is difficult to distinguish between

strictly propagandistic material, in the traditional sense in which the word has been used, and the less blatant type. In commercial circles the dichotomy would be the "hard sell" and the "soft sell."

RECEIVER'S PERSPECTIVE

It seems necessary, too, to look at persuasive communication more from the point of view of the receiver than the sender. It is the receiver who not only is expected to react but perhaps actually does. Therefore, if he is going to look at a given subject as perhaps being propagandistic, then he is going to deal with it against the background of such a premise. It has been said that if a person defines a given situation as being real, it is real to him in its consequences. We are therefore concerned here with such reality, regardless of whether an "objective" observer defines it as such or not. This is also an avenue for research which has not so far been tackled systematically in the international arena except insofar as cross-national "images" are concerned.

The speed with which communication can take place today has made it possible for any active propaganda to have some effect in large parts of the world. Similarly, any item of news or information also has a way of reaching large numbers of people in widespread areas of the world.

The printed media, and other media as well, carry three broad types of persuasive content. All of these may not fall readily into any strict definition of propaganda. However, as we have already indicated, the very fact that they can be persuasive makes them suspect in the eyes of a sensitive audience. This audience in the developing countries is not the mass of the people, whose interest in such matters is extremely limited in any case, but the leaders in these countries.

The three types of persuasive content of printed media have been delineated as: (1) advertisement; (2) intentional advocacy—editorials, editorial cartoons, signed columns, and interpretive articles intended to cause the reader to reach a conclusion; (3) content which is intended primarily as entertainment or information but of which persuasion may be a by-product.

Peterson, Jensen, and Rivers, among many others, have come to the conclusion that

the informational content of the media is probably more influential on public opinion than the avowedly persuasive. That is, news stories may be a greater force in shaping public attitudes than editorials and political columns.[5]

This is why, as the techniques of propaganda have been sharpened, as professional information specialists have learned from the conclusions of behavioral scientists, and as public relations personnel have been increasingly recruited to advise individuals and institutions there has been a greater effort made to "plant" seemingly informational items in newspapers and magazines. Similarly, persuasion has been carried on not only by what is said or printed but, even more important, by what is withheld. The recent furor over the Pentagon Papers is a case in point.

In his book on the elite press, Merrill quotes James Reston:

We have no right to twist the mass of facts into forms which are exciting but misleading; to take out of it that portion that conforms to our prejudices, to preserve the shocking or amusing, and to leave out the dreary but important qualifications which are necessary to essential truth.[6]

Merrill adds that the popular press "calls the people of the world to play. It does not call them to think, to assess, to become concerned, involved, or empathic."[7] This is what the leadership in the developing countries wants the public to do—to be concerned, to become involved in the national effort toward social change, and to think.

Perhaps the leaders want the public to think as they do and perhaps this is not the "correct" way. But the fact remains that the leaders are getting terribly wary. And it is this aspect of the situation which must cause concern to those who argue for a free flow of information. It is not enough to point a finger at those who would like to place barriers in the way of such free flow; it is also important that those who are better endowed with the means to fill the channels of communication, stop and endeavor to get some idea of the reactions of the receiving countries. It is up to the scholars of international communication to investigate the causes of the reactions and come up with constructive suggestions, which then need to be fed to those who are clogging those channels now with "unhealthy" and perhaps unnecessary information. It would be far better if some self-control were exercised now, for later it may be too late because such control would by then have come from outside.

SOCIAL CHANGE

It is possible for scholars to view more accurately such a phenomenon, and the interrelatedness of human thought and behavior, if they look at these from the point of view of the developing countries. Such communities, being in the process of bringing about quick and easy social, economic, and political change, necessarily expose themselves to a great deal of international contact arising from international assistance and international expertise.

While benefiting from such contacts and discourse, these communities have also, with varying degrees of sophistication, become aware of the possibilities for international propaganda—using the term in its "evil" connotation. Such awareness has had its concomitant reactions, often illogical and even irrational and of a virulent kind.

The power game can be played by more than one. The developing countries have increasingly become conscious of this. And much of this consciousness has resulted from communication with and from the more advanced countries, especially those which have highly developed media networks and the resources to enlarge these networks outside their national boundaries, whether through satellites, cables, or distribution facilities for printed material. For a long time, it was considered that free flow of information is of itself a good thing. The quantity or quality of such information was to be determined by the "rational" potential receiver. However, the economics of the situation is such that most of this free flow of information has been moving in only one direction—from the developed countries to the developing.

The fear in the developing countries is not only that the information may be biased but also that the entertainment content and the triviality may have an effect on their societies which may not be in consonance with the kinds of change their leaders are striving for, in the social, economic, cultural, and political spheres. The implication of this for international propaganda seems to be fairly clear. Suspicion feeds on suspicion and a point is soon reached where all non-indigenous influences, direct and indirect, are taboo. Whether the world is moving in that direction, back to square one, is a moot point. It cannot be denied, however, that there are signs that it indeed is. One needs only to live and work in a developing country to feel such a danger.

The developing countries, generally speaking, are in a dilemma. Their leaders, however conscientious at their best and however illogically sensitive and chauvinistic at their worst, do recognize the fact that they cannot develop their countries without some international contact and discourse. They also recognize that for any development to take place, the communication facilities have to be expanded all the way from microwave links to teleprinter circuits to newsprint.

This process of mass media development, once initiated for national purposes, begins to develop a momentum of its own. Apart from an increase in the number of radio receivers, television sets, and films, there is also an increase in the number and circulation of newspapers, magazines, books, and the like. Meanwhile, educational development increases the demand for reading material. It also expands the horizon of the reading public. To meet this demand, the printed media are now forced to fill more and more space and to cater to the wider interests of their readers. To do this, just as the broadcasting networks import old movies and documentaries produced by major film companies and major U.S. broadcasting networks, newspapers and magazines are forced to subscribe to syndicated feature services, international news agencies, and so on. It is not uncommon to see frequent and spacious spreads on hot pants and mini-skirts in the newspapers and magazines of sari-wearing India or sarong-wearing Malaysia!

Does this constitute international propaganda? Perhaps not. Maybe it is easier to talk of international propaganda only in terms of the publications of the U.S. Information Agency or of the news reports and feature articles coming from TASS. However, it seems impossible to disregard the effects of material which is not blatantly propagandistic or political. This is the dilemma of the developing countries. Where does one draw the line? Is it, in fact, practical or feasible to want to have one's cake and eat it, too?

A CASE IN POINT

A clear-cut answer to this question was given recently by the Prime Minister of Singapore in a talk to the general assembly of the International Press Institute in Helsinki. Mr. Lee Kuan Yew said; "The underdeveloped have no choice. Whatever the side effects of importing Western science and technology, not to do so will be worse." Looking at it from the point of view of the "exporters," Mr. Lee had this to say:

Few viewers and readers of the mass media in new countries know of the tormer amongst Western intellectuals. Some Americans question where their bureaucratised science and technology, their military/industrial complex, are leading them

Singapore, a small, multiracial city state, has in the last decade made a deliberate choice, forced by the very nature of its small urban population and entrepôt trade, to modernize. While accepting the need rapidly to model itself in the image of an affluent, developed state, it now finds itself, midway in this thrust, challenged by some of the attendant evils of such a speedy process.

"Fortunately, we have not gotten to the stage of mod style, communal living, drugs, and escapism," Mr. Lee mused. The Prime

Minister also wondered aloud whether the mass media could affect a people to the extent that over a sustained period they determine not only social behavior but also political action:

Censorship can only partially cut off this influence. It is more crucial that the local production of films and publication of newspapers should not be surreptitiously captured by their proxies.[9]

The latter reference was to foreign financiers.

Although in most new countries radio and television are controlled by the state, Mr. Lee felt that the problem was that the economics of operation make it necessary to buy foreign programs. At their best, he said, these programs can entertain without offending good taste. At their worst, they can undo all that is being inculcated in the schools and universities. The newspapers, even if nationalized, carry reports from the well-organized worldwide news agencies of the West. There is also a whole range of American and British-language magazines and journals to cater to all tastes. And if people cannot afford them, USIS and the British Information Services provide ample facilities.

The fear of the leaders in the developing countries regarding the one-way flow of information through the print media is not based entirely on hearsay. The concern that most of the news comes from the four big international wire services and that much of the feature material comes also from internationally syndicated services is a real one.

Although the Singapore Prime Minister's feelings and fears, especially about the media, may be but one man's, there are increasing indications that they are widely shared in many of the developing countries—and to some extent even perhaps in the developed countries.

The case of *The New York Times* and the Pentagon Papers may perhaps be looked upon as a national issue, but in these days of international communication it does have its international implications as well. And these implications are not confined to the possible "image" which they may project of America abroad. Dwight D. Eisenhower is reputed to have said: "I believe the United States is strong enough to expose to the world its differing viewpoints."[10] That these viewpoints range in subject matter from freedom of the press to war and peace or to drugs and hippies is common knowledge; and Americans are as concerned about the international publicity for such matters as the leaders in the developing countries are concerned about its implications for their own national plans and programs, values and beliefs.

THE PRINT MEDIA

Insofar as the printed media in the developing countries are concerned there are certain specific factors which one can discuss as leading to an international intercourse which is neither planned nor propagated deliberately. It is difficult, in the absence of any systematic study, to point out how much of this international intercourse is "propaganda" and how much is nonpersuasive content affecting thought and behavior. To the extent that in many of these countries a relatively free press does exist and that outright censorship does not exist, there is scope for a considerable amount of international flow of information. But there are other factors within the structure of the printed media themselves which lead to a situation where a great deal of non-indigenous material comes in. These factors are worthy of consideration.

The post-colonial era left a number of newspapers in the hands of foreign investors and of expatriate editors and editorial staff who gained their experience during the colonial period. We are not now dealing with those newspapers which printed surreptitiously and perhaps provoked people into rebellion or some other manifestation of an anti-colonial nature leading thereby to independence. We are talking only about those newspapers which were economically viable and which have continued to publish after the countries gained independence. The editorial staffs of these papers have continued, generally speaking, as the "Westerners" did. They have continued to belong to an elite group which is invariably far removed from the mass of the people; they have continued, by and large, to talk a certain "language"—which is usually the language of *The Times* of London or the *Daily News* or the *Daily Express*. These have been the newspapers which the average journalist in the developing countries still tries to emulate, whether or not he has the benefit of the audience of, say, *The New York Times*. This has led to a certain professional conformity which is international. It has also limited their appeal, viewed in the context of communities where broad-based governments and political structures are now generally the rule. This has left the newspapers catering only to a small minority, however important that minority may be in the decision-making process.

Another factor leading to such conformity is both economic and professional in nature: the presence of the big international news agencies, and in many ways their stranglehold on the newspapers of the developing countries. It is professional because of the quality and the convenience which these agencies provide; it is economic because most of the newspapers cannot afford to have correspondents in the major news centers of the world. An additional reason is that many of the developing countries cannot afford to have national news agencies of any reasonable size; and even where these exist, such agencies in turn have to subscribe to one or more of the international agencies for their inflow of world news.

The pressure toward "objectivity" and accuracy to satisfy a mixed clientele—including governments, commerce, and industry, as well as news media of varying political beliefs—has already led to conformity among the newspapers in the industrially advanced countries, where it is increasingly common to have only one newspaper in each town. Although not quite to the same extent, a similar situation seems to be developing in other parts of the world. In the absence of human and material resources to support competing newspapers, news agencies, or feature services, the content of newspapers is becoming increasingly standardized.

SPECIALIZED AUDIENCES

In the case of magazines, however, the situation is perhaps slightly better, but only slightly. While these publishers do aim at more specialized audiences—youth, women, the educated elite, the business community, and so on—even they are finding it more convenient and cheaper either to subscribe to syndicated material from abroad or to buy regional rights to publication of new books in serialized form.

Even where book publishing is concerned, it is becoming increasingly common for publishing firms to establish similar relationships with publishers abroad. One need only to go into a book shop or a stationery shop in a developing country to find this uniformity of taste (innate or developed) extending to such things as posters and phonograph records.

Among the widely circulated magazines, *Time, Newsweek, Life* and the *Reader's Digest* come immediately to mind as those which have special editions for specific regions, with local advertising and well-organized distribution systems. Newspapers like the international edition of the *Herald Tribune,* the Sunday *New York Times,* or the weekly English edition of *Le Monde,* reach the far corners of the earth within a day or two of publication. And books, whether they be *The Death of a President, The Ugly American,* or *Candy,* are to be found on the bookshelves of the rest of the world at almost the same time as they reach the homes of Americans.

It is obvious, therefore, that, for good or bad, international intercourse made possible through the ever-expanding channels of communication has indeed led to a certain amount of commonness and uniformity through the printed media, even as it has led to the same result through the non-print media.

One must note, however, that insofar as the developing countries are concerned, this commonness and uniformity, internationally speaking, have so far been generally confined to small minorities—minorities which are well educated and relatively high up in the socio economic scale. It is only a matter of time before these tastes, these values and beliefs, percolate downward and begin to affect the major ities. This will happen as intra-national communication networks begin to function as effectively as the international channels perform today. The tragedy in many of the developing countries is that it is easier, in both a practical and a psychological sense, for a person in a capital city to communicate with London or Paris or New York or Moscow than with someone in a smaller town or rural community in his own country.

The recognition of this phenomenon in the developing countries has been fairly recent. Fears are being expressed openly by the leaders in these countries that the process has already gone so far that it cannot be reversed. The question now is: should efforts be made in fact to reverse it, or is it the inevitable result of development and modernization? After all, these are, in most cases, the same leaders who only a few years ago not only recognized the need for international intercourse but also insisted upon it. The price, if indee it is a price, had to be paid. If pressures are growing for a reversal of the process, these pressures are being exerted, by and large, by the senior citizens, to whom such change has perhaps been too rapid for adjustment and too intense for emotional comfort. Where such a feel ing of going too far has been felt by the leaders themselves, it is very political in nature, and only social and cultural to a lesser degree. Foreign investment, welcomed in other fields, has been seen as a threat—a political threat—when it impinges upon the media. There has been a growing concern about expatriates owning and/or operating the media, for fear that public sentiment may be swayed in favor of political ideologies repugnant to the basic tenets of the present leaders.

One of the more cogent arguments of the leaders of developing countries today is that political stability is perhaps more important than political philosophy—and especially the freedoms that go with it—and that a country cannot afford the luxury of a clash of ideas or a clash of interests while it is dealing with the more fundamental problems of food and shelter.

As far as the printed media are concerned, the pressure is towar more conformity—not conformity with international standards or international symbols but with national aspirations, with national needs and national priorities, and therefore with national governments. The printed media therefore are standing today amid a great deal of talk about international intercourse, and are on the brink of disaster, for the very reason that in their shortsighted quest for internationalism—admittedly propounded by their own national leadership at an earlier stage—they are paying the price for neglecting their own national roles.

It has been said repeatedly in the literature of communication that a country's media networks and media content are but a reflection of the country's own structure, its own values, beliefs, and aspirations, and its own stage of development. To the extent that the printed media are in the throes of intellectual ferment, they do reflect the mood of their countries. The media as producers have been found wanting; the media as importers have been shortsighted. By importing material to satisfy their own immediate needs and by not making efforts meanwhile to develop their own production capacities, they are in danger of neither producing nor being allowed to import further.

The implication of such a state of affairs, viewed from an international point of view, propagandistic or otherwise, is frightening. This discussion has dealt with the problem deliberately and almost exclusively from the point of view of the developing countries because the more developed countries have had such intercourse for a long time and have built their own safeguards and their own forms of attack. The United States and the Soviet Union, for example, have worked out a fairly convenient way of exchanging publications, such as *America Illustrated* and *Soviet Life.* The number of copies, the content, and the like, are all fairly well standardized. No overtly propagandistic material is permitted, but each knows what type of content may subtly influence the readers.

The developing countries are new at this game. But they are beginning to learn the rules and it would be a great shame if, because of their own lack of experience and lack of foresight, they were to stop playing the game altogether. Propaganda used in its broadest and healthiest connotation can add greatly to a society's education and experience. The political aspects of it can perhaps be controlled if all parties concerned can achieve some kind of understanding in a spirit of give and take. But to lose sight of the social and cultural advantages accruing from international exchange of information, and so to reject them, is tantamount to throwing out the baby with the bath water.

In his oft-quoted discussion on *Political Propaganda,* Bartlett said as long ago as 1940 that

today propaganda is in the air and on it. There is no escaping from its insistent voice. Even were it only half as effective as it is often claimed to be its power would be enormous. . . . It is at work to fashion the education of the child, the ambitions of youth, the activities of the prime of life, and it pursues the aged to the grave.[11]

It is this fear of propaganda, right or wrong, that the leadership in the developing countries shares.

NOTES

1.   Quoted in John C. Merrill, *The Elite Press* (New York: Pitman Publishing Corporation, 1968), p. 5.

2.   Robert E. Elder, *The Information Machine* (Syracuse: Syracuse University Press, 1968), p. vii.

3.   F. C. Bartlett, "The Aims of Political Propaganda," in Katz et al., eds., *Public Opinion and Propaganda* (New York: Holt, Rinehart and Winston, 1954), p. 464.

4.   *International Encyclopedia of the Social Sciences,* s.v. "propaganda."

5.   Theodore Peterson et al., *The Mass Media and Modern Society* (Holt, Rinehart and Winston, 1965), p. 167.

6.   Merrill, op. cit., p. 5.

7.   Ibid, pp. 5–6.

8.   As quoted in *The Manila Chronicle,* June 11, 1971.

9.   Ibid.

10. Quoted by Frank Stanton, President of the Columbia Broadcasting System, in an address to the International Radio and Television Society, New York, November 25, 1969.

11. F. C. Bartlett, op. cit., p. 463.

The International Commercialization of Broadcasting *

HERBERT I. SCHILLER

HERBERT I. SCHILLER is Professor of Communication
of the Third College, University of California, San Diego.
He was formerly editor of the Quarterly Review of Economics and Business. His numerous articles and reviews
have appeared in leading periodicals. He is the author of
Mass Communications and American Empire and The
Mind Managers.

The United States communications
presence overseas extends far beyond the facilities owned, the exports, and the licensing agreements secured by major American
broadcasting companies and electronics equipment manufacturers,
considerable as these are. Equally, if not more important, is the
spread of the American system, the commercial model of communications, to the international arena. How readily a large and growing
part of the world community has succumbed to communications
arrangements patterned after the United States style and how these
developments have been engineered is a story of relatively current
vintage.

The electronics revolution that has transformed communications

*Reprinted from Herbert I. Schiller, *Mass Communications and American Empire* (New
York: A. M. Kelley, Publishers, 1969), pp. 93–107. Used by permission of the publisher
and the author.

since the first world war also has provided the instrumentation of saturation advertising. Radio and television, almost from their inception in the United States were preempted to fulfill the sales objectives of the business community. Though cautioned in the 1920's by Herbert Hoover not to disfigure the exciting potential of the new natural resource that had been discovered, commerce unhesitatingly turned radio into its untiring pitchman.

Twenty years ago, against the advice and judgment of those who wanted to experiment carefully with the new medium and to discover its most fruitful capabilities, television prematurely was hurried into the economy by impatient equipment manufacturers and broadcasting networks, eager to sell sets and screen time.[1] To no one's surprise, television followed closely in radio's commercial footsteps.

THE GLOBAL COMMERCIALIZATION OF COMMUNICATIONS SYSTEMS

In the pre-television era, the United States stood alone amongst advanced industrialized nations in having its radio broadcasting unabashedly commercial. In no other society did advertisers pay the bill and direct the destinies of the medium so completely. State broadcasting authorities in Europe were the rule and the American arrangement was the exception.

With the advent of television, but not because of it, many national broadcasting structures adopted one or another variants of the American style. Dizard, author of *Television: A World View,* has written about this shift:

Television has developed primarily as a commercial medium. This was to be expected in the United States and a few other countries, notably in Latin America where broadcasting was traditionally a private venture. Elsewhere, however, broadcasting was a state monopoly without commercial connections. Theoretically, television should have followed in the established pattern; significantly it did not. . . . At present, television systems in over fifty countries are controlled, in whole or in part, by private interests under state supervision. Commercial advertising is carried by all but a handful of the world's ninety-five television systems.[2]

For the new countries the emerging pattern is the same. Dizard notes "the virtual domination of local television in developing nations by commercial interest."[3] Unesco reports the same finding. A 1963 study concludes, after presenting evidence that television has been less subject to state control than radio that "this might seem to show that the tendency towards commercial operation is becoming more accentuated in television services than in radio broadcasting."[4]

Even strong, industrialized nations have been forced to modify their longtime stabilized broadcasting services and accept commercial operations. Britain yielded in 1954. France teetering on the edge of advertising-sponsored support for years has just moved across the line. The Russians, a special case to be sure, advertise in American newspapers their willingness to accept commercial material over their state-owned TV system.[5]

What has powered this almost universal push toward commercialization in the electronic communications media? Its advocates claim that commercial broadcasting is the most satisfactory method of meeting the financial and programmatic needs of the new media. Dizard, for instance, asserts that "The change [to commercialization] confirmed the effectiveness of American-style broadcasting both as a revenue producer and as a highly acceptable form of entertainment and persuasion."[6]

The revenue-producing capabilities of commercial broadcasting cannot be disputed. The acceptability of the entertainment offered is another matter that will be considered further along. But neither reason faintly suggests the more fundamental forces that are operating. *Nothing less than the viability of the American industrial economy itself is involved in the movement toward international commercialization of broadcasting.* The private yet managed economy depends on advertising. Remove the excitation and the manipulation of consumer demand and industrial slowdown threatens. *Broadcasting* magazine puts it this way: "In this country, where production capacity exceeds consumer demand, advertising has become more than an economic force—it is an influence on our quality of life."[7]

The continuing and pressing requirements of United States manufacturers to reach annually higher output levels to sustain and increase profit margins activate the process that is relentlessly enveloping electronic (and other) communications in a sheath of commercialization. What happens, of course, is a continuing interaction. The direct intrusion of American influence catalyzes developments in the affected nations. Also, those countries with similar industrial structures and organization feel corresponding, if at first weaker, impulses themselves in the same direction.

The international dynamics resulting from the explosive force of private enterprise industrialism's market requirements find expression in ordinary trade accounts. *Television Magazine,* for instance, describes the interconnections between the advertising, manufacturing and broadcasting industries:

About 1959 a gentle curve representing the expansion of American advertising agencies overseas started an abrupt climb which hasn't yet levelled off. . . .The growth of television abroad had something to do with this upsurge, since the

head-start American agencies had in dealing with the medium commercially has
given them a highly exportable know-how. But television wasn't the prime mover
That role belongs to the client: The American consumer goods industry.

The magazine explained this process with a simple illustration:

Take a giant corporation like Proctor and Gamble with sales over $2 billion a
year. Its position on the open market is based partly on the corporation's growth
rate. But to add, say, 10% in sales each year becomes increasingly difficult when
already over the two billion mark. *Where do you find that additional $200 mil-
lion? The answer, for more and more American corporations, is overseas.*[8]

American companies have been crossing the oceans regularly,
either through direct acquisition or new plant expansion or leasing
arrangements or combinations thereof. United States private direct
investments in manufacturing across the globe have spurted in the
twenty-four years beginning in 1943, from $2,276 millions to $22,05
millions. In this period in Western Europe alone, manufacturing investments have increased from $879 millions to $8,879 millions. To
assist in marketing the output of their expanding foreign facilities,
U.S. advertising agencies have been accompanying the industrial
plants overseas. McCann-Erickson has 70 offices employing 4,619
persons in 37 countries. J. Walter Thompson, "the grand-daddy of
international operations," has 1,110 people employed in its key London office alone. England has 21 American-associated ad agencies,
West Germany has 20 and France 12. In Latin America, Brazil has
15 American ad agencies and Canada has more U.S. agencies than
any other nation. Even the developing world has begun to be pene-
trated. "Three enterprising U.S. agencies have tackled the huge market of India. . . . [and] Africa, too, may be part of a future wave of
agency expansion overseas."[9]

The advertising agencies rely on the communications media to
open markets for their patrons—the American and Western European
consumer goods producers. The state-controlled broadcasting structures which resist commercialization are under the continuous siege
of the ad-men and their cohorts in public relations and general image
promotion.

Once the privately-directed manufacturing enterprises have begu
their goods production, all energies are concentrated on securing the
public's ever-widening acceptance of the outpouring commodity
streams. The insistence of powerful American sellers, temporarily
allied with their local counterparts, on obtaining advertising outlets
abroad is overwhelming state broadcasting authorities, one after
another. The successful campaign to introduce commercial television
in England was largely a matter of industry ad-men manipulating

complex political wires. The former director of the BBC's television explained with some understatement, what happened in Britain:

... there was an unusually strong demand from large sections of British industry in the early nineteen fifties for more opportunities for advertising their goods. Wartime restrictions especially on paper had only recently been lifted, and a real boom in consumer goods was developing, but industry felt that there were insufficient opportunities for telling the public about the large range of new goods which were becoming available. Television was obviously an excellent medium for this, and industry was not averse to harnessing the television horse to the industrial chariot.[10]

Raymond Williams, also generalizing from the British experience, writes that "It is almost a full-time job to work for democratic communications against the now fantastic economic and political pressures of managed capitalism."[11]

What is emerging on the international scene bears a striking resemblance to the routine in the United States, of uncoordinated expansion of goods production, their promotion through the communications media, higher sales, further plant expansion and then the cycle's repetition. The symptoms that Fromm finds endemic in America are spreading across oceans and continents. Industrial society's troubled individual who seeks release in goods consumption is appearing throughout the expanding orbit of the international free market. According to Fromm,

Twentieth century industrialism has created this new psychological type, *homo consumens*, primarily for economic reasons, i.e., the need for mass consumption which is stimulated and manipulated by advertising. But the character type, once created, also influences the economy and makes the principles of ever-increasing satisfaction appear rational and realistic. Contemporary man, thus, has an unlimited hunger for more and more consumption.[12]

The man in the market economy has become a message receiver beyond all imagination. This individual is the target of the most effective communications media devised by modern technology. Bombarded in the United States by an estimated 1,500 advertising messages a day,[13] and exposed to 4,000 hours of TV viewing before arriving in grade school[14] "contemporary men" are multiplying rapidly in the North Atlantic community. In fact, *homo consumens* is beginning to be discovered as well in Africa, Latin America and Asia. In fourteen industrial private enterprise countries in 1964, twenty-one billion dollars were spent on advertising, two-thirds of which were expended in the United States.[15] Financing much of this staggering budget for global commercial message-making are the powerful multi-national corporations whose plants and service installations are spread over several countries. The major United States advertisers are, as might be expected, the most prominent consumer goods producers. Tobacco, drugs, cosmetics, beer, automobiles, gasoline, and food products are the chief sponsoring industries of commercial television in the United States. Table 1 is an abbreviated listing of the largest American TV advertisers in 1966.

TABLE 1. Television Advertising Expenditures of U.S. Companies, 1966[16]

1. Proctor & Gamble	$179.2 million
2. Bristol-Myers	93.6
3. General Foods	93.3
4. Colgate-Palmolive	67.1
*5. Lever Brothers	58.0
6. American Home Products	57.1
7. R. J. Reynolds	49.8
8. Gillette	41.9
9. Warner-Lambert	41.3
10. American Tobacco	40.8
11. General Mills	39.1
12. Sterling Drug	39.0
13. Coca-Cola Co./Bottlers	38.8
14. General Motors	38.4
15. Kellogg	35.1

*Lever Brothers is British-owned.

The engines of commercialization in the West are these "big spenders." Long ago they captured the radio spectrum in the United States. Now they are waging successful campaigns to extend their conquests to Europe, Africa and Asia. One advertising agency predicts that in 1976, American advertisers will be spending as much abroad as they do in the United States.[17] *Television Age's* annual survey of television around the world, offers country by country progress reports of the multi-national companies' advertising penetration. For example, in Argentina, "gasolines and automobile manufacturers, such as Shell, Esso, General Motors, Ford . . . are major advertisers. . . . Ponds, Philips, Gillette, Nestle and Colgate are also heavy advertisers. . . ." In Australia, "Coca-Cola and Chemstrand are major advertisers along with Ford, Lever Brothers, Alcoa, Ansett Air lines, The Australian Biscuit Co., Beecham Products, and Bristol-Myers." In Finland, "Ford, Coca-Cola and General Motors are about as active here as they are in the U.S."[18] Wherever big company influ-

ence penetrates, electronic communications are subverted to salesmanship.

Three soap companies [Fred Friendly notes] Proctor & Gamble, Colgate-Palm-
olive, and Lever Brothers, account for about 15 percent of the nation's total
television sales. This is one reason why Americans know more about detergents
and bleaches than they do about Vietnam or Watts. The three great printing
presses in their seven-day-a-week continuous runs are so oriented to advertising
and merchandise that after a single day of viewing television, a visitor from
another planet could only infer that we are bent on producing a generation
of semiliterate consumers. [19]

It is not only a matter of the ubiquitous, jarring commercial.
The entire content that illuminates the home screen is fitted to the
marketeer's order. "TV is not an art form or a culture channel; it
is an advertising medium," states an American TV writer. Therefore,
". . . it seems a bit churlish and un-American of people who watch
television to complain that their shows are so lousy. They are not
supposed to be any good. They are supposed to make money . . .
(and) in fact, 'quality' may be not merely irrelevant but a distrac-
tion." [20]

Admittedly, the situation of radio-television in the United States
is the extreme case. In Western Europe, the tradition of state broadcasting authorities exercising some social responsibility has not yet
been demolished. But the striving of the consumer goods producers
to gain the attention of large audiences is unrelenting, and as Fromm
observes, once the contact is made, the audience itself searches out
further stimuli. If commercials are still controlled and compressed
into special slices of the viewing time in some national systems
abroad, the shows themselves often follow the dictates, directly or
indirectly, of their sponsors. Certainly, this is the case in the popular
and widely shown American productions where the advertising agency may have sat in at each stage of a script's development. Consider
this account of a show's gestation: "The writing of a half-hour script
takes approximately three weeks. As a first step, Baer (responsible
for such shows as "Petticoat Junction," "The Munsters," and "Bewitched") submits several basic ideas for the plot to the producer.
If the latter likes one of them, he gives the signal to go ahead. The
next step is a five or six-page outline. This is read by the producer,
the story editor and sometimes representatives from the advertising
agency. On some shows the advertising people only read the fin-
ished script."

Whether in at the beginning of the "creative" process or at its
conclusion, the advertiser's influence in American programming is
paramount. Inevitably, "the writer feels that some of his best and

most meaningful ideas have not reached the air because they were not considered commercial enough. Sponsors and producers do not want too radical a departure from what has been done before. Since the financial stake is so large, they want to play it safe."[21]

All the same, American shows, written exclusively to serve the ends of goods producers, are gobbling up the international TV market. ABC, NBC and CBS send their packaged programming to all continents, charging what the freight will bear. In low-income areas in Africa and Asia, old U.S. films and shows are dumped at low prices to secure a foothold in emerging markets, regardless of the relevance or appropriateness of the "entertainment"

In Western Europe, the most stable non-commercial broadcasting structures of sovereign states are unable to resist the forces that are arrayed against them. Here is one description of how "commercials" defy national boundaries, especially in the geographically compact North Atlantic region:

Of course, the continued expansion of commercial television, despite powerful opposition, is playing a major role in making unity of diversity. Although many important countries, particularly in Europe, still forbid TV advertising, there is a certain "spillover" effect that tends to spread commercials even to those countries that originally were adamant. Only this year did the 11-year-old government-controlled Swiss TV service permit commercials on its three regional networks. The move was in large part prompted by the concern of Swiss manufacturers who knew their customers were viewing Italian and German TV across the border. The same process is expected to unfold in the Netherlands, a large part of which is also open to German programming and advertising messages. If Netherland TV goes commercial, then Belgium is expected to follow shortly thereafter. Then France and Scandinavia will be the last big holdouts. ... If French television goes commercial, an executive at J. Walter Thompson remarks, then there truly will be a common market for the TV advertiser.[22]

The pressure on the noncommercial European TV networks to incorporate private programming and commercials is mounting and the same forces are at work in radio broadcasting. France was compelled to shift the programming patterns on one of its biggest radio networks, France-Inter, because of the competition of foreign station close to the border. "The change was forced on the non-commercial network when it realized that it was losing its young listeners to the Luxembourg Radio and Europe Number One, two stations situated on the borders of France that adhere to the American-style diet of pop music interspaced with commercials and newscasts."[23]

If "legitimate" infiltration and demolition of non-commercial state systems of broadcasting is inapplicable for one reason or another, less sophisticated techniques are available. Consider the bizarre charades of the pirate radio stations which were located off the coast of England and some even in the Thames estuary. These illegal transmitters completely disregarded international frequency allocation agreements. They broadcast pop music interlaced with commercials to European and English audiences who are apparently hungering for the entertainment and not at all displeased with the accompanying consumer messages. Though the pirates were small-scale broadcasters, behind them stood large-scale interests. In England, until the government actively intervened, both the Institute of Practitioners in Advertising and the Incorporated Society of British Advertisers lent indirect support to the pirates. A director of the ISBA stated: "We recognize they fulfill a need. We would be happier, though, if they were on-shore and permanent."[24]

Reacting to an impending governmental regulatory bill, one of the pirates, Radio London, commented: "We expect to get sufficient advertising from overseas to enable us to continue. We have four million overseas listeners, *and much of our revenue is from international companies who would not be affected by British legislation.*"[25] Even after Parliament acted against the offshore broadcast facilities, the international connections of commercial broadcasting—the multinational companies, their advertising agencies, wealthy free-booters, and broadcast and record companies—continued to support the pirates in their efforts to weaken the state broadcasting authority.

Piracy apart, programming cannot be contained under present laissez-faire conditions within national frontiers. The flashy show with its lowest common denominator emotional features, styled expressly by commerce for the mass audience, cannot be kept out of one country if presented in another nearby. However questionable the "domino theory" may be in analyzing political developments in Southeast Asia, it is certainly an apt explanation for the march of commercial radio and television in Western Europe. Once a commercial inroad has been made electronically, technology and geography can be relied upon to exploit the advantage in depth.

A similar progression is beginning to appear in Asia. All-India Radio, reversing a thirty-year policy, has acceded, with governmental approval, to commercial advertising. The explanations for the decision are familiar. The government needed revenue, and, more persuasive, "Indian companies have been placing advertisements on the Ceylon Radio, whose light, commercial-studded programs can be heard throughout India." The parallel is striking: "Ceylon, an island a few miles off India's southern coast, has been compared in this respect to the pirate radio stations that beam commercial programs to Britain. . . ."[26]

Successfully securing control of communications across a good part of the earth's surface, commerce now has turned its attention to conquering space. At the White House Conference on International Cooperation in the winter of 1965, the National Citizens Commission's Committee on Space (whose chairman incidentally was Dr. Joseph Charyk, the president of Comsat), listed as the *first* application of communications satellites their future impact on "trade and commerce." The committee's report stated: "It is possible to foresee use of closed circuit television by major companies doing a worldwide business to link together their offices and affiliates in order to kick off a new sales campaign or to demonstrate a new product or to analyze a new marketing situation in the far corners of the world."[27] Admittedly, other applications were proposed but priority went to business.

Similar sentiment exists in other influential places. The London *Economist* views communications satellites as the chosen business medium of the future. Lamenting the British Government's reluctance to participate more actively in ELDO (European Launcher Development Organization), the Europeans' sole hope of matching American communications technological advances, the magazine commented: "But is there only an American or a Russian or a Chinese way of life to be propagated around the world? Will Britain (and Europe) even be able to sell its goods around the world if it cuts itself out of *the advertising medium of the 1970's*?"[28]

Sir John Rogers, president of London's Institute of Practitioner in Advertising and deputy chairman as well of J. Walter Thompson Co., Ltd., an affiliate of the world's largest advertising agency, is more hopeful. Before the 1967 annual meeting of the American Association of Advertising Agencies he declared: "I believe as far as Europe is concerned, where the advertisers need a medium, and the public wants them to have it, they will eventually get it. . . . And the projected increase in satellite communications will probably speed both this and the increasing internationalism of advertising in Europe."[29]

Even more indicative of the way utilization of communications satellites is shaping up are the perspectives of two recent conferences concerned with the matter. In December 1965, Unesco assembled representatives from 19 member states and other interested international organizations to consider the use of space satellites for informational and cultural purposes. A few months later, at the 18th World Congress of the Advertising Association in Mexico City, *World vision*, a network including 62 television stations in 25 countries, organized by the American Broadcasting Company's international subsidiary, ABC International, ran a three-day workshop demonstrating how "international advertisers could use TV right now." In the words of Donald W. Coyle, president of ABC International, "Global television is not something that we are going to have to wait for a far-off future to implement. It is upon us now."[30]

The contrast in the two approaches to the use of space communications is depressing. Unesco's vision of international control of communications satellites for cultural use is *in the future*. *Worldvision's* program for commercial utilization of space media *already has begun.* Business and the PR world have swung into action and economic consultants are canvassing clients and informing them of global communications possibilities in marketing their products. A senior vice-president of Young and Rubicam, another giant American advertising agency, explained the new dynamics of selling this way: "I think the time is now, if it hasn't been already," he said, "to consider selling your product everywhere. Not in one country or on one continent, but all over. . . . Now with subtitles, when you've a good television campaign or a selling idea, and it works in one place, whether England or the United States, Japan, or whatever, then you don't have to test-market it any more, you go right to global marketing immediately and this could happen now."[31]

It is a mistake to view these developments as evidence of an international cabal seeking the global commercialization of communications. The forces are openly at work and the success of "consumerism" rests on a varied mix of human and institutional pressures which are at present very powerful. "Both a consumer oriented economy and commercial television seem to have things going for them at this moment of history in a good part of the globe," is the way one broadcasting publication puts it.[32]

If conspiracy is absent in the American commercial electronic invasion of the world, there is all the same a very clear consciousness present of how to utilize communications for both highly ideological and profitable ends. Professor Ithiel de Sola Pool of the Massachusetts Institute of Technology told a congressional committee inquiring into "Modern Communications and Foreign Policy" that "the function that American international communications can serve is to provide people with things for which they are craving but which are not readily available to them." He mentioned world news as one example and added "Another thing that people crave is simply to see what a modern way of life is like—seeing *commodities,* seeing how people live, or hearing popular music." Dr. Joseph Klapper of the Columbia Broadcasting System expanded on the musical theme for the Committee: ". . . the broadcasting of popular music is not likely to have any immediate effect on the audience's political attitude," he noted, "but this kind of communication nevertheless provides a sort of entryway of Western ideas and Western concepts, even though these concepts may not be explicitly and completely stated at any one particular moment in the communication."[33]

The deprivations imposed by the protracted depression of the 1930's in the Western world and the war years shortages of the 40's created a huge longing in Europe and America for goods. The failure of basic social reform in Western Europe after the war to change the motivation and thrust of the national economies toward a public orientation permitted the reconsolidation of the private goods producers' interest. In America, the business system had already recaptured its confidence and authority before the United States entered the war in 1941. Advertising, on behalf of the private interest, whipped the appetite of consumerism higher still. The world outside the industrial North Atlantic enclave has followed the impulses originating in the wealthy core area.

The efforts to hold back the accelerating push toward commercialization of broadcasting communications in Western Europe have relied on the existence of national traditions of propriety unobserved in the United States and even some exclusion or limitation on American programming. Canada and Great Britain, for example, have tried, not too successfully, to keep the proportion of American to domestic shows within certain limits.

Yet the attempts to exclude United States programming and to limit the number and length of national commercials are unlikely to be effective in any one country no matter how influential that society may be in its own region. The subject matter that is denied local transmission reappears in and is broadcast from neighboring states, with transmitters sometimes deliberately established for this specific purpose. Then too, the business system in Western Europe, Canada, Japan and Australia supports the general principle of commercialization and accordingly throws its weight wherever possible behind an advance of salesmanship. After all, the marketing problems in these privately organized industrial states, if not yet at American levels, are approaching them rapidly.

As for the universe of the global poor, the "have-not" nations stand practically defenseless before a rampaging Western commercialism. Impoverished as they are, many developing states are able to afford the new communications complexes only by accepting commercial packages which "tie" their broadcasting systems to foreign programming and foreign financial sponsorship. Time-Life's Vice President Sig Mickelson asserts bluntly: "The various underdeveloped countries are having to permit commercials because they can't afford a television system otherwise."[34] In this way their economic developmental paths are set, regardless of the intentions and designs of their planners, by the pull of market-directed consumerism. Expectations of new roads to national development which *might* foster motivations and behavior different from contemporary Western styles are being dashed in their infancy.

The gloomy and bitter words of Japanese economist, Shigeto Tsuru, seem to take on universality before Western market enterprise's electronic communications offensive:

In this world of high-powered communications we may even have to speak of a new kind of "self-alienation" for citizens living under capitalism. If there were a society on this earth somewhere which would make full use of the highly developed techniques of communication of today for the sole purpose of its inhabitants' autonomous cultural needs, it would be an experience of a lifetime for us to visit there—for us who daily, even hourly cannot escape from the onslaught, either subtle or crude, of modern commercialism in a capitalist society.[35]

NOTES

1. "Television Network Procurement," Report of the Committee on Interstate and Foreign Commerce, 88th Congress, 1st Session, House Report No. 281, March 3, 1963, U.S. Government Printing Office, Washington, 1963, p. 49 and footnote 9.

2. Wilson P. Dizard, *Television: A World View,* Syracuse University Press, 1966, Syracuse, New York, p. 12-13.

3. Dizard, *op. cit.,* p. 13.

4. Unesco, *Statistics on Radio and Television, 1950-1960,* 1963, Paris, France, p. 20.

5. *The New York Times,* January 16, 1967.

6. Dizard, *op. cit.,* p. 13.

7. *Broadcasting,* June 26, 1967.

8. Ralph Tyler, "Agencies Abroad: New Horizons for U.S. Advertising," *Television Magazine,* September 1965, p. 36. (Italics added.)

9. *Ibid.,* p. 65. In 1967, according to *Printers Ink,* there were "at least 46 U.S.-based ad agencies abroad, with a total of 382 branch offices beyond the U.S. boundaries." Forty of these agencies, reported *Advertising Age,* claimed overseas billings of $1,138 millions.

10. Gerald Beadle, *Television: A Critical Review,* 1963, George Allen and Unwin, Ltd., London, p. 82.

11. Raymond Williams, "Britain's Press Crisis," *The Nation,* April 10, 1967, p. 467.

12. Erich Fromm, "The Psychological Aspects of the Guaranteed Income" in *The Guaranteed Income,* edited by Robert Theobold, Doubleday and Co., Inc., New York, 1966, p. 179.

13. *The Wall Street Journal,* November 3, 1965.

14. *Television Magazine,* July, 1967, p. 37.

15. "Advertising Investments Around the World," *International Advertising Association,* October, 1965.

16. *Broadcasting*, April 17, 1967, p. 38.

17. *Ibid.*, December 19, 1966, p. 23.

18. *Television Age*, July 3, 1967, pp. 33 and 61.

19. Fred Friendly, *Due to Circumstances Beyond Our Control*, Random House, 1967, New York, pp. 294-295.

20. Daniel Karp, *The New York Times Magazine*, "TV Shows are Not Supposed To Be Good," January 23, 1966.

21. *The New York Times*, December 12, 1965.

22. *Television Magazine*, September, 1965.

23. *The New York Times*, February 26, 1967. See also, *Variety*, "Rising Tide of Monied Interests May Yet Swing 3rd French TV Web," February 15, 1967, p. 38.

24. *The Sunday Times*, London, June 19, 1966.

25. *The Times*, London, July 2, 1966. (Italics added.)

26. *The New York Times*, January 29, 1967.

27. *The White House Conference on International Cooperation.* National Citizens' Commission, Report of the Committee on Space, November 28-December 1, 1965, Washington, D.C., p. 27.

28. *The Economist*, London, June 11, 1966, p. 1167. (Italics added.)

29. *Broadcasting*, April 24, 1967, p. 75.

30. *The New York Times*, May 15, 1966.

31. Ralph Tyler, "Television Around the World," *Television Magazine*, October, 1966, p. 61

32. *Television Magazine*, September, 1965.

33. "Modern Communications and Foreign Policy," Committee on Foreign Affairs, House of Representatives, 90th Congress, 1st Session, May 4, 1967, Washington, D.C., pp. 63-64. (Italics added.)

34. *Television Magazine*, October, 1966, p. 61.

35. Shigeto Tsuru, *Has Capitalism Changed?*, Tokyo, 1961, p. 56.

Selective
Bibliography

This bibliography is not meant to be exhaustive.
It does, however, suggest reading to supplement
the topics covered in this book. Its organization
follows approximately that of the volume; a section on general works is added and Third World
development concerns receive separate treatment.
For more complete bibliographical references the
reader may consult regular up-to-date listings in
Journalism Quarterly and the International Communications Bulletin. William A. Hachten has
compiled a highly valuable 121-page listing for
Africa, Mass Communication in Africa: An Anno-
tated Bibliography (Madison: University of Wisconsin, Center for International Studies, 1971).
The Asian Mass Communication Research and
Information Center (Ming Court Hotel, Tanglin
Road, Singapore 10) publishes occasional documentation lists for Asia. Finally, for global broadcasting, Lawrence Lichty's compilation, World and
International Broadcasting (Washington, C.D.:
Association for Professional Broadcasting Educa-
tion, 1971), may be useful.

GENERAL WORKS ON INTERNATIONAL MASS MEDIA

Benn's Guide to Newspapers and Periodicals of the World. 119th issue. London: Benn Brothers, 1970. 1058 pp.

Dizard, Wilson P. *Television: A World View.* Syracuse, N.Y.: Syracuse University Press, 1966.

Edelstein, Alex S. *Perspectives in Mass Communications.* Copenhagen: Einar Harcks, Forlag, 1966.

Educational Television International, Journal of the Centre for Educational Television Overseas. London.

Emery, Walter B. *National and International Systems of Broadcasting: Their History, Operation and Control.* East Lansing: Michigan State University Press, 1969.

Green, Timothy. *The Universal Eye.* London: Bodley Head, 1972.

Hancock, Alan. *Mass Communication.* London: Longman Group, 1970.

Merrill, John C., Carter R. Bryan, and Marvin Alisky. *The Foreign Press.* Baton Rouge: Louisiana State University Press, 1970.

Mowlana, Hamid. "Toward a Theory of Communications Systems: A Developmental Approach." *Gazette,* 17, no. 1/2, 1971, pp. 17-28.

Nixon, Raymond B. "Freedom in the World's Press: A Fresh Appraisal with New Data." *Journalism Quarterly,* 42, no. 1, pp. 3-14, 118-19.

Nixon, Raymond B., and Tae-Youl Hahn. "Concentration of Press Ownership: A Comparison of 32 Countries." *Journalism Quarterly,* 48, spring 1971, pp. 5-16.

Schiller, Herbert I. *Mass Communications and American Empire.* New York: Augustus M. Kelley, 1969.

———. "The Electronic Invaders." *Progressive,* 37, no. 8, August 1973, pp. 23-25.

Siebert, Fred S., Theodore Peterson, and Wilbur Schramm. *Four Theories of the Press: The Authoritarian, Libertarian, Social Responsibility and Soviet Communist Concepts of What the Press Should Be and Do.* Urbana: University of Illinois Press, 1956.

Tebbel, J. "World Press and the Teaching of Journalism: Helsinki Convention," *Saturday Review,* 54, September 11, 1971, pp. 64-65.

Unesco. *World Communications: Press, Radio, Television, Film.* New York: Unesco, 1964.

World Radio TV Handbook 1969. 23rd ed. Hellerup, Denmark: World Radio-Television Handbook Company, 1968.

DEVELOPED COUNTRIES: WESTERN EUROPE, JAPAN, AND THE COMMUNIST BLOC

Briggs, Asa. *The History of Broadcasting in the United Kingdom.* Vol. 1, *The Birth of Broadcasting;* Vol. 2, *The Golden Age of Wireless.* London: Oxford University Press, 1965.

British Broadcasting Corporation. *BBC Handbook, 1972.* London: BBC, 1972.

Broman, Barry M. "Tatzepao: Medium of Conflict in China's 'Cultural Revolution'." *Journalism Quarterly,* summer 1969, pp. 100-104.

Browne, Don. "The BBC and the Pirates: A Phase in the Life of a Prolonged Monopoly." *Journalism Quarterly,* Spring, 1971, pp. 85-99.

Colitt, Leslie R. "Television" [on East German television]. *Nation,* November 11, 1968, pp. 508-10.

EBU Review, European Broadcasting Union, Geneva.

Emery, Walter B. "Five European Broadcasting Systems." *Journalism Monographs,* no. 1. Austin, Tex.: Association for Education in Journalism, 1966.

Gould, Jack. "What Public TV Can Be: Britain's BBC." *Columbia Journalism Review,* July/August 1972, pp. 16–20.

Hamsik, Dusan. *Writers against Rulers.* New York: Vintage, 1971.

History of Broadcasting in Japan. Tokyo: NHK, 1967.

Independent Television Authority. *ITV 1972: Guide to Independent Television.* London: ITA, 1972.

Krosney, Herbert. "TV Comes to Israel." *Nation,* October 6, 1969, pp. 339–43.

Lowenstein, Ralph L. "The Daily Press in Israel." *Journalism Quarterly,* summer 1969, pp. 325–31.

Markham, James W. *Voices of the Red Giants: Communication in Russia and China.* Ames: Iowa State University Press, 1967.

Motte, Michelle. "How Dutch Television Goes Its Own Way." *Atlas,* 20, February 1971, p. 487.

Paulu, Burton. "American News on the Soviet Television Screen." *Journalism Quarterly,* fall 1971, pp. 459–65.

———. *British Broadcasting in Transition.* Minneapolis: University of Minnesota Press, 1961, pp. 7–17.

———. *Radio and Television Broadcasting on the European Continent.* Minneapolis: University of Minnesota Press, 1967.

Radio, Television. Review of the International Radio and Television Organization, Prague.

Schalk, A. "Putting the Starch in the German Press." *Saturday Review,* 55, March 25, 1972, pp. 80–82.

Toogood, Alex. "The Canadian Broadcasting System: Search for a Definition," and "The Mixed Private-Public Structure of Canadian TV." *Journalism Quarterly,* summer, 1971, pp. 331–36.

MASS MEDIA IN AFRICA, ASIA, AND LATIN AMERICA

Ainslie, Rosalynde. *Press in Africa.* Rev. ed., New York: Walker, 1968.

Austin, Alvin E. "Infringements on Freedom of the Press in Latin America." *North Dakota Quarterly,* spring 1969, pp. 60–71.

Brown, Trevor. "Free Press Fair Game for South Africa's Government." *Journalism Quarterly,* spring 1971, pp. 120–27.

Carter, Roy E., Jr., and Orlando Sepulveda. "Some Patterns of Mass Media Use in Santiago de Chile." *Journalism Quarterly,* 41, no. 2, spring 1964, pp. 216–24.

Chilcote, R. H. "The Press in Latin America, Spain and Portugal." *Hispanic American Report,* August 1963 (special issue).

Davies, Derek, et al. "The Asian Press." *Far Eastern Economic Review,* October 9, 1971, pp. 21–28.

Dowry, Dennis T. "Radio, T.V. and Literacy in Mexico." *Journal of Broadcasting,* spring 1970, pp. 239–44.

Emery, W. "Broadcasting in Mexico." *Journal of Broadcasting,* 8, 1964, pp. 257–74.

Erlandson, E. "The Press in Mexico: Past, Present, and Future." *Journalism Quarterly*, 41, 1964, pp. 232-36.

Estrada, Luis P., and Daniel Hopen. "The Cultural Value of Film and Television in Latin America." Paris: Unesco, July 9, 1968.

Frappier, J. "The U.S. Media Empire in Latin America." *NACLA Newsletter*, 11, no. 9, January 1969, pp. 1-11 (North American Congress on Latin America, New York).

Hachten, William A. "Moroccan News Media Reflect Divisive Forces While Unifying." *Journalism Quarterly*, spring 1971, pp. 100-110.

Hachten, William A., and Harva S. Hachten. *Muffled Drums: The News Media in Africa.* Ames: Iowa State University Press, 1971.

Lent, John A. "Mass Media in the Netherlands Antilles." *Gazette*, 17, no. 1/2 1971, pp. 51-73.

"Looking at the TV." *Pakistan Economist*, August 14, 1971, pp. 18-27.

Mujahid, Sharif al. "After Decline during Ayub Era, Pakistan Press Strives, Improves." *Journalism Quarterly*, fall 1971, pp. 526-35.

Nam, Sunwoo. "Editorials as an Indicator of Press Freedom in Three Asian Countries." *Journalism Quarterly*, 48, winter 1971, pp. 730-40.

Schiller, Herbert I., and Dallas Smythe. "Chile: An End to Cultural Colonialism." *Society*, March 1972, pp. 35-39, 61.

Sommerlad, E. Lloyd. *The Press in Developing Countries.* Sydney: Sydney University Press, 1966.

Unesco. *Mass Media in the Developing Countries.* Paris: Unesco, 1961.

Whiting, Gordon C., and J. David Stanfield. "Mass Media Use and Opportunity Structure in Rural Brazil." *Public Opinion Quarterly*, spring 1972, pp. 56-68.

COMMUNICATION, MODERNIZATION, AND ECONOMIC DEVELOPMENT

Deutsch, Karl W. "Social Mobilization and Political Development." In Jason L. Finkle and Richard W. Gable, eds., *Political Development and Social Change.* New York: Wiley, 1966.

Deutschmann, Paul J., et al. *Communication and Social Change in Latin America.* New York: Praeger, 1968.

Fliegel, F. C., J. E. Kivlin, and G. S. Sokhon. "Message Distortion and the Diffusion of Innovations in Northern India." *Sociologia Ruralis*, 11, 1971, p. 2.

Grunig, James E. "Communications and the Decision Making Process of Colombian Peasants." *Economic Development and Cultural Change*, 19, no. 4, 1971, pp. 580-97.

Lerner, Daniel. "Communication Systems and Social Systems." In Wilbur Schramm, ed., *Mass Communications.* Urbana: University of Illinois Press, 1960.

———. *The Passing of Traditional Society.* New York: Free Press, 1958.

———. "Toward a Communication Theory of Modernization." In Lucian W. Pye, ed., *Communications and Political Development.* Princeton, N.J.: Princeton University Press, 1963.

Lerner, Daniel, and Wilbur Schramm, eds. *Communication and Change in the Developing Countries.* Honolulu: East-West Center Press, 1967.

Maddison, John. *Radio and Television in Literacy.* Paris: Unesco, 1971.

Mishra, Vishwa M. "Mass Media Variables Related to Urbanization and Modernization in Developing Areas." *Journalism Quarterly*, 48, no. 3, 1971, pp. 513-18.

Oshima, Harry T. "The Strategy of Selective Growth and the Role of Communications." In Daniel Lerner and Wilbur Schramm, eds., *Communication and Change in the Developing Countries*. Honolulu: East-West Center Press, 1967.

Rao, Y. V. Lakshmana. *Communication and Development, a Study of Two Indian Villages*. Minneapolis: University of Minnesota Press, 1966.

Rogers, Everett M. "Mass Media Exposure and Modernization among Colombian Peasants." *Public Opinion Quarterly*, 29, no. 4, 1965-66, pp. 614-25.

Rogers, Everett M., and L. Svenning. *Modernization among Peasants: The Impact of Communication*. New York: Holt, Rinehart and Winston, 1969.

Schramm, Wilbur. "Communication Development and the Development Process." In Lucian W. Pye, ed., *Communications and Political Development*. Princeton, N.J.: Princeton University Press, 1963.

———. *Mass Media and National Development*. Stanford, Calif.: Stanford University Press, 1964.

Schramm, Wilbur, and W. Lee Ruggels. "How Mass Media Systems Grow." In Daniel Lerner and Wilbur Schramm, eds., *Communication and Change in the Developing Countries*. Honolulu: East-West Center Press, 1967.

de Şola Pool, Ithiel. "Communications and Development." In Myron Weiner, ed., *Modernization: The Dynamics of Growth*. New York: Basic Books, 1966.

———. "Mass Media and Politics in the Modernization Process." In Lucian W. Pye, ed., *Communications and Political Development*. Princeton, N.J.: Princeton University Press, 1963.

Wells, Alan. *Picture Tube Imperialism? Development and Television in Latin America*. Maryknoll, N.Y.: Orbis Books, 1972.

Whiting, Gordon C., and J. David Stanfield. "Mass Media Use and Opportunity Structure in Rural Brazil." *Public Opinion Quarterly*, spring 1972, pp. 56-68.

INTERNATIONAL COMMUNICATION AND PROPAGANDA

Cherry, Colin. *World Communication: Threat or Promise?* New York: Wiley-Interscience, 1971.

Davison, W. Phillips. *International Political Communication*. New York: Praeger, 1965.

Goodfriend, Arthur. "The Dilemma of Cultural Propaganda: 'Let it Be.' " *Annals*, 398, November 1971, pp. 104-12.

Hayes, Harold. "International Persuasion Variables Are Tested across Three Cultures." *Journalism Quarterly*, fall 1971, pp. 714-23.

Hester, Al. "An Analysis of News Flow from Developed and Developing Nations." *Gazette*, 17, no. 1/2, 1971, pp. 29-43.

Kruglak, Theodore E. *The Two Faces of TASS*. Minneapolis: University of Minnesota Press, 1962.

Maddox, Brenda. "Intelsat on Ice?" *New Republic*, May 16, 1970, pp. 10-11.

Manvell, Roger. *This Age of Communication*. Glasgow and London: Blackie, 1966.

McNelly, John T., and Julio Molina R. "Communication, Stratification and International Affairs Information in a Developing Urban Society." [Peru] *Journalism Quarterly*, 48, no. 2, summer 1972, pp. 316-26, 339.

Moulton, E. J. "Satellite over Africa." *Africa Report,* 12, May 1967, pp. 13–19.

Schramm, Wilbur, and Lyle Nelson. *Communication Satellites for Education and Development—the Case of India.* Washington, D.C.: U.S. Agency for International Development, August 1968.

Siebert, Fred. "Property Rights in Materials Transmitted by Satellites." *Journalism Quarterly,* spring 1971, pp. 17–32.

Smith, Don. "Some Effects of Radio Moscow's North American Broadcasts." *Public Opinion Quarterly,* winter 1970-71, pp. 539–51.

Sparks, Kenneth R. "Selling Uncle Sam in the Seventies." *Annals,* 398, November 1971, pp. 113–23.

"Telecommunications and Education." *Telecommunication Journal,* 37, July 1970, pp. 315–27.

Unesco. *Communication in the Space Age: The Use of Satellites by the Mass Media.* Paris: Unesco, 1968.